Routledge Revivals

Mauryan Public Finance

First published in 1935, *Mauryan Public Finance* by M.H. Gopal explores the economic administration of the Mauryan Empire through the lens of modern economics. Drawing primarily from Kautilya's Arthashastra and comparing it with ancient Athens, Gopal examines revenue sources like land, mines, and taxes, alongside expenditures on governance, education, irrigation, and defense. This insightful study highlights the Mauryan Empire's fiscal sophistication, making it essential for scholars of Indian economic history and Indian Economics.

Mauryan Public Finance

M. H. Gopal

Routledge
Taylor & Francis Group

First published in 1935
by George Allen & Unwin Ltd.

This edition first published in 2026 by Routledge
4 Park Square, Milton Park, Abingdon, Oxon, OX14 4RN

and by Routledge
605 Third Avenue, New York, NY 10158

Routledge is an imprint of the Taylor & Francis Group, an informa business

A Library of Congress record exists under LCCN: 35021890

ISBN: 978-1-041-38153-2 (hbk)
ISBN: 978-1-042-01160-5 (ebk)
ISBN: 978-1-041-38154-9 (pbk)

Book DOI 10.4324/9781042011605

MAURYAN PUBLIC FINANCE

by

M. H. GOPAL
M.A., Ph.D. (Econ. Lond.)
Assistant Professor of Economics,
University of Mysore, Mysore

LONDON
GEORGE ALLEN & UNWIN LTD
MUSEUM STREET

FIRST PUBLISHED IN 1935

PRINTED IN GREAT BRITAIN BY
UNWIN BROTHERS LTD., WOKING

CONTENTS

PREFACE

THE present book was drafted in the summer of 1927, and has been revised and rewritten in view of materials in London and on my return home.

I am greatly indebted to Dr. M. H. Krishna, M.A., D.Lit.(Lond.), Professor of History and Director of Archaeology in Mysore, Dr. L. D. Barnett of the British Museum, Professor F. W. Thomas of Oxford, Dr. Gilbert Slater, late of the London School of Economics, Mahamahopadhyaya Panditaratnam L. Srinivasacharya of Mysore, Pandit R. Chakravarthy, and Mr. L. Narasimhacharya of the Mysore Archaeological Department for various kinds of help. But the responsibility for interpretations and conclusions found in the book is entirely mine.

I am also indebted to Dr. Shāma Śāstry for his excellent translation of the *Arthaśāstra*, which I have liberally made use of in the following pages.

M. H. GOPAL

INTRODUCTION

SINCE the discovery of the Kauṭilīya *Arthaśāstra* so much has been written about it and the Mauryan period that some apology seems necessary for one more addition to that literature. But the *Arthaśāstra* is a mine which has not yet been exhausted, and it "will continue to give occupation to scholars for a long time to come from many points of view."

The Mauryan period may roughly be said to comprise the years between the last quarter of the fourth century and the first quarter of the second century B.C. The principal sources relied upon for information during this period are Kauṭilya's *Arthaśāstra*, Aśōka's edicts, the accounts of the Greeks, and stray references in later writers, Hindu, Buddhist, and Greek.

There is much controversy about the date of the *Arthaśāstra* and the conditions which it describes. There are scholars like Winternitz,[1] Jolly,[2] and Hildebrandt who ascribe the work to the third century after Christ. Others, like Fleet,[3] Shāma Śāstry,[4] R. K. Mookerjea,[5] and Jacobi, ascribe the work to the last quarter of the fourth century B.C. There are also some scholars[6] in whose opinion the *Arthaśāstra* describes pre-Mauryan policy.

[1] *Some Problems of Indian Literature*, p. 109.

[2] *Arthaśāstra*, edited by J. E. Jolly, vol. i, p. 29.

[3] Introductory Note in Shāma Śāstry's translation of the *Arthaśāstra*.

[4] *Arth. Trans.*, Preface, p. ix.

[5] Introductory Essay in N. N. Law's *Studies in Ancient Hindu Polity*. The same view is found in *Mahā-mahōpādhyāya* Gaṇapati Śāstri's preface to vol. ii of his edition of the *Arthaśāstra* and in K. V. Rangaswamy Aiyangar's Introduction in his *Considerations on some Aspects of Ancient Indian Polity*. A lucid and interesting discussion of the subject is found in Hemachandra Ray Chauduri's articles in the *Indian Antiquary*, 1925. See also Shāma Śāstry's article in the *Calcutta Review* of 1925.

[6] *Early History of India*, p. 145.

Without entering into discussion about these questions, I have followed the view of F. W. Thomas. He writes:[1] "Concerning the condition and organization of the vast Mauryan empire, the Greeks have provided us with a considerable body of valuable information; and as the *Artha-śāstra* furnished the means of describing the complete polity existing at the time, its land system, its fiscal system, its administrative system, its law, its social system, with some view of literature and religion, we shall not forgo the opportunity so rare in Indian history—we must wait for the time of Akbar and the *Ain-i-Akbari*—of dwelling a little on the picture." A discussion of the date of the great work is unnecessary for our present purpose; the general conclusion that it describes the conditions existing in the Mauryan period has been accepted in this book.

Next arises the question whether what Kauṭilya describes is an ideal or what was existing actually. According to Thomas, "the *Arthaśāstra* furnishes the means to describe the complete polity existing at the time." Jolly thinks that the *Arthaśāstra* is thoroughly realistic and worldly,[2] but that its author was not a statesman but a theoretician[3] and is opposed to strict idealism. A study of the work of Kauṭilya suggests to me that the author is describing only the state as he found—perhaps made—it at the time. Of course it cannot be expected of any writer, much less of a great creative personality like Kauṭilya, that his writings would be free from his own ideas and ideals. Kauṭilya may and does describe here and there what a state ought to be. But the description is too graphic and the details too minute and numerous to indicate that the conditions described were only ideal. The corroborative evidence of the Greeks as regards some facts and the parallels found in ancient Greek and Indian states for some others strongly

[1] *Cambridge History of India*, vol. i, p. 474.
[2] *Op. cit.*, vol. i, p. 2.
[3] *Op. cit.*, vol. i, p. 47.

suggest that the *Arthaśāstra* deals largely with the organization of the state as existing in the Mauryan period.

There is no necessity to consider the question whether the work is the product of an individual or of a school.

The present book is an attempt to study the public finance of the Mauryan period from a modern point of view. The ancient ideas are presented in the light of modern economics, and wherever necessary they are compared with modern principles and conditions. They are also compared with those of the ancient world, specially Athens, and some striking parallels are found: for example, the tax on prostitutes. These similarities will be noted in detail in their proper places.

But some important differences between the Mauryan and the Athenian states must be remembered. There was the great difference in size between a small city state like Athens and a vast empire like the Mauryan. Athens, again, was a democratic republic, and the will of the people determined financial principles. Mauryan India, on the other hand, was, at best, a benevolent despotism, and the policy of public administration was influenced by the teachings of the *smṛitis* and the notion of *dharma*, as well as by the condition of the times. In Athens there was little of standing army, and in times of war the state expenses, for example, of equipment and the like of the national *militia*, were ignorable, as every citizen furnished his own arms; in India there was a huge standing army equipped and maintained by the state. Lastly, the period of Greek history with which we have compared the Mauryan conditions is generally pre-Mauryan. These are no doubt important considerations to be borne in mind, but we cannot but feel surprised at some peculiar outstanding similarities.

Another explanation is perhaps not out of place. Ancient Indian administrations have much in common. In this book Mauryan financial principles have been often compared with those mentioned by a few of the ancient thinkers, and also with what actually prevailed in the Indian states even as late as the tenth century after Christ. But no detailed comparison is made, as this book deals with a particular period.

To acquaint ourselves with the financial system of the Mauryan period "we must consider in what manner her finances were administered, what were the wants of the state, what revenues the state had for the supply of the same and whether they were sufficient for the purpose and even furnished a surplus, and what extraordinary means of aid were employed upon the occurrence of pecuniary embarrassment. We confine ourselves in the consideration of the subject, excluding subordinate communities and corporate bodies, to the administration of the state itself."

PART I

REVENUE

CHAPTER I

GENERAL CONSIDERATIONS

Importance of finance—Peculiar features—Application of modern canons of taxation

A GREAT finance minister of modern India, James Wilson, once observed: "Finance is not arithmetic; finance is a great policy; without sound finance no sound government is possible; and without sound government no sound finance is possible." Indeed, finance is the very life-breath of the state. In modern society its all-absorbing importance is unquestionably established.

While dealing with an ancient state, the first question to be considered is whether the ancient—for our purposes the Maurya—financiers considered finance of the same importance as we do, and, if so, how far it was organized. The profound truth of Wilson's statement is, indeed, as old as the day when states and governments were first formed. The Mauryas fully recognized the extraordinary importance of finance. In Kauṭilya's words, "All undertakings depend upon finance. Hence foremost attention shall be paid to the treasury."[1] Again, "Thus, when both the receipts and expenditures are properly cared for, the king will never find himself in financial or military difficulties."[2] Finance was considered to be one of the elements of sovereignty itself. "The king, the minister, the country, the fort, the treasury, the army, and the friend are the elements of

[1] *Arth.*, Bk. II, ch. 8:

Kōśapūrvāssarvārambhāḥ
Tasmātpūrvaṃ Kōśamavēkshēta.

[2] *Arth.*, Bk. V, ch. 3:

Ēvamavēkshitāyavyayaḥ kōśadaṇḍavyasanaṃ nāvāpnōti.

Compare *Kāmandaka*, v, 61.

sovereignty."[3] Even among them finance and the army were marked out as the most important, and of these two the palm was given to the former. Nay, it was considered to be the basis of virtue even. To quote Kauṭilya: "But finance was the chief means of observing virtuous acts and of enjoying desires. Owing to a change in place, time, and policy, either finance or the army may be a superior power; for the army is sometimes the means of securing the wealth acquired; but wealth is always the means of securing both the treasury and the army. Since all activities depend upon finance, financial troubles are more serious."[4] It was more important than virtue, not because "as a robe conceals a woman's nakedness, so does wealth conceal sin,"[5] but because "religious merit springs from the treasury, O! son of Kunti; and it is through the treasury that the roots of the kingdom extend."[6] Or, as Kauṭilya puts it, charity and desire depend upon wealth for their realization,[7] and "finance is the chief means of observing virtuous acts."[8] It was because that finance was considered so important that it was, along with the army, under the direct control of the king.[9] Both of them were required to be located in one place, although their actual administration was under two trust-

[3] *Arth.*, Bk. VI, ch. 1, *Svāmyamātyajanapadadurgakōśadaṇḍa-mitrāṇi prakṛitayaḥ*. This idea of the seven elements of sovereignty was very common in ancient India. *Yājñavalkya*, i, 13, 353; *Vishṇu*, iii, 33; *Kāmandaka*, i, 18.

[4] *Arth.*, Bk. VIII, ch. 1, *Kōśō dharmakāmahētuḥ*, etc. See also *Arth.*, Bk. IX, ch. 8, where Kauṭilya says that wealth is to be secured prior to even virtue and enjoyment. Compare what Hopkins says (*J.A.O.S.*, vol. xiii) of a passage in the *Rāmāyaṇa*: "The possibility of the kingdom existing without taxation seems specially to irritate the compilers of the epic. They revert to the subject again and again and prove that the king must have wealth—his army, his happiness, his virtue depend upon it."

[5] Hopkins, *op. cit.*

[6] *Śāntiparva*, ch. cxxxiii.

[7] *Arth.*, Bk. I, ch. 7, *Arthamūlau hi dharmakāmāviti*.

[8] *Arth.*, Bk. VIII, ch. 1, *Kōśō dharmakāmahētuḥ*. Cf. *Kāmandaka*, v, 61; xiv, 21, 32–3. *Śukranīti*, iv, 2, 5–6; 28 ff.

[9] *Arth.*, Bk. VIII, ch. 2, *Kōśadaṇḍaśaktimātmasamsthāṃ kurvīta*.

worthy persons and elaborate departments.[10] It is interesting to note that Śukra also pays the same importance to this subject. According to him, the king was to collect funds by any means to maintain the commonwealth, the army, and the sacrifices.[11]

As will be seen in the course of this book, the wants of the state, as well as the sources of income, were so varied and numerous that they would do discredit to few modern countries, although some of the means of raising revenue, especially in financial difficulties, may not be ethically commendable.

A peculiar feature of most ancient countries was the identification of the king with the state, and, consequently, the absence of any difference between the private purse of the monarch and the public purse. In the Mauryan days also this appears to have been the case. But, as will be seen presently, there was an efficient administrative organization under the king and a council of ministers who were all largely guided by the established notions of justice and virtue. Where, however, the needs of the state imperatively demanded—as in a calamity—funds, all possible means, fair and foul, were adopted.[12]

A fair idea of the revenue resources of the Mauryan state can be had from Kauṭilya's description of the ideal country.[13] The ideal country was one productive of subsistence not only to its own people but also to outsiders on occasions of calamities, containing fertile lands, mines, timber and elephant forests, and pasture grounds full of cattle, not depending upon rain for water, possessed of land- and water-ways, rich in various kinds of commercial articles, capable of bearing the burden of a vast army and heavy

[10] *Arth.*, Bk. V, ch. 6, and Bk. II, chs. 12, 13, etc. Cf. *Yājñavalkya*, i, 13, 327.

[11] *Śukranīti*, iv, 2, 3–4; also see 28–9. Contrast *Yājñavalkya*, i, 13, 340.

[12] *Infra*, Chapter IX.

[13] *Arth.*, Bk. VI, ch. 1. Cf. *Kāmandaka*, iv, 7, 49 *seq.*

taxation, and inhabited by agriculturists of good and active character. Here are found the sources of revenue such as lands, mines, forests, taxes, and others.[14] According to Kauṭilya, the country must have the capacity to bear heavy taxation, and a study of the taxes of that period indicates that taxation must have been as heavy as the people could bear, and perhaps heavier than to-day.

The Mauryan taxes were greatly similar to those enumerated by Dowell as being used by the Romans. The following were the principal Roman taxes in use at different times and in different parts of the state: tributes from lands, poll taxes, income taxes on senators, tradesmen and others, taxes on successions, houses and animals, indirect taxes like duties on exports and imports, and taxes on commodities sold at auction or in the public market. With these may be compared land revenue, poll tax, income tax on prostitutes and others, taxes on houses and animals, tolls and octroi duties (perhaps customs duties also), and sales tax of the Mauryan period.

The variety of taxes is a compliment to Maurya financiers, for it must have been a great help in distributing equitably the burden of taxation, and incidentally in yielding the state great income, as more persons contributed to the public purse with less harm to their own interests.

A peculiar feature of Mauryan finance was the different forms of paying the taxes. Taxes were paid in gold, coin, cattle, grains, raw material, and personal service. This must have been of great convenience to the people, although somewhat embarrassing to the state. Some villages supplied soldiers in lieu of taxation, others supplied free labour, and still others dairy produce.[15] No doubt there were coins, and gold was widely used, but taxes were received in various

[14] Cf. *Kāmandaka*, iv; 8, 77–8.

[15] *Arth.*, Bk. II, ch. 35, *Samāhartā . . . grāmāgram parihārakamāyudhīyam dhānyapaśuhiraṇyakupyavishṭikara pratikaramidaṃ ētāvaditi nibandhayēt.*

forms. This feature, though common in olden days, is rarely to be found to-day.

A respectable revenue system in a modern state is expected to conform itself to certain canons of taxation, the first of which is the canon of convenience. It implies that a tax should be levied at the time and in the manner most convenient for the contributor to pay it, e.g. when he has the funds to make the payment. This principle holds good not only in the case of taxation, but with regard to every kind of revenue which the state gets from its subjects.

This canon was not new to the Mauryan financiers. Chāṇakya expresses this principle very picturesquely when he says: "Just as fruits are gathered from a garden as often as they become ripe, so revenue shall be collected as often as it becomes ripe. Collection of revenue or of fruits, when unripe, shall never be carried on, lest their source may be injured, causing immense trouble."[16] It clearly indicates that Chāṇakya was aware that collection of revenue must be made at times when the people have the capacity to pay.

Nor does it seem that the canon of economy was unknown in those days. Shortly, the maxim means that the tax should thus take out of the pockets of the people as little as possible over and above what it brings into the public treasury. That is to say, the cost of collection should be small and production and consumption should not be injuriously affected. "Thus a wise Collector-General," says Kauṭilya, "shall conduct the work of revenue collection, increasing the income and decreasing the expenditure."[17]

[16] *Arth.*, Bk. V, ch. 2:

Pakvam pakvamivārāmāt phalaṃ rājyādavāpnuyāt
Āmachchēdabhayādāmaṃ varjayet kōpakārakaṃ.

Gaṇapati Śāstri (*op. cit.*, vol. ii, p. 201) reads the third quarter of the verse as *ātmachchēdabhayādāmaṃ*, while Jolly has *āmachchēdabhayādāmaṃ*. Cf. *Kāmandaka*, v, 8, 83; *Śukranīti*, i, 420; iv, 2, 222–3; *Manu*, viii, 129, 139.

[17] *Arth.*, Bk. II, ch. 6. Jolly (*op. cit.*, vol. ii, p. 19) interprets it as "Restraining government servants." See also Gaṇapati Śāstri, *op. cit.*, i, p. 152.

Moreover, in a state where retrenchment of government servants was known,[18] it is but natural to expect this principle of economy in operation.

The other aspect of the principle of economy, viz. that production and consumption should not be injuriously affected, was perhaps not forgotten by the state which recognized that financial prosperity depended on public prosperity, abundance of harvest, and prosperity of commerce among other things,[19] and that people can be well off and commerce can flourish only when production and consumption are not hampered.

Adam Smith explains the canon of certainty in these words: "The tax which each individual is bound to pay ought to be certain and not arbitrary. The time of payment, the manner of payment, the quantity to be paid, ought all to be clear and plain to the contributor, and to every other person." The Mauryas were aware that uncertainty of any kind was greatly troublesome, to both the state and the subject. So they had fixed the amount of land revenue, water rate, and other kinds of payments. According to Kauṭilya, taxes on commodities intended for sale were to be prescribed once for all.[20] As regards the time of payment, collection of revenue at a season when people were unable to pay was forbidden because it injured the source and caused immense trouble.

If this principle is violated and the taxes to be paid are uncertain, then "every person subject to the tax is put more or less in the power of the tax-gatherer, who can either

[18] *Arth.*, Bk. II, ch. 6:

Ēvaṃ kuryātsamudayaṃ vṛiddhiṃ chāyasya darsayēt
Hnāśaṃvyayasyachaprājñaḥ sādhayēchcha viparyayaṃ.

[19] *Arth.*, Bk. II, ch. 8. *Sasyasampatpanyadbāhuḷyaṃ*. Cf. *Śāntiparva* lxxxviii, 15 *seq*; *Kāmandaka*, v, 8, 77–8, iv, 7, 48; *Śukranīti*, ii, 345–6, 351–2.

[20] *Arth.*, Bk. II, ch. 12, *Ēvaṃ sarvēshu paṇyēshu sthāpayēn mukhasamgrahaṃ*. Compare *Śukranīti*, iv, 2, 214: "Duties are to be levied on goods only once"—*Vāstujātasyaikavāraṃ śulkam grāhyaṃ paryantaḥ*.

aggravate the tax upon any obnoxious contributor, or extort by the terror of such aggravation, some present or perquisite to himself." To safeguard against this evil of over-collection by the revenue collectors, punishments were inflicted. "Whoever doubles the revenue, eats into the vitality of the country. If he brings in double the amount to the King, he shall, if the offence is small, be warned not to repeat the same; but if the offence be grave, he should proportionately be punished."[21] There were numerous officers to find out any mismanagement in revenue collection.

As for the principle of sufficiency or adequacy,[22] the revenue collected by the Mauryas appears to have been not only sufficient but much in excess of what was needed for the ordinary expenses of the state. In modern times the revenue is determined by the ordinary expenditure, and for extraordinary expenditure like war or famine, generally borrowing is largely resorted to. Balanced budgets are to-day much in fashion, and enormous continued surpluses are looked down on as bad finance. It was otherwise with the Mauryan financiers. Revenue was determined by expenditure including extraordinary expenditure which could be foreseen. As a precaution against wars, large surpluses were accumulated, and the people were not generally taxed much specially for war. Thus, in a state where surpluses were common,[23] the question of sufficiency of revenue does not at all arise.

The principle of variety means that because a particular tax or a few taxes tend to bear unjustly upon one class or two, it is necessary that there should be a variety of taxes so as to distribute the burden equitably. The principle

[21] *Arth.*, Bk. II, ch. 9, *Yassamudayam dviguṇamudbhāvayati sa janapadaṃ bhakshayati*, etc. Doubling the revenue must not be taken too literally, but must be understood to mean over-collection. Cf. *Śukranīti*, i, 617–18.

[22] Seligman (*Studies in Public Finance*, p. 131) terms this canon the principle of adequacy.

[23] *Infra*, pp. 134 *seq*.

source of revenue in the Mauryan days was no doubt land, but there were other sources of income also, e.g. taxes on commodities, octrois, tolls, customs duties, excise duties, sales and income taxes, etc. Thus the principle of variety, too, was recognized.

But how far the canon of equity was put into practice by the Mauryas cannot be determined.

CHAPTER II

CLASSIFICATION OF REVENUE HEADS

Kauṭilya's classifications—Modern classifications—Mauryan items of revenue under modern heads—Appendix—Some revenue terms: *vāstu, vāstuka, kara, rajjū,* and *chōrarajjū*

A CLEAR classification of revenue, as of expenditure, is important from the academical as well as the administrative standpoint; and it is indispensable for a correct and scientific understanding of finance. We shall, therefore, first note the classifications of revenue given by Kauṭilya, next consider present-day classifications, and then try to arrange the Mauryan heads of income under a modern classification, so that the ancient sources of revenue can be conveniently compared with the modern ones.

Kauṭilya mentions three different classifications of public income. The first is based upon the sources from which revenue is derived.[1]

1. FORTS (*durga*)[2]

This included revenue from the following sources:

Tolls, octrois, and perhaps customs duties (*śulka*).[3]
Fines (*daṇḍa*).
Weights and measures (*pautava*).[4]

---

[1] *Arth.*, Bk. II, ch. 6, *Samāhartā durgaṃ rāshtraṃ khaniṃ sētuṃ vanaṃ vrajam vaṇikpathaṃ chāvēkshēta.*

[2] *Durgaṃ* does not seem to mean only the capital as P. N. Bannerjea takes it in his *Public Administration of Ancient India*, p. 175. It probably denotes fairly big and perhaps fortified towns, e.g. the district towns, provincial capitals, and the like, where the same system of administration as in the capital, Pāṭalīputra, was perhaps instituted.

[3] This item and others following which are not explained in the footnotes in this chapter are discussed in detail in the book later on.

[4] This appears to be the revenue from the department of weights and measures in the form of charges for stamping, and thus authen-

City-Superintendent (*nāgarika*).[5]
Mint (*lakshaṇādhyaksha*).
Visa fees (*mudrādhyaksha*).
Excise from liquor (*surā*).
Slaughter of animals (*sunā*).[6]
Threads (*sūtra*).[7]
Oils (*taila*).
Ghee (*ghṛita*).[8]
Sugar (*kshāra*).[9]
State goldsmith (*sauvarṇikā*).[10]
Warehouse of merchandise (*paṇyasamsthā*).[11]
Prostitutes (*vēśyā*).
Taxes on houses and building sites (*vāstuka*).[12]
Guilds of artisans and handicraftsmen (*kāruśilpigaṇāḥ*).[13]

---

ticating the correctness of weights and measures used by private persons. *Arth.*, Bk. II, ch. 19. An income from this source, which, according to Seligman (*Studies in Public Finance*, p. 287), is a fee, exists in many of the French colonies. Or could the income mentioned by Kauṭilya be the same as the tax on weights mentioned in *Ep. Ind.* v, no. 9, and *South Indian Inscriptions*, ii, no. 22, and the *tulya-mēya* in *Ep. Ind.*, vii, no. 22? Kielhorn says that the technical meaning of *tulyamēya* is not certain, but that its exact translation is "things to be weighed and to be measured."

5 Shāma Śāstry (*Arth. Trans.*, p. 63) translates *nāgarika* as town clerk. This does not appear as good as the one adopted here and suggested by Jolly (vol. ii, p. 17) specially in view of the description of magistrates given by Megasthenes. Moreover, in *Arth.*, Bk. II, ch. 36, Shāma Śāstry himself translates *nāgarika* as city-superintendent. Cf. Bhaṭṭaswami's interpretation, *J.B.O.R.S.*, vol. xii, part 2, p. 205.

6 This was a sort of tax in kind whereby a certain proportion of animals captured by private persons was taken by the state.

7 This was perhaps income from the state department of weaving.

8 Gaṇapati Śāstri (*op. cit.*, i, p. 136) explains these as the value realized from their sale.

9 Gaṇapati Śāstri (*op. cit.*, i, p. 136) explains these as the value realized from their sale.

10 This appears to be the income obtained by the manufacture of gold and silver articles for private persons. See *Arth.*, Bk. II, ch. 14. Revenue from mint is separately enumerated,

11 Could this be a kind of charge for keeping private goods in the state warehouse? See Gaṇapati Śāstri (*op. cit.*, i, p. 136).

12 *Infra*, Appendix.

13 *Kāruśilpigaṇāḥ* appears to include mechanics, artisans, and artists. Apte (*Sans-Eng. Dic.*, p. 397) quotes the following verse to enumerate the occupations generally coming under this head:

Superintendent of gods (*dēvatādhyakshā*).[14]
Poll taxes on undesirable foreigners, i.e. *bāhirikas*.[15]

II. COUNTRY PARTS (*rāshṭra*)

This included:

Revenue from crown lands (*sītā*).
Land revenue (*bhāga*).
Bali.[16]
Kara.[17]
Merchants (*vaṇik*).[18]
Superintendent of rivers, ferries, boats, and ships (*nadīpalastaronāvaḥ*).[19]
Towns (*paṭṭaṇa*).[20]

Takshāścha tantravāyaścha nāpitō rajakastathā.
Pañchamaścharmakāraścha kāravaśśilpinōmatāḥ.

i.e. carpenters, weavers, barbers, the fifth class (?), cobblers, and artisans. Could the revenue from this source be a kind of fee for the recognition of the guilds, or for special privileges granted to them, like the "fines," licences, concessions, and franchises of mediaeval Europe? (*infra*, p. 94).

[14] It is not clear what income this was. This appears to have included a tax on people congregating, perhaps for worship, upon the appearance of a spirit. This tax was not unknown in ancient India (*infra*, p. 143). It may have included other items also. Could it indicate any kind of tax on the income of the temples given by the devotees or got from the temple property? It may be pointed out that in financial difficulties (*infra*, Chapter IX) temple property was sometimes confiscated. Could there have been in ordinary times any tax on the property?

[15] This appears to have been a kind of poll tax (*infra*, p. 99).

[16] *Infra*, p. 116.

[17] *Infra*, Appendix.

[18] It is not certain what this was, for there were many taxes which business men paid. Perhaps this refers to the trade taxes, sales tax, and the like.

[19] This included tolls and revenue from mercantile marine (*infra*, p. 125).

[20] It is uncertain what kind of revenue this was. Gaṇapati Śāstri, who alone attempts at some explanation of it, says, *paṭṭanaṃ alpanagaralabhyaṃ* (*op. cit.*, vol. i, p. 136), which explanation does not take us any further, for what was this income from small *nagara* or town? Could this be some kind of contribution from towns towards the imperial budget?

Pasture ground (*vivita*).[21]
Road cess[22] (*vartanī*).
Rajjū.[23]
Chorarajjū.[24]

III. MINES (*khani*)

This included:[25]

Gold.
Silver.
Diamonds.
Gems.
Pearls.
Corals.
Conch shells.
Metals.
Salt.
Other minerals extracted from plains and mountain slopes.

IV. IRRIGATION (*sētu*)[26]

This included revenue from:[27]

[21] This was perhaps some charge levied for the privilege of using the pasture grounds for grazing the cattle.

[22] *Infra*, pp. 77 and 90.

[23] *Infra*, Appendix.

[24] *Ibid.*

[25] *Arth.*, Bk. II, ch. 6, *Suvarṇarajatamaṇimuktāpravāḷaśaṅkhalōhalavaṇabhūmiprastararasadhātavaḥ.*

[26] Shāma Śāstry (*Arth. Trans.*, p. 63) translates the word as buildings and gardens, and Gaṇapati Śāstri (*op. cit.*, vol. i, p. 137) interprets it as *pushpavāṭādayaḥ*, i.e. flower gardens and the like, while Kauṭilya himself explains it (*Arth.*, Bk. III, ch. 8), though in a different connection, as *karṇakilāyāsasambandhō anugṛiham sētuḥ*, i.e. the fastening of the roof of a house to the transverse beams by means of iron bolts is called (*sētuḥ*). All these interpretations (including Kauṭilya's own) appear unsuited here. The details enumerated under this head deal only with cultivation. Neither buildings nor any other public work (as Bannerjea interprets the word in his *Public Administration in Ancient India*, p. 175) is mentioned, nor is it confined to gardens only, while the details carefully omit dry lands. It appears, therefore, better to interpret it as revenue from irrigation, which though an important source of income detailed by Kauṭilya elsewhere has not been mentioned anywhere in this classification.

[27] *Arth.*, Bk. II, ch. 6, *Pushpaphalavātashaṇḍakēdāramūlavāpaḥ sētuḥ.*

Flower gardens.
Fruit gardens.
Vegetable gardens.
Wet field lands.
Lands where crops are grown by sowing roots for seed (e.g. sugar-cane).

V. FORESTS (*vana*)

The income from this source[28] was derived from:

Game forests.
Timber forests.
Elephant forests.

VI. HERDS (*vraja*)[29]

This included:[30]

Cows.
Buffaloes.
Goats.
Sheep.
Asses.
Camels.
Horses.
Mules.

VII. ROAD OF TRAFFIC (*vaṇikpatha*)

Land and waterways (*sthalapathō vāripathaseha*).

Another Classification of Revenue is as follows:[31]

[28] *Arth.* Bk. II, ch. 6. *Paśumṛigadravyahastivanaparigrahō vanaṃ.* Compare *Vishṇu,* iii, 16, *nāgavana. Infra,* p. 120.

[29] Bannerjea (*op. cit.*, p. 175) takes *vraja* to mean pasture lands. This appears to be incorrect because income from pasture lands has already been mentioned under "country parts." The revenue from herds was probably in the shape of the yield of cows and buffaloes and the like, and in the increase in the number of camels, horses, etc., which were used for military purposes among others.

[30] *Arth.*, Bk. II, ch. 6. *Gōmahishamajāvikaṃ kharōshṭramaśvās-vatarāścha vrajaḥ.*

[31] *Arth.*, Bk. II, ch. 6.

(1) Capital (*mūla*).[32]
(2) Share (*bhāga*).[33]
(3) Premia (*vyāji*).[34]
(4) *Parigha* (?).[35]
(5) Fixed taxes (*klṛipta*).
(6) Premium on coins (*rūpika*).
(7) Fines (*atyaya*).

Neither of these classifications is exhaustive. Many kinds of revenue mentioned in the *Arthaśāstra* cannot be classed under these heads; for instance, extraordinary income like presents and treasure troves.

[32] *Mūla* appears to be the value of the output—for example, of state monopolies like mining—of perhaps the yield of crown lands, and of state undertakings like manufactures. Compare Bhaṭṭaswāmi's interpretation, *J.B.O.R.S.*, vol. xi, p. 58. Gaṇapati Śāstri (*op. cit.*, i, p. 137) thinks that *mūla* is the value realized by the sale of grains, fruits, and the like. Cf. *Śukranīti*, ii, 717.

[33] *Bhāga* is the share in kind paid to the state specially land revenue. It is improbable that other payments in kind are also included, e.g. imported salt paid one-sixth portion to the king (*Arth.*, Bk. II, ch. 12, *Āgantulavaṇam shaḍbhāgaṃ dadyāt*). Here *bhāga* appears to be used in the restricted technical sense denoting land revenue.

[34] *Vyāji* is the premium in kind or in cash realized on account of the difference between the royal and market measures and weights. Kauṭilya explains the term thus, *vikrayē paṇyānām arghavṛiddhirūpaja mānōnmānaviśēshō vyāji*. See Bhaṭṭaswāmi's interpretation of the word (*Bhaṭṭaswāmi*, f. 34). In view of these explanations Jolly (*op. cit.*, ii, pp. 18, 23) does not appear to be correct in regarding it as "the name of a certain tax." Also see *Arth.*, Bk. II, ch. 15, and *infra*, Chapter VII.

[35] The nature of this source of revenue is uncertain. Bhaṭṭaswāmi the commentator is himself doubtful (*Bhaṭṭaswāmi*, f. 34). He says: *parighaḥ pārīkshikamiti kēchit. Dhātusamuththitānām tadjanatakarmāntēshu prayōgallabdhaviśēsha ityapare.* Shāma Śāstry follows, in *Arth. Trans.*, p. 97, the first interpretation and regards *parigha* as the testing charge of coins, while he merely notes the second explanation that it was the profit realized by the manufacture of goods from minerals. But in *ibid.*, Preface, p. xxii, he translates it as a tax. Jolly also explains it as the name of a certain tax, though he does not explain what kind of a tax it was (*op. cit.*, ii, p. 18). Sohrabji suggests if *parigha* could mean investment (*Notes*, p. 11). According to Gaṇapati Śāstri it means ferry dues—*ātaradravyam* (*op. cit.*, i, p. 137); while the same scholar interprets the word elsewhere (*op. cit*, i, p. 208) as *pārīkshikam*.

The Third Classification is as follows:[36]

I. CURRENT (*vartamānaḥ*), i.e. receipts from day to day.[37]

[36] *Arth.*, Bk. II, ch. 6.

[37] Śukra also (ii, 645 ff.) suggests four classifications:

(i) A. Last year's surplus.
  B. Current receipts.

(ii) A. Annual.
  B. Monthly.
  C. Daily.

(iii) A. New.
  B. Old.

(iv) A. *Belonging to others.*
  1. Deposits (*aupanidhika*).
  2. Gifts (*yāchita*).
  3. Loans (*auttamarṇika*).

 B. *Wealth with unknown owners*, i.e. (*asvāmika*). Gems and jewels found in street.

 C. *Belonging to oneself.*
  1. Normal (*sāhajika*), i.e. regularly increasing daily, monthly, or yearly—non-quasi economic receipts according to B. K. Sarkar (*Śukranīti Trans.*, p. 95).
   (*a*) *Terrestrial* (*pārthiva*), i.e. coming from land.
    Natural waters.
    Artificial waters.
    Cities.
   (*b*) *Non-terrestrial* (*itara*).
    Śulka.
    Fines (*daṇḍa*).
    Royalties on mines (*ākara*).
    Presents and contributions.

  2. *Adhika* (increase), i.e. quasi-economic receipts.
   (*a*) *Terrestrial.*
    Natural waters.
    Artificial waters.
    Villages.
    Cities.
   (*b*) *Non-terrestrial.*
    Duties.
    Fines.
    Royalties from mines.
    Presents and contributions, etc.

II. LAST BALANCE

This includes:

(*a*) Balance of previous year (*paramasamvatsarika*).
(*b*) Whatever is in the hands of others (*paraprachāra*).[38]
(*c*) Whatever has changed hands (*sankrānta*).

III. ACCIDENTAL (*anyajāta*)[39]

This consists of:

(*a*) Property lost and forgotten by others (*nashṭaprasmṛitam*).
(*b*) Fines on government servants (*ayuktadaṇḍaḥ*).
(*c*) Excess profits tax (*pārśvam*).
(*d*) Compensation for damage (*pārihīṇikam*).[40]
(*e*) Presents (*aupayānikam*).
(*f*) Unclaimed property (*ḍamaragatasvamaputrakaṃ*).[41]
(*g*) Treasure trove (*nidhiḥ*).

Let us now briefly consider modern classifications of revenue. "Differing classifications of public revenue have been almost as numerous as the writers who have made them."[42] We shall, however, note those given by Adams[43] and Seligman.[44]

[38] This may be government revenue not yet credited to the state. Jolly, however, suggests (*op. cit.*, ii, p. 18) that it may be "what has been brought forward from last year." This suggestion appears incorrect as the balance of a previous year is already mentioned. Sohrabji accepts Shāma Śāstry's translation (which is followed here) and asks if it could mean arrears (*op. cit.*, p. 12).

[39] Accidental revenue (*anyajāta*) is also mentioned in *Arth.*, Bk. II, ch. 15. The details enumerated, e.g. presents, unclaimed property, and the like, are often referred to in the *Arthaśāstra*. These, however, will be discussed in detail later on.

[40] The interpretation of Jolly (*op. cit.*, ii, p. 18) as "lost property" is unacceptable because it has been already mentioned under the name *nashṭaprasmṛitam*. Sohrabji (*op. cit.*, p. 12) suggests if it could mean confiscation. *Infra*, p. 130.

[41] Jolly (*op. cit.*, ii, p. 18) translates *ḍamaragatasvaṃ* as "the property of one who has fled in a riot (or in times of war)." Could this refer to the property of a rebel or coward who does not stand by the state? *Infra*, p. 130.

[42] Ely and Wicker, *Elementary Principles of Economics*, p. 361.

[43] *Science of Finance*, pp. 219 ff.

[44] *Essays in Taxation*, ch. xiv.

H. C. Adams divides revenue into three groups:

I. *Direct Revenue.*
(i) Public domains.
(ii) Public industries.
(iii) Gratuities, gifts, and treasure troves.
(iv) Confiscation and indemnities.

II. *Derivative Revenue.*
(i) Taxes.
(ii) Fees, assessments, fines, and penalties.

III. *Anticipatory Revenue.*
(i) Sales of bonds and other forms of commercial credit.
(ii) Treasury notes.

E. R. A. Seligman's classification[45] is as follows:

1. Gratuitous, e.g. gifts.
2. Contractual public properties and industry, e.g. prices.
3. Compulsory:
   (i) Eminent domain-expropriation.
   (ii) Penal power-fines and penalties.
   (iii) Taxing power:
      (*a*) Fees.
      (*b*) Special assessments.
      (*c*) Taxes.

We shall now place side by side classified modern Indian revenue heads, with the Mauryan incomes classified under similar heads:

MODERN INDIAN REVENUE HEADS[46]	MAURYAN REVENUE UNDER MODERN HEADS
A. Tax Revenue.	*A. Tax Revenue.*
I. *Direct.*	I. *Direct.*
Land revenue.	Land revenue.
Income tax.	Various taxes, e.g. income tax, poll tax, etc.
Provincial rates.	
Tributes from state.	

[45] *Essays in Taxation*, ch. xiv, p. 430.
[46] Shirras, *Science of Public Finance*, p. 632.

MODERN INDIAN REVENUE HEADS (*cont.*)	MAURYAN REVENUE UNDER MODERN HEADS (*cont.*)
A. Tax Revenue (cont.).	*A. Tax Revenue* (cont.).
II. *Indirect.*	II. *Indirect.*
Opium.	Salt.
Salt.	Excise.
Excise.	Customs, Tolls, Octrois.
Stamps.	
Registration.	
Customs.	
B. Non-tax Revenue.	*B. Non-tax Revenue.*
III. *Government or public undertakings.*	III. *Government undertakings.*
Railways.	Mercantile marine.
Irrigation.	Irrigation.
Other public works.	Mines.
Posts and telegraphs.	Manufactories.
Mint.	Trading.
Forests.	Mint.
Stationery and printing.	Forests.
Scientific and miscellaneous.	Crown lands.
IV. *Other Sources.*	IV. *Other Sources.*
Interest.	Treasure troves.
Military receipts.	Compensations.
Exchange.	Unclaimed property, etc.
Superannuation.	Miscellaneous.
Miscellaneous.	

APPENDIX

SOME REVENUE TERMS

IN Sanskrit treatises on Government, specially in the Kauṭilīya *Arthaśāstra*, there are some revenue terms the exact significance of which is by no means clear. An attempt has been made below to explain a few such words, viz. *vāstuka*, *kara*, *rajjū*, and *chōrarajjū*.

Vāstuka

Under the head *durga*[1] is mentioned a source of revenue called *vāstuka*, which word has been translated by Shāma Śāstry[2] as building sites, and explained by Gaṇapati Śāstri[3] as *āvasathanirmātārastakshādayaḥ*.

Before determining what kind of income it was, we shall ascertain the meaning of the word, and also of the word *vāstu*, with which *vāstuka* is very closely connected; for it is by no means easy to know what the words exactly signify.

Vāstu has been defined by Kauṭilya[4] as *gṛiham kshētra-mārāmassētubandhastaṭākamādhārō vā vāstuḥ*, i.e. "Houses, fields, gardens, buildings of any kind [*sētubandhaḥ*], lakes, and tanks are each called *vāstu*."[5] But Kauṭilya himself appears to use the word in various senses, often with a restricted meaning. In the passage[6] *kṛishṭākṛishṭasthala-kēdārārāmashaṇḍavāṭavanavāstuchaityadēvagṛiha*, etc., *vāstu* evidently stands for houses only, as the irrigation works, fields, and gardens mentioned in Kauṭilya's definition of

[1] *Arth.*, Bk. II, ch. 6.

[2] *Arth. Trans.*, p. 63.

[3] *Op. cit.*, i, p. 136.

[4] *Arth.*, Bk. III, ch. 8.

[5] *Arth. Trans.*, p. 204. As regards the word *sētubandhaḥ*, Jolly (*op. cit.*, ii, p. 37) says that it may denote irrigation works here as it is followed by *taṭāka* and *ādhārō*. This interpretation appears more correct than Shāma Śāstry's, which is quoted above.

[6] *Arth.*, Bk. II, ch. 35. Shāma Śāstry, in his translation, p. 173, appears to omit the word *vāstu*.

vāstu are separately enumerated. Again, the word is used in this restricted sense of house in the chapter on "Sale without ownership."[7] It is also used in the sense of fields.[8] It denotes a site in the passage *vāstukapraśastavāstuni.*[9] Likewise in *vāstuvibhāgaḥ,*[10] i.e. demarcation of ground.

The same kind of difficulty is evident as regards *vāstuka.*[11] Kauṭilya says, *Vāstukapraśastē dēśē,* and Shāma Śāstry translates[12] it, "On a site naturally fitted for that purpose." Jolly's translation[13] is very much the same, but he adds, "Or *vāstuka* may denote the art of building like *vāstuvidyā,* the meaning being that the harem should be erected on a site recommended by the rules of architecture." This suggestion of Jolly finds support in the chapter entitled *Gṛihavāstuka,*[14] which deals with the rules of construction of houses. But the word *vāstuka* is also used in the sense of house or building.[15] For instance, in the passage[16] *sarvavāstukayōḥ prākshiptakayōrvā śālayōḥ kishkurantarikā tripadī vā,* it means,[17] "Between any two houses or between the extended portions of any two houses, the intervening space shall be 4 *padas* or 3 *padas.*" Again, sometimes the word is so used as to include all the items mentioned in

[7] *Arth.,* Bk. III, ch. 16, *Vimśativarshōpēkshitam anuvasitam vāstunānuyuñjīta. Jñātayaśśrōtriyāḥpāshaṇḍā vā rājñāmasannidhau paravāstushu vivasanto na bhōgēna harēyuḥ.* The phrase *vāstuvikrayaḥ* in the closing sentence in Bk. III, ch. 9, stands for sale of buildings, while, as the title of the chapter, it includes, if we assume that it is used to denote all the items in the chapter and not that it is only a short heading, as Shāma Śāstry obviously and correctly also takes it in his translation (title of ch. 9 in Bk. III), all the items found in the definition of *vāstu.* In the passage *pāṃsuviśēshēṇa vāstuchchhidraṃ vā pūrayēt* (Bk. II, ch .3), *vāstu* stands for ramparts, i.e. building.

[8] *Arth.,* Bk. III, ch. 9.

[9] *Arth.,* Bk. X, ch. 1. Here *vāstu* stands in the place of *dēśa* in the passage *vāstukapraśastē dēśē* in Bk. II, ch. 3.

[10] *Arth.,* Bk. II, ch. 4.

[11] *Arth.,* Bk. II, ch. 3, and Bk. I, ch. 20.

[12] *Arth. Trans.,* p. 42.

[13] Jolly's Edition, ii, p. 12.

[14] *Arth.,* Bk. III, ch. 8.

[15] *Ibid.* Also Bk. II, ch. 3.

[16] *Arth.,* Bk. III, ch. 8.

[17] *Arth. Trans.,* p. 205.

Kauṭilya's definition of *vāstu*. For example, in the passage while concluding some chapters,[18] *iti dharmasthīyē vāstukē vāstuvikrayaḥ*. The chapters deal with houses, fields, irrigation works, and the like.

In the *Jātakas*,[19] *vatthu* (*vāstu*) denotes site. Likewise, in the Damodarpur copperplate inscription of the fifth century after Christ,[20] *vāstu* is used in the same sense. It says: "Application had been properly made (by him) for *vāstu* [land] to be given to him in the neighbourhood of those cultivated lands for the purpose of building temples and store-rooms."

In the light of the foregoing discussion, it may be perhaps not incorrect to take *vāstu* to mean sites, and *vāstuka*, house or building.[21]

What, then, is the revenue from *vāstuka*? Even accepting Kauṭilya's definition of *vāstu* as including houses, fields, and gardens and irrigation works, we find that the mention of revenue from *vāstuka* leads us to take it as buildings and sites; for income from land is mentioned under country parts and that from irrigation under *sētu*. Further revenue from land and irrigation cannot be expected from forts. Therefore the income from *vāstuka* appears to be from houses and sites.

Next arises another question: Of what particular kind was this income? The revenue from houses and sites may take various forms. It may denote revenue from letting out buildings and sites owned by the state. This suggestion arises because a state which owned lands, mines, and manufactories—in short, was itself a private capitalist—may have owned houses and leased them out, even as it

[18] *Arth.*, Bk. III, chs. 10 and 11.

[19] *Jātaka*, no. 257.

[20] *Ep. Ind.*, xv, no. 7 (4).

[21] According to Monier-Williams' *Sans.-Eng. Dict.*, p. 908, *vāstu* means "the site or foundation of a house, ground suitable for building a house, a building place, building ground, site, ground, a house habitation, abode, region, a kind of vegetable [*vāstuka*]." *Vāstuka* is explained as the potherb *Chenopodium album.*

did its ships and boats. Moreover, a similar instance is found in ancient Athens,[22] where the state owned houses which it leased out to private persons.

Or it may denote the value realized from the sale of government houses and sites, just as in modern days states and municipalities do sell building sites.

A third alternative is that it may be in the nature of a tax on the sale or transfer of private houses and sites. This finds some support in the fact that the Mauryan state actually levied a tax on the sale of articles,[23] and also on the sale of land.[24] It would, therefore, be nothing uncommon to find one on the sale of houses and sites.

But the greatest probability appears to be in favour of the last alternative, viz. that it was a house tax like the inhabited house duty of England and a tax on building sites as is common in modern days. This suggestion finds support in the *Śukranīti* and the later inscriptions. Śukra observes that the king should receive taxes from houses and abodes[25] as from lands and from shopkeepers.[26] Taxes on houses and shops are mentioned in the inscriptions. The Bankarpur inscription of Sōmēśvaradēva I of A.D. 1055[27] mentions house taxes along with petty taxes, fines, etc. An inscription from Hottur (A.D. 1064)[28] mentions the grant of a tax of a *paṇa* and a quarter on the . . . house belonging to the magistracy of Poṭṭiyūr and the petty (?) tax on houses under the seigniorial authority. Again, the Kyasanur inscription of Nityavarsha Amōghavarsha of A.D. 970[29] says: "For a *mettal* (the tax is to be) four *damma*, for an . . . three,

[22] Boeckh, *The Public Economy of the Athenians*, p. 140.

[23] *Arth.*, Bk. II, ch. 22.

[24] *Arth.*, Bk. III, ch. 9.

[25] *Śukranīti*, iv, 2, 256, *Gṛihādyādhārabhūśulkaṃ*. B. K. Sarkar translates *bhūśulkaṃ* as rent (*Śukranīti Trans.*, p. 149), but it appears better to take it as tax.

[26] *Śukranīti*, iv, 2, 257, *Tathāchapaṇikēbhyastu paṇyabhūśulkamāharēt*. Here Sarkar translates *bhūśulkam* as land tax.

[27] *Ep. Ind.*, xiii, no. 14.

[28] *Ep. Ind.*, xvi, no. 11.

[29] *Ep. Ind.*, xvi, no. 21.

for a house two, the *damma* in houses (is to be) one gold." The house and shop taxes are also mentioned in the Arthuna inscription of the Paramāra Chāmuṇḍarāja of A.D. 1079.[30]

A rather doubtful piece of evidence is found in the *Arthaśāstra* itself. Kauṭilya says[31] that one of the duties of the *gōpa* was to number the houses as tax-paying (*karada*) and non-tax-paying, and to collect from each house gold, free labour, *śulka* (which we shall interpret not as toll but as tax), and fines. This applied to the country as well as the city. It suggests that these may have been taxes on houses. But the point of doubt is that while *vāstukaṃ* is mentioned under forts only and not under country parts, this passage from Kauṭilya refers to the country parts also, and would imply that there was the house tax in the country also.

However, it appears that *vāstukaṃ* is the revenue from taxes on houses, and perhaps on building sites also.

Kara

The correct interpretation of the word *kara* is very important, specially for a true understanding of the question of land ownership because of the frequent use of the word in connection with land.

In the *Arthaśāstra* the word appears to have been used in different senses, one of which at least denotes a particular tax. This use is found in the enumeration of *kara* as a particular form of revenue.[32] Shāma Śāstry interprets the word in one place[33] as "taxes paid in money," while in

30 *Ep. Ind.*, xiv, no. 21. This inscription says: "Under this constitution there was assigned on every house of the whole population a *dramma*, on the gambling (house) two *rūpakas*." Also see *Ep. Ind.*, xix, no. 4, where a corporation of *Vīra-Baṇajigas* levies house and shop taxes and assigns them to two temples. See also *Ep. Ind.*, v, no. 9, where a tax on residence within the village is mentioned.

31 *Arth.*, Bk. II, ch. 35, *Gṛihāṇāñcha karadākaradasaṅkhyānēna*, etc.

32 *Arth.*, Bk. II, chs. 6 and 15.

33 *J.B.O.R.S.*, vol. xi, part 3, pp. 83–4, *Karaḥ prativarshadēyaḥ, bhādrapadika vāsantikādyam pādāvam.*

another,[34] where the same word is used in the same sense, translates it as "taxes or subsidies that are paid by vassal kings and others," perhaps on an interpretation of commentator Bhaṭṭaswāmi's explanation of the word as *vāsantika* and *bhādrapādika.*

The first interpretation cannot be accepted, although the word has that meaning also,[35] because it implies that the other items of income mentioned along with *kara* were in kind. But it is highly probable that the revenue from merchants and the road cess, as well as the *piṇḍakara* and the *utsaṅga,* were in money. The second interpretation not only contradicts the first, but appears to be an uncommon use of the word.

Gaṇapati Śāstri[36] is at least consistent in his explanation that *kara* is *phalavṛikshādisambandham rājadēyam.* This meaning appears quite new to the word *kara.*

The difficulty in the interpretation of the word is to a certain extent due to Kauṭilya himself. He seems to use the term in various contexts. As remarked above, in Bk. II, chs. 6 and 15, he mentions it as a distinct source of revenue coming from country parts (*rāshṭra*), along with *sītā* (income from crown lands) and *bhāga* (land revenue) and other items. This clearly indicates that not only was *kara* a particular tax and not the general name for tax, but also that it was an income from country parts only. Were it the name for taxes paid in money, as Shāma Śāstry contends, it ought to have been mentioned under forts also, where a host of taxes in money is found.

However, when Kauṭilya says[37] *karadēbhyaḥ kṛitakshētrāṇyaikapurushikāṇi prayachchhēt,* the *karadas* referred to appear to be the crown tenants, and *kara* therefore denotes *sītā.*[38]

[34] *J.B.O.R.S.*, vol. xi, part 3, p. 109.

[35] *Vide* the interpretations of *Manu*, viii, 307, by Mēdhātithi and Sarvajñanārāyaṇa (*Mandalik*, vol. ii, p. 1057).

[36] *Op. cit.*, i, pp. 136, 230.

[37] *Arth.*, Bk. II, ch. 1.

[38] Gaṇapati Śāstri (*op. cit.*, vol. i, p. 111) takes it as the king's share (*rājabhāga*). When in the same chapter (*Arth.*, Bk. II, ch. 1)

In Bk. III, ch. 10, which deals with the alienation of lands, we find *karadāḥ karadēshvādhānam vikrayam vā kuryuḥ brahmadēyikā brahmadēyikēshu*, etc. This perhaps refers to all lands other than crown lands.[39] If it refers to all lands, as it does, *kara* obviously indicates *bhāga*, though it is probable that other taxes also are included, because of the succeeding reference to tax-free villages and to the *brahmadēya* lands which were exempt from all taxes.

Again, in the passage *gṛihāṇāñcha karadākarada saṅkhyānēna*,[40] etc., *kara* may have reference to taxes in money.

Another use of the word *kara* is found when the king is said to protect agriculture from *daṇḍavishṭikarābādhaiḥ*.[41] This protection obviously extended to all agriculture and both crown and "private" lands. *Kara* would, therefore, include *sītā* as well as *bhāga*. But the use of *kara* in Bk. II, chs. 6 and 15, in the particular sense clearly shows that there at least neither *bhāga* nor *sītā* is denoted by the word, for they are separately enumerated.

Lastly, when *brahmadēya* lands are referred to as *akaradāḥ*, *kara* seems to denote all kinds of taxes.

This confusion in the use of the term gets confirmed by its employment in Manu and the inscriptions. Manu says,[42] *yōrakshanbalamādhattē karam śulkam cha pārthivaḥ*. *Kara* excludes *śulka* and *bali*. Manu's commentators[43] do not agree on the meaning of the term in the foregoing connection. According to Mēdhātithi, *kara* denotes *dravyādānam*,

brahmadēya lands are *adaṇḍakarāṇi*, the *kara* included, among other taxes, *sītā*; if, as it is contended, though incorrectly, the second book deals with crown lands only, then the *brahmadēya* lands would be only crown lands.

39 If crown lands are included, it would imply that even the mere tenant-cultivator had the right of alienation. This is contradicted by the passage quoted above (Bk. II, ch. 1), where lands are said to be leased not only for life, and, moreover, is opposed to common sense that a person who merely cultivates another's land could alienate it.

40 *Arth.*, Bk. II, ch. 35.

41 *Arth.*, Bk. II, ch. 1.

42 *Manu*, viii, 307.

43 *Mandalik*, vol. ii, pp. 1056–7.

and according to Sarvajñanārāyaṇa it means *tadvat* [i.e. *dhānyādibhagavat*] *bhūminiyatam dēyaṃ hiraṇyaṃ*. Rāghavānanda regards it as given monthly by villagers (*grāmavāsi*), while Rāmachandra explains it as *gulmadāyikaṃ*. These interpretations are not supported by Manu's own explanation. "Let the king make the common inhabitants of his realm who live by traffic pay annually some trifle which is called a tax (*kara*)."[44]

In the Girnar[45] inscription, Rudradāman's treasury is said to have been filled by *baliśulkabhāgaiḥ* "tributes [*bali*], toll [*śulka*], and shares," while the dam is said to have been built without oppressing the people with *kara*, forced labour (*vishṭi*), and benevolences. The use of *bali* in one place and *kara* in another seems to indicate that both cannot stand for tax in general.[46]

In the Gaya copperplate of Samudragupta[47] it is mentioned that the tax-paying cultivators and artisans should not be allowed to settle in a certain gift village. The mention of artisans as tax-paying indicates that *kara* is used to denote all the taxes, including those paid by the cultivator as well as the artisans. Likewise, in the Chammak copperplate of Pravarasēna,[48] *akaradāyi* denotes taxes in general, but the details of remissions enumerated in the grant include contributions other than taxes. In another inscription[49] *kara* stands for all kinds of contributions other than land revenue (*bhāga*) and *bhōga* (?), and yet in another[50] it excludes *śulka*, *bhāga*, *bhōga*, and *hiraṇya* (? gold).[51]

[44] *Manu*, vii, 137, *Yatkiñchidapivarshasya dāpayētkarasajñitam; vyavahārēṇa jīvantām rajā rāshṭrē pṛithagjanaṃ*. Compare the interpretations of Mēdhātithi, Sarvajñanārāyaṇa Kulluka, Rāghavānanda, Nandana, and Rāmachandra. *Mandalik*, vol. ii, pp. 820–1.

[45] *Ep. Ind.*, viii, no. 6.

[46] In this sense the word is used in *Ep. Ind.*, xiv, no. 27, and xv, no. 1, and some others.

[47] *Gupta Inscriptions*, no. 60.

[48] *Gupta Inscriptions*, no. 55.

[49] *Gupta Inscriptions*, no. 26.

[50] *Gupta Inscriptions*, nos. 27 and 28.

[51] Also see *Ep. Ind.*, i, no. 11, *Bhāgabhōgakarahiraṇyādi*. Kielhorn (*Ep. Ind.*, vii, no. 22) translates *karahiraṇya* as "payments

In the Khalimpur plate of Dharmapāladēva,[52] Kielhorn takes *kara* as "payments in money," because he interprets *piṇḍaka* as "payments in kind."

The *prākṛit* grant of the Pallava king, Śivaskandavarman,[53] appears to use the word *kara* in two different senses. It says, "*chilerekakodumkavaṭṭakam akarayollakavinesikhaṭṭāvāsam adūdhadadhigahanam araṭṭhasamvinayikam alonagulachchōbhaṃ akaraveṭṭhikonjallam*," etc., and this is translated by Bühler thus:[54] ". . . this garden in *Chillerakakodumka* which belongs to brahmans (is to be) *free from taxes* . . . free from the taking of sweet and sour milk, free from all troubles about salt and sugar, *free from taxes*, forced labour . . . free from the taking of oxen in succession, free from the taking of grass and wood, free from the taking of vegetable and flowers," etc.

Bühler's translation of *kara* in both places as tax appears incorrect. For if the word were intended to indicate tax in general there would have been no necessity for using it twice. Moreover, *kara* is enumerated along with other taxes, e.g. those on oxen, grass, wood, etc. Therefore it seems that the word is used in two senses—probably the first *kara* stands for tax in general, while the second denotes a particular tax, perhaps like the one mentioned by Kauṭilya; or it may even denote the taxes in money if the taxes on oxen and the like were, as is quite possible, in kind.

in money, "evidently taking *kara* by itself simply as "tax," just as Barnett has taken *karadhanaṃ* (*Ep. Ind.*, xiii, no. 23), while in *Ep. Ind.*, xii, no. 8, Rādhāgovinda Basak interprets the same phrase as "*kara and hiraṇya* tributes," taking the two as separate tributes. Basak's interpretation is supported by *Ep. Ind.*, xvi, no. 2, where instead of *karahiraṇyādi* is found *bhāgabhōgapaśuhiraṇyakaraśulkādi*. This interchange of the words, the use of *hiraṇyaṃ* instead of *hiraṇya*, and the mention of the two terms along with (tax on) cattle (*paśu*) and *śulka*, appear to confirm that *hiraṇya* and *kara* are two different contributions and that, as *śulka* and perhaps *hiraṇya* also were in money, Kara does not refer to money taxes but only to a particular kind of tax. It is, however, uncertain if *hiraṇya* indicates royalty on mining.

[52] *Ep. Ind.*, iv, no. 34, *Samuchita karapiṇḍakādi sarvapratyāyōpanayaḥ*. See Kielhorn's explanation of *piṇḍaka*.

[53] *Ep. Ind.* i, no. 1.

[54] *Ibid.*, pp. 8–9.

The one peculiar use of *kara* is found in the sixth Pithapuram plate of Vīrachōḍa,[55] where it appears to have been used in the sense of land revenue. The passage "*pratisamvatsara atra pratibhāgaṃ sārdhaṃ nishkam ka* [*ram*] *parikalpya*," etc., is translated by H. Krishna Sastri as "having fixed an annual assessment of one and a half *nishka* on each of these shares." Perhaps a like usage is found in the Palitānā plate No. 1 of Dhruvasēna I,[56] which mentions the grant of "the *karada* field (formerly) enjoyed by the brahman, Visākha." Sten Konow[57] explains that "karada perhaps means tribute-paying." Thus in this inscription also *kara* appears to denote land revenue.

Thus even in the inscriptions the word is used in different senses, and the uses in the *Arthaśāstra* find support in one or the other of the edicts. In short, as remarked above, in *Arth.*, Bk. II, chs. 6 and 15, it is almost certain that *kara* is a particular tax. The commentator explains it as taxes collected annually in the months of *Bhādrapada* (April and May) or *Vasanta* (August and September). But the exact nature of this tax is not known.

Rajjū and Chōrarajjū

These are mentioned[58] as sources of revenue from country parts (*rāshṭra*). Great difficulty has been felt in the correct interpretation of these words, especially of *rajjū*. Shāma Śāstry translates[59] *rajjū* as "ropes," and writes in the footnote that the precise meaning of the word is not known. Jolly[60] writes that "the *rajjūs* by name correspond to the officials in the Aśōka inscriptions whose functions are rather those of the *Sthānikas* of the *Arthaśāstra*." Gaṇapati Śāstri[61] says, "*rajjūḥ vishayapālādēyaṃ ityāhuḥ*," i.e. the revenue from district officers (*vishayapāla*).

The real explanation of *rajjū* is indicated in the *Artha*-

[55] *Ep. Ind.*, v, no. 10.
[56] *Ep. Ind.*, xi, no. 9.
[57] *Ep. Ind.*, xi, p. 111.
[58] *Arth.*, Bk. II, ch. 6.
[59] *Arth. Trans.*, p. 63.
[60] *Op. cit.*, ii, p. 17.
[61] *Op. cit.*, i, p. 136.

śāstra itself. *Rajjū* is mentioned[62] as a length used for measuring lands. Its length is given as follows:

6 *kamas* or 192 *aṅgulas* = 1 *daṇḍa* used in measuring such lands as are gifted to the brahmans.
10 *daṇḍas* = 1 *rajjū*.
2 *rajjūs* = 1 *pandesa* (square measure).
3 *rajjūs* = 1 *nivartana* (square measure).
The same 3 *rajjūs* plus two *daṇḍas* on one side only = 1 *bāhu* (arm).
10 *dhanas* = 1 *goruta*.
4 quarters = 1 *yōjana*.

Thus are the lineal and square measures dealt with. It is thus evident that *rajjū* was a standard of measure. Shāma Śāstry[63] calculates 96 *aṅgulas* as equal to 6 feet, and this gives the following measurements:

Each *aṅgula* is equal to three-quarters of an inch.
1 *daṇḍa* or 196 *aṅgulas* are equal to 12 feet.
10 *daṇḍas* or a *rajjū* is equal to 120 feet.

Each *rajjū* therefore denotes a length of 120 feet.[64]

The exact length of the *rajjū*, however, does not matter for the discussion. It is enough to know that it was a land measure. This conclusion is supported by the fact that in the *Kurudhammajātaka*[65] is mentioned an officer called *rajjū gāhaka amacco*, who appears to be the settlement officer and who measured land by means of a cord (*rajjū*). Moreover, the *rajjukas*,[66] who were officers of a very high grade under Aśōka, appear to have been settlement officers. Further, Strabo has perhaps the *rajjukas* in view when he speaks of

[62] *Arth.*, Bk. II, ch. 20.
[63] *Arth. Trans.*, p. 128, footnote.
[64] C. V. Vaidya (*Medieval India*, vol. i, p. 133), however, gives a different length. He calculates the *nivartana* as equal to 120 cubits = 180 feet = 60 yards. The *rajjū*, then, would be 60 feet or 20 yards, i.e. half of what Shāma Śāstry gives.
[65] *Jātaka*, no. 276 (*Fausboll*, vol. ii, p. 376), "... *sō pi ēkadivasaṃ janapade khittam minantō rajjini daṇḍake bandhitvā ēkaṃ kōtim khettasamikena gahopetvā ēkam attema aggahesi.* . . ." *Vide* the description of the *rajjukas* in Fick's *Social Organization in North-East India in Buddha's Time*, pp. 148 ff.
[66] *Rock Edicts III*, *IV*, etc.

magistrates superintending the rivers and measuring the land as in Egypt.[67]

The *rajjū* was probably some kind of revenue from the land, but of what kind exactly is uncertain. It was something other than the income from crown lands and land revenue, for both *sīta* and *bhāga* are mentioned along with *rajjū* under country parts.

As regards *chōrarajjū*, Shāma Śāstry[68] translates it as "ropes to bind thieves." Jolly[69] writes that "the *chōrarajjukas* recur in iv, 13, as certain police officers responsible for robberies committed in their district." Sohrabji[70] notes what Shāma Śāstry has to say, and remarks: "The word *chorasnāyu* is to be found, and Wilson has explained it as the Lecahirta (see Mon. Wm's *Dic.*, *Chōrasnāyu*). The word again occurs in Bk. IV, p. 232, l. 10, *avinītānām chōrarajjukaḥ*. The word *rajjū* preceding seems unnecessary." Gaṇapati Śāstri[71] explains it as "*chōrarajjūḥ chōragrāhakāya grāmadēyamityāhuḥ*." Hultzch,[72] too, is of the same opinion. He says: "In the Kauṭilīya, the two terms '*chōra-rajjū* (p. 60) and *chōra-rajjuka*' (p. 232) seem to mean something like 'police' and 'police officer' respectively. Cf. I. J. Sohrabji, *Notes on the Arthaśāstram*, p. 10 f., and Jolly in *Z.D.M.G.*, 71, 228."

Gaṇapati Śāstri's interpretation appears to be the correct one, as is evident below. According to Kauṭilya,[73] if merchants lost their goods in villages through theft or otherwise, the headman of the village had to make good the loss. "Whatever of their merchandise is stolen or lost in the intervening places between any two villages," says Kauṭilya,[74] "shall the superintendent of pasture lands make good. If there are no pasture lands (in such places) the

[67] *Strabo*, xv, 50.
[68] *Arth. Trans.*, p. 63.
[69] *Op. cit.*, ii, p. 17.
[70] *Notes*, pp. 10–11.
[71] *Op. cit.*, i, p. 136.
[72] *Corp. Ins. Ind.*, vol. i, p. 5.
[73] *Arth.*, Bk. IV, ch. 9.
[74] *Arth. Trans.*, p. 283. Cf. *Āpasthambha*, ii, 10, 26, 8; *Vishṇu*, iii, 66–7.

officer called *chōrarajjuka* shall make good the loss. If the loss of merchandise occurs in such places or parts of the country as are not provided even with such security, the people in the boundaries of the place shall contribute to make up the loss. If there are no people in the boundaries, the people of five or ten villages of the neighbourhood shall make up the loss."

This passage clearly indicates that the *chōrarajjukas* were a sort of police officers responsible for loss of goods. But as to why the superintendent of pasture lands was primarily liable for the loss, and the *chōrarajjukas* only in his absence, is not clear. Did these police officers exist only where the superintendent of pasture lands was not found? At least there were some places in the country where the *chōrarajjukas* were not instituted, because, according to Kauṭilya,[75] in places with no such security (i.e. a *chōrarajjuka*) the people of the neighbourhood made up the loss.

However, that the *chōrarajjukas* were police officers is proved by the fact that they were responsible for the security of the kingdom. Further interesting evidence supporting the above view is available from some inscriptions of a later period.[76] Some of the inscriptions, while granting lands, mention officers called *chaurōddharaṇikas*[77] and revenue called *chaurōddharaṇa*.[78] For instance, the Rampal copperplate of Śrīchandradēva[79] grants a piece of land: "*sadaśāparādhā sachaurōddharaṇā parihṛitasarvapīḍā*." This indicates that *chaurōddharaṇa* was some kind of revenue due to the state but transferred to the grantee. It is not, as R. D. Bannerjea translates,[80] "the right of extirpation of robbers," for this right is a responsibility involving expenditure, and, therefore, is obviously out of place where liabilities exempted from and rights to revenue conferred

[75] *Arth.*, Bk. IV, ch. 13.
[76] *Ep. Ind.*, xi, no. 5; xii, nos. 8 and 18; xiv, no. 23; xvii, no. 17.
[77] *Ep. Ind.*, xi, no. 5; xii, no. 8; xvii, no. 17.
[78] *Ep. Ind.*, xii, no. 18; xiv, no. 23; xvii, no. 17.
[79] *Ep. Ind.*, xii, no. 18.
[80] *Ep. Ind.*, xiv, no. 23.

upon are enumerated. On the contrary it is, as Rādhāgōvind Basak[81] hesitatingly translates, "police taxes (?)," for the above sentence evidently means "with (the fines on) the ten offences, with the police taxes, without any liability."

Moreover, Śukra states[82] that the police were to be main tained out of money raised from the householders of the locality where they are instituted. This clearly means a special tax for the upkeep of the police.

In the light of the foregoing evidence it appears that *chaurōddharaṇa* indicates police tax and *chaurōddharaṇika* police officer. Likewise it is probable that *chōrarajjuka* denotes police officer and *chōrarajjū* police tax, and not either "ropes to bind thieves," as Shāma Śāstry puts it, or "police," as Hultzch explains. For *chōrarajjū* is mentioned as a source of revenue, and mere police cannot be a source of income. It is a kind of contribution for the maintenance of the police, a tax perhaps, like the modern punitive police tax imposed on a turbulent locality which requires extra police help.

From the fact that the police officers may not have been in all parts of the country, as is indicated by Kauṭilya, it may be that the tax was not imposed universally in the kingdom, but only where the police were instituted.

[81] *Ep. Ind.*, xii, p. 142.

[82] *Śukranīti*, i, 581.

CHAPTER III

REVENUE FROM LAND AND IRRIGATION

I. *Land Revenue:* The ownership of land—Examination of current views—Conclusion—Survey of land—Forms of settlement—Amount of revenue. II. *Irrigation Revenue:* Was there an irrigation cess?—Different rates of cess—Comparison with modern Indian rates.

I. LAND REVENUE

AT all times and in almost every country the revenue from land has been an important source of income to the state. In our own country it was until recently the mainstay of Indian finance, yielding a large part of the revenue. Mauryan finances also seem to have depended a great deal, perhaps more than the British Indian finances ever did, upon this source of income.

At the very outset it may be observed that revenue from land was received from two distinct sources—as income from royal domain, and from taxation of non-crown lands. Royal or public domain or crown lands mean in this book lands owned and often cultivated by the state. The non-crown lands denote the land in the possession—the question of ownership will be discussed at length presently—of the people. In this chapter is considered the problem of "non-crown" lands, the income from which source is called land revenue.

THE OWNERSHIP OF LAND

Before examining this question of ownership, it should be noted that there can be little dispute about the existence of crown lands.[1] The only question is whether the non-crown

[1] *Infra*, Chapter VII.

lands which were in the people's possession were in any sense owned by the state.

There are three distinct views on this subject. The first one, represented by V. A. Smith, is definite on the point that there was state-landlordism, i.e. that the state was the owner of all lands. "The native law of India," writes Smith,[2] "has always regarded agricultural land as being crown property." The second view, championed by K. P. Jayaswal, takes us to the other extreme. To quote Jayaswal:[3] "Some of these writers have confidently asserted that property in the soil, according to the Hindu view, always vested in the Hindu sovereign. The fact, on the other hand, is that it is exactly the reverse of the Hindu theory on the subject. The writers unconsciously read their own feudal law into Hindu jurisprudence. Nothing is so distant from Hindu law as this theory. Anyone who is conversant with the general tendency of the principles of Hindu law in constitutional matters would not believe his eyes even if he were given a *ślōka* in support of the feudal theory." F. W. Thomas represents the third view—qualified state-landlordism—that the land belonged to the state under certain conditions. Says Thomas:[4] "Apart from the royal domains, which must have been considerable, the ultimate property in the land appertained, in the sense which has since prevailed, to the king; that is to say, the king was entitled to his revenue therefrom, and in default could replace the cultivator in his holding."

I shall consider how far each of these views is tenable, making where necessary a detailed examination of the text of the *Arthaśāstra*.

[2] *Early History of India*, pp. 137 ff.

[3] *Hindu Polity*, part ii, pp. 174 ff. Also see P. N. Bannerjea, *Public Administration in Ancient India*, p. 179, where he writes: "The king, however, was never regarded as the owner of the land, and he never claimed a right to the unearned increment of the land." For a criticism of the latter idea, i.e. about unearned increment, *infra*, p. 112.

[4] *Cambridge History of India*, vol. i, p. 475.

The theory of absolute state-landlordism is based upon the following pieces of evidence. Megasthenes, who was the Greek ambassador in the Mauryan court for a number of years, says:[5] "They [the husbandmen] pay a land tribute to the king because all India is the property of the crown, and no private person is permitted to own land. Besides the land tribute, they pay into the royal treasury a fourth part of the produce of the soil." Again, Bhaṭṭaswāmi, a commentator of the *Arthaśāstra*, quotes[6] a verse in support of state proprietorship of land:

Rājā bhūmeḥ patirdṛishṭaḥ śāstrajñairudakasyacha.
Tābhyāṃ anyattu yaddravyaṃ tatra svāmyaṃ kuṭumbināṃ.

This *ślōka* means, "Those who are well versed in the *Śāstras* admit that the king is the owner of both land and water, and that the people can exercise their right of ownership over all other things except these two."[7]

[5] *Diodorus*, ii, 40. In *Ancient India as described in Classical Literature*, p. 48, footnote, where Diodorus is quoted, we find land *rent* instead of land *tribute*. Also see *Strabo*, xv, 1, 40. McCrindle translates the passage thus: "The whole of the land belongs to the crown, and the husbandmen till it on condition of receiving as wages one-fourth of the produce." Also see McCrindle's footnote on this passage. Dr. L. D. Barnett has kindly supplied me with a literal translation of the original Greek. The second half of the sentence literally means "they work it for hire, at the rate of fourth (part) of the produce." I shall deal with this passage in detail presently.

[6] *Bhaṭṭaswāmi*, f. 78.

[7] *Arth. Trans.*, p. 140, footnote. Also see Jolly, *op. cit.*, vol. ii, p. 29, and for the *ślōka* Gaṇapati Śāstri, *op. cit.*, vol. i, p. 287. Jolly says in this connection: "This rule agrees with the theory of the code of Manu that the king is the *owner* of the soil (*Manu*, viii, 39)." This idea of ownership does not appear to be warranted by the *ślōka* referred to. Manu says:

Nidhīnāntu purāṇānām dhātunāmēva cha kshitau.
Ardhabhāgrakshaṇādrājā bhūmēradhipatirhisaḥ.

This is translated by Bühler (*Sacred Books of the East*, vol. xxv, p. 259) as follows: "The king obtains one-half of ancient hoards and metals (found) in the ground by reason of (his riving protection) (and) because he is *the lord of the soil.*" Burnell and Hopkins also

In the *Arthaśāstra* itself one or two pieces of indirect evidence are found. Kauṭilya says[8] that lands prepared for cultivation should be given to taxpayers (*karada*) only for life, and that unprepared lands should not be taken away from those who are preparing them for cultivation. This means that the state gave the land to the cultivator for life, which indicates the ownership of the state. Further, if land was private property, why take unprepared land? When the state gave the land to another cultivator, it appears very improbable that he acquired its ownership because he was prepared to cultivate.

Let us now examine each of these arguments. The evidence of Megasthenes has been rejected on the ground that the statements found in Diodorus and Strabo differ materially from and contradict each other.[9] According to Diodorus, the

(*Ordinances of Manu*, p. 183) translate the last quarter of the verse—which is the point in discussion—as "since he is *the lord of the earth*."

But Bühler writes in the footnote: "I take the last clause which might be translated '(and) because he is the lord of the earth' as a distinct recognition of the principle that the ownership of all land is vested in the king." In other words, *Bühler's own interpretation* is that the king was the *owner* of the soil. But Manu definitely states (ix, 44) that the land belongs to him who cleared it. Bühler refers to this *ślōka* in *Ep. Ind.*, i, no. 11 (p. 74, footnote), and says: "The ultimate sense of the expression is, therefore, that the land in question is made over to the donee with the same full right of ownership which the first cultivator would have possessed who reclaimed it." Therefore, to infer from the above verse that, according to Manu, the king was the owner of the land appears too far-fetched. Moreover, Bühler himself translates another verse (viii, 239) as follows: "(The owner of the field) shall mark a hedge over which a camel cannot look," etc.

[8] *Arth.*, Bk. II, ch. 1:

Karadēbhyaḥ kṛitakshētrānyaikapurushikāni prayachchēt.
Akṛitāni kartṛibhyaḥ nadēyāt.

As regards the interpretation of the word *kara*, on which depends a great deal, see Appendix, *supra*, p. 41.

[9] This contradiction was pointed out as early as the beginning of the last century by Major Wilks in his *History of Mysore*. In view of my interpretation in these pages I have not considered it necessary to deal with K. M. Gupta's views on land ownership and the Greek passages (K. M. Gupta, *The Land System in South India*, chs. iv and v).

cultivator paid the fourth part of the produce to the state, whereas, according to Strabo, *the state paid as wages to the cultivator* the fourth part. This contradiction has been the principal ground for rejecting Megasthenes' evidence.

As pointed out above, the original Greek passage from Strabo literally means,[10] "They [i.e. the cultivators] work it for hire, at the rate of fourth [part] of the produce." McCrindle's version is, therefore, not exactly literal. However, the original passage lends itself to two interpretations. It may indicate that the cultivators hired the *land, paying to the state* as hire one-fourth of the produce, for it is not definite whether the fourth part was paid by them to the state as rent or whether they received it as the hire (wages) for their labour. If the former meaning is accepted, then there is no such material difference or contradiction between Strabo and Diodorus. If, on the other hand, the passage is interpreted as McCrindle does, i.e. that the cultivators *received the fourth part as wages*, even then there is no contradiction. As will be seen presently, the statements of Strabo and Diodorus, instead of being contradictory, appear to be in reality complementary to each other, the former referring to crown lands and the latter to non-crown lands.

Diodorus, it may be noted, refers to two taxes—one the land tribute and the other a tax involving one-fourth of the produce. The former was, of course, the land revenue, and the latter seems to have been the irrigation cess. Kauṭilya also mentions two taxes—the *bhāga* (land revenue) and the *udakabhāga* (water rate).[11] The land revenue was one-sixth of the produce, while the irrigation cess varied between one-third and one-sixth of the produce, although one-fourth seems to have been the common rate. The latter tax appears to have been paid by the non-crown lands.[12] Megasthenes, therefore, probably refers to the irrigation

[10] I am indebted to Dr. L. D. Barnett for this translation of Strabo.

[11] *Infra*, pp. 71 ff.

[12] *Ibid.*

cess of one-fourth. He mentions only one-fourth, and neither one-third nor one-fifth, perhaps because the fourth appears to have been the most common rate, and so it is natural that he should mention it, instead of going into details.

While Diodorus thus refers to non-crown lands, Strabo deals with crown lands or royal domain. As discussed in a later chapter,[13] when the royal domain was more than could be cultivated by the state, some part of it was leased out to private cultivators, who received one-half of the yield if they employed their own capital, one-fourth or one-fifth if the state supplied the capital. In other words, the price paid for their labour, i.e. their wages, was one-fourth or one-fifth of the produce. The fourth was probably the common rate paid to such cultivators. It is to this that Strabo alludes in the passage that the husbandmen till it on condition of receiving as wages a fourth part of the produce. He does not mention any other payment, because the crown lands do not seem to have paid either the land revenue or the water cess.

Thus the facts that Diodorus mentions *two* taxes, while Strabo refers only to one contribution, i.e. wages paid by the state, and that according to one the cultivator paid the taxes, and according to the other *the state paid the wages*, clearly suggest that between Strabo and Diodorus there is neither confusion nor contradiction, and that Diodorus speaks of the land revenue of one-sixth and the water rate of one-fourth, while Strabo refers to the wages received by the cultivators of the royal domain.

Of course, it may be pointed out that the passages occur in the same connection, viz. while describing the "second caste" of husbandmen; but this by itself does not show that the reference is to the same kind of land.

Therefore the objection that the evidence of Megasthenes cannot be accepted because of the contradiction between his two chroniclers does not appear to be weighty. The Greek

[13] *Infra*, pp. 126 ff.

ambassador's statement may be accepted as broadly true.

As regards the verse quoted by Bhaṭṭaswāmi the commentator, it must be noted that Jayaswal gives a different reading of the *ślōka*. He writes: "I have obtained a copy of the manuscript of the commentary which is at the Government Oriental Library, Madras, made under the supervision of the librarian through the kind agency of Professor S. Kṛishṇaswāmi Aiyangar. The original couplet reads as follows:

Rājā bhūmeḥ patirdṛishtaḥ śāstrajñairudakasya cha
Tābhyāmanyattu yaddravyam tatra sāmyaṃ kuṭumbinām.

A mere reading of this *ślōka* will convince those who are familiar with Hindu law that the translation is not what the *ślōka* says. The natural, unforced meaning of the *ślōka* is: "The king is the protector (*pati*) according to the opinion of the learned in the *śāstras* of the *bhūmi* (land) and water. Excepting those two, whatever property there may be, private persons have sameness of right therein."[14] In other words, the difference between the two interpretations of the *ślōka* is in the meaning of the words *pati* and *kuṭumbinām*, and whether in the fourth quarter the word is *sāmyam* or *svāmyam*.

The *ślōka* is thus liable to two different interpretations. And Jayaswal's translation that the verse refers to the rights of the family of a ruler and that "a kingdom is not divisible, because according to the *śāstras* it is not the property of the king," is plausible, though, as will be seen presently, this meaning appears far-fetched. Moreover, the evidentiary value of the verse is a matter of doubt in view of its unknown authorship and unknown date, especially when Jayaswal has tried to show in his valuable book that there was private ownership of land in ancient India.[15]

[14] *Hindu Polity*, part ii, p. 182.

[15] *Hindu Polity*, ch. xxxiv. Also see R. Shāma Śāstry, *Evolution of Indian Polity*, Appendix C.

As for the difference in the reading of the verse, there seems to be little doubt that the term in question is *svāmyam*.[16] Further, the word *pati* means an owner, possessor, proprietor, as much as it means a governor, master, or even a protector. Finally, although *kuṭumbinām* may be taken as private persons as well as members of a family, Kauṭilya uses the word at least once in the sense of private persons and not members of family.[17]

On the whole, the interpretation of the supporters of state-landlordism appears more correct and probable.

As regards the passage from the *Arthaśāstra* quoted above in support of state-landlordism, it appears probable, though by no means certain, that the lands referred to in Bk. II, ch. 1, are crown lands. The statement that lands which were not cultivated may be cultivated by employing village labourers and others and the general trend of the chapter point to this conclusion. Further, it appears that Bk. II of the *Arthaśāstra* deals generally with matters concerning the state, unlike Bk. III, for instance, which treats also of transactions between private people.[18] Moreover, the correct meaning of the passage quoted above and of passages quoted below remains uncertain until the meaning of the

[16] I have myself referred to the manuscript of Bhaṭṭaswāmi's commentary to be found at Mysore and also to a specially made copy of the relevant part of the manuscript at Madras, and I am satisfied that the word is *svāmyam*. Moreover, I. J. Sohrabji, who has made use of "a carefully made copy" (*Notes*, p. ii) of the manuscript at Madras, has the reading *svāmyam* (*Notes*, p. 55). Finally, Shāma Śāstry (*Arth. Trans.*, p. 140), Jolly (*op. cit.*, ii, p. 29), and Gaṇapati Śāstri (*op. cit.*, i, p. 287) have adopted the term *svāmyam*.

[17] *Arth.*, Bk. II, ch. 25.

[18] But without entering into details it may be observed that in Bk. III there are many references to matters concerning purely the state, just as in Bk. II there are many details about purely private transactions. For instance, in the very first chapter of Bk. II we find reference to elders acting as guardians to minors, to punishment for neglecting to maintain dependents, to the age for becoming ascetics, and so on.

word *kara* is definitely known.[19] If, for instance, *kara* here means land revenue (*bhāga*), the objection that this passage refers to crown lands loses its force. But, tentatively, crown lands may be taken to be referred to here.

Further, even if the passage refers to all lands, there are other passages in the *Arthaśāstra* indicating a kind of private ownership.

In support of the theory of private ownership can be adduced two important considerations. First, Jayaswal[20] has tried to prove by means of various pieces of evidence that land in ancient India—not particularly in the Mauryan period—was owned by the people. Macdonell and Keith[21] are of opinion that "the position of the king with regard to land is somewhat obscure"; that the Greek notices are inconsistent and not completely trustworthy;[22] that the evidence from the Vedic literature, Manu, and the *Mahābhārata* is inadequate to prove what is sought (i.e. state-landlordism) and is not supported by the evidence of the Aryan peoples.

Apart from the general theory that there was no state-landlordism in ancient India as a whole, some passages in the *Arthaśāstra* itself indicate private ownership. To begin with, Kauṭilya mentions that people had the right to alienate lands, and he gives detailed rules about alienation. Kinsmen, neighbours, and rich persons had, in that order, the right to purchase land.[23] Right of alienation implies to a certain extent the right of ownership. Again, Kauṭilya says that taxpayers (*karadāḥ*) could sell or mortgage their lands to taxpayers alone, and that brahmans could sell or mortgage their *brahmadēya* or gift lands only to those who

[19] Appendix, *supra*, p. 41.

[20] *Hindu Polity*, part ii, pp. 174 ff.

[21] *Vedic Index*, vol. ii, pp. 214–15.

[22] As regards the "contradiction," *supra*, pp. 54 ff.

[23] *Arth.*, Bk. III, ch. 9, *Jñātissāmantadhanikāḥ kramēṇa bhūmiparigrahān krētum abhyābhavēyuḥ.*

are endowed with such lands.[24] The restriction on the right of transfer, however, needs an explanation. Lands were divided into revenue-paying and revenue-free lands like *brahmadēya* and gift lands. If a revenue-paying land were transferred, for instance, to a brahman who was exempted from paying revenue, the state lost its income, and, therefore, a limitation was necessary to prevent evasion of taxes and to ensure revenue to the state.[25]

A very important piece of evidence in support of private ownership is that Kauṭilya definitely uses the word *svāmyam* or its equivalent in connection with land: "*asvāmipratikrōśē chaturvimśatipaṇō daṇḍaḥ*"[26]—"Bidding for land in the absence of its owner shall be punished with a fine of 24 *paṇas*."[27] The objects of sale include fields (lands and other holding-*bhūmi*), gardens, lakes, and the like. Again, we have the passage, "*Tadubhayam parōktam vāstu rājā harēt, praṇashṭasvāmikañcha ethōpakāram vā vibhajēt*," meaning, "If both these methods fail, the holding under dispute shall be taken possession of by the king. The same rule

[24] *Arth.*, Bk. III, ch. 10, *Karadāḥ karadēsvādhānam vikrayam vā kuryuḥ, brahmadeyikā brahmadeyikēshu, anyathāpūrvassahasa daṇḍaḥ*. Here, also, as noted before, the correct meaning depends on the significance of *kara*. Whatever its meaning, there appears to be a contradiction between this passage and the one in Bk. II, ch. 1, quoted above. For while the present passage empowers taxpayers (*karadāḥ*) to sell their lands—which implies a sort of ownership—the other passage says that lands should be given to taxpayers (*karadāḥ*) only for life, which indicates a life tenancy. Each of these passages supports one of the two extreme views about ownership of land. As hinted above, the possible explanation which can reconcile the two extreme views about ownership is that one refers to crown lands and the other to non-crown lands.

[25] Compare what the Gaya copperplate record of Samudragupta of A.D. 320 (*Gupta Inscriptions*, no. 60) says after granting a village as a gift. "And from this time forth, the tax-paying cultivators, artisans, etc., of other villages, etc., should not be introduced by the *Agrahārika* of this (village) (for the purpose of settling in it and carrying on their occupations); (for) otherwise there would certainly be a violation of (the privileges of) an *agrahāra*."

[26] *Arth.*, Bk. III, ch. 9.

[27] *Arth. Trans.*, p. 207.

shall hold good in the case of a holding for which no claim is forthwith coming, or it may be beneficially distributed among the people."[28] *Śvāmikam* can be better translated as *ownership*. Thus Kauṭilya himself, while speaking of disputes about fields, mentions that there were lands owned by private persons. Another passage to the same effect, where a fine of twelve *paṇas* is inflicted on persons who drive cattle through a field without intimating the owner:

"*Svāminaśchanivēdya chārayatō dvādaśapaṇō daṇḍaḥ.*"[29]

A different kind of support is from building and sites. Kauṭilya mentions[30] *parabhūmi* while speaking of constructing buildings on sites *belonging to others*. There is also evidence that gardens were privately owned.[31] Could it be that people who owned buildings and garden land did not own fields and other lands?

[28] *Arth. Trans.*, p. 208. In this connection it may be mentioned that Shāma Śāstry's translation of *akṛishantaḥ* in the following passage is misleading. Bk. II, ch. 1, says, "*akṛishantō apahīnam dadyuḥ,*" which Śāstry translates "lest these *owners* who do not properly cultivate them might pay less." The use of the word owner is misleading and perhaps superfluous, for the passage has no reference to *ownership*, and those who cultivate may not at all own the land, but may be mere tenants. Further, the correct meaning of the passage appears to be that those who do not cultivate should pay more (*apahīnam*). Again, Śāstry (*Arth. Trans.*, p. 208) uses the word owner while translating the passage in Bk. III, ch. 9, *Kedārārāmassētubandhānām parasparahimsāyām himsādviguṇō daṇḍaḥ*. The use of the word owner here again is misleading, as the original does not appear to warrant it.

Once again, Śāstri's translation of *svasētubhyaḥ* in the following passage (Bk. II, ch. 24) is not happy: "*Svavīryōpajīvinōvā chaturthapañchabhāgikāḥ yathēshṭamanavasitaṃ bhāgaṃ dadyuḥ, anyatra kṛichchhrēbhyaḥ svasētubhyaḥ. Hastaprāvartimam udakabhāgaṃ pañchamaṃ dadyuḥ.*" Śāstry translates *svasētubhyaḥ* as private lands. It is doubtful if the word can mean private lands. It appears to mean irrigation works constructed by private persons, and often referred to in the *Arthaśāstra*. Cf. Bhaṭṭaswāmi's explanation, *svayam kṛita taṭākādibhyaḥ* (*J.B.O.R.S.*, vol. xii, part ii, p. 137). Gaṇapati Śāstri (*op. cit.*, vol. i, p. 286) takes *svasētubhyaḥ* along with the next sentence and he appears to be correct.

[29] *Arth.*, Bk. III, ch. 10.

[30] *Ibid.*

[31] *Arth.*, Bk. III, ch. 9.

It must be admitted that the right of alienation which is one of the main supports of Jayaswal's view implies to a great extent ownership for all practical purposes. It cannot, however, always imply absolute ownership,[32] but only a kind of proprietary right conditional upon paying revenue or upon the performance of some other obligation. The passages quoted above from the *Arthaśāstra* restrict the right of alienation. "Lands may be confiscated from those who do not cultivate them and given to others," says Kauṭilya,[33] thus indicating that the cultivator was not at liberty to do with the land what he liked. This restriction was placed probably because non-cultivation meant loss of income to the state, as the land revenue was a portion of the produce and so dependent upon cultivation. Even in British India lands making default in paying revenue are liable to be sold by public auction.

Viewing the discussion as a whole, it is difficult to come to any definite conclusion on the question as to who was the owner of the land. However, it appears that the views of both Smith and Jayaswal are incorrect. F. W. Thomas's view noted already appears to be the safest conclusion on the evidence before us. The land belonged to both the state and the cultivator, and both of them were only conditional owners. The state was entitled to land revenue, and so long as it was paid it could not lawfully eject the cultivator. But the moment default was made in paying it the state asserted its latent right and actually became the owner and holder. Likewise, so long as he paid the land tax, the cultivator owned the land. But his property in it ceased when he ceased to pay revenue. In other words, it was a sort of perpetual lease held on the annual performance of an obligation.[34] For all purposes including alienation the

[32] See practice in ancient Greece quoted below.

[33] *Arth.*, Bk. II, ch. I, *Akṛishatāmāchchhidyānyēbhyaḥ prayachchēt.*

[34] A close parallel to this kind of double ownership, if it can be so called, is found in the case of mines in ancient Greece. "*The people or the state was the proprietor of the mines,* but they were never worked

lessee is the owner and considers himself as such, and the lessor has the right of only demanding performance of the obligation. But when once the lessee fails to do his duty, the lessor's ownership asserts itself. In short, what an eminent economist writes of the present position in India may very well be applied to the Mauryan days. "The balance of reasoning seems to be in favour of regarding the possession of the Indian cultivator as a sort of conditional ownership, conditional upon the payment of the dues to the state."[35]

Uncultivable and uncultivated land appears to have belonged to the state, for compensation was levied in the shape of grains for any damage done by the cattle to the crops (*pārihīṇakam*)[36] that grew on uncultivated lands. Pasture grounds were required to be maintained by the

on the public account, nor were they ever let, as other landed property in leasehold, but were *all granted in fee form to private persons and they passed from one to another by inheritance, sale and in brief, every legal method of alienation*. The *poletae* had the charge of the sale of the mines, that is, of the right to work them. For this once for all a price was paid beside which the tenant was bound to pay the *twenty-fourth part of the produce as a perpetual tax*" (Boeckh, *op. cit.*, Bk. III, ch. 3). "The right of the state was strictly guarded. . . . The mines were also exempt from extraordinary taxes . . . *because they were considered as the property of the state, the use of which was enjoyed in return for a definite payment like the duties and tolls by* the farmers general" (Boeckh, *op. cit.*, p. 417).

This disproves the argument that right of alienation implies absolute ownership. Moreover, it shows how the kind of land proprietorship described above as existing in the Mauryan period was possible.

[35] The Government view, at least of some officials, appears to be to regard the state as the ultimate owner of all land, as is evident from the *Imperial Gazetteer of India*, vol. iv. "The peculiarity of Indian rents lies, therefore, in this fact, that whereas in most countries the land revenue is an assignment made by the landowner to the government, in India the net rent is, historically speaking, a relinquished part of the profits of land by the government to the landowners."

[36] *Arth.*, Bk. II, ch. 15. Shāma Śāstry's explanation (*Arth. Trans.*, p. 109), that the crops referred to were those that grew on uncultivated waste land, may be accepted. As the state property was injured, compensation had to be paid (*infra*, p. 131).

state between any two dangerous places and in uncultivable tracts; and there was also a superintendent of pasture lands (*vivītādhyaksha*).[37] Even in British India the state is the owner of all waste and unoccupied land in general

SURVEY OF LAND

In many parts of modern India each field is measured up, and the soil of each survey number is classified according to the quality of the soil in various grades, and the details of the fields and the crops grown are kept by the officials. The same system appears to have existed under the Mauryas. It was the duty of the revenue collector to classify villages according to their rank, "first, middle, and lowest (*jyēshṭhamadhyamakanishṭha*)."[38] The village officer (*gōpa*) had to number plots of ground as "cultivated, uncultivated, plains, wet lands, gardens, vegetable gardens, fences," and so on.[39] That there was a systematic survey of land there appears to be little doubt. Even in the age of the *Mantras* a survey of the land is said to have existed.[40] The Greeks state that the Mauryan officers measured the land

[37] *Arth.*, Bk. II, chs. 2 and 34, *Akṛishāyāṃ bhūmau paśubhyō vivītāni prayachchhēt bhayāntarēshu cha vivitaṃ sthāpayēt.*

[38] *Arth.*, Bk. II, ch. 35. Compare *Śukranīti*, iv, 2, 220–1, "Having ascertained the amount of produce from the measured plots of land, whether great, middling, or small," etc.

[39] *Arth.*, Bk. II, ch. 35.

[40] Compare the system prevalent in the time of the *Mantras*. P. T. Srinivasaiengar observes, in his *Life in Ancient India in the Age of the "Mantras,"* p. 60, "Life in the age of the *Mantras* was sufficiently organized for lands to be measured (*R.V.*, ii, 15, 4) with measuring rods (*R.V.*, iii, 38, 3) classified as barren (*khila*, *A.V.*, vii, 115, 4), waste, (*dhanva*, *A.V.*, vii, 117, 1), forest (*araṇya*, *A.V.*, xii, 1, 11), and cultivated land (*urvara*, *R.V.*, vii, 80, 60), and for fields to be definitely marked out (*R.V.*, i, 110, 5). The *Atharva Vēda* mentions two units of measurements, the *abhiśu* (lit: rein), evidently a short measure, and the *vyama*, the space between the tips of the fingers when the arms are extended (vi, 137, 2)." Also *Kama Jātaka*, no. 467 (*Fausboll*, vol. iv, p. 169), *Rājakammikā khēttappamanagahanatthaya* . . ." Also *Kurudhanma Jātaka*, no. 276. *Supra*, p. 47.

as in Egypt.[41] Kauṭilya definitely mentions the standards by which land was measured.[42] And the *rajjukas* mentioned by Aśōka were very probably settlement officers.

Without entering into details of land survey and measurement, it may be mentioned that the survey of land was perhaps as much for the purposes of the collection of land revenue as for furnishing a record like the one undertaken by William the Conqueror of England in his Domesday Book.

FORMS OF SETTLEMENT

There are various methods of levying land revenue.[43] In the Mauryan days, as in ancient India generally, land revenue was levied according to the produce of the land, and hence was in kind. The very use of the word *bhāga* for land revenue indicates that it was in kind. The Greeks[44] also observe that, "Besides the land tribute they pay into the royal treasury one-fourth part of the produce of the soil."[45] It was not a fixed amount, but a fixed proportion of what was grown on the land. This was a common system in both pre- and post-Mauryan days, and was not peculiar to the Mauryas.[46]

This form of revenue collection had many advantages. As it was a share of the gross produce, the calculation of the cultivator's share was simple. Nor was there any com-

[41] *Strabo*, xv, 1, 50.

[42] See for details *Arth.*, Bk. II, ch. 20, and Appendix, *supra*, p. 47.

[43] They may be enumerated as follows:

(*a*) Taxation on the capital value of the land.
(*b*) Taxation on area, e.g. taxes on *Jugera* in Rome.
(*c*) Taxation according to produce.
(*d*) Taxation on the sale value of the land.
(*e*) Taxation of the net income.

[44] *Diodorus*, ii, 40; *Strabo*, xv, 1, 40. *Supra*, p. 53.

[45] This is merely to illustrate that the payment was a certain proportion of the produce; the question of the exact proportion is discussed later on.

[46] Compare the practice described in the *Jātakas*. Fick's *Social Organization in North-East India in Buddha's Time*, pp. 116 ff.

plication about the costs of production or about the relative value of the land. There was also no trouble about the productiveness of the seasons. The calculation was simple and easy both to the state and to the cultivator. Both knew that one was to get and the other to give a certain part of the produce. Whatever the land produced lay on the threshing floor, and the revenue officer took away the share of the state. In times of drought and famine the cultivator paid little or nothing, and the question of remissions and other means of famine relief did not arise. For when the crop was little, the state took little. The remission was automatic and in proportion to the misery of the cultivator.

But the system must have had also its defects, specially in connection with public revenue. Agriculture depends on fickle Nature, and it is very difficult to forecast the next harvest. Revenue, being thus dependent upon an unknown factor, was itself uncertain. It was only after the harvest that the state could know what its revenue from this source would be. But this defect did not perhaps affect the ancient state much, because the state always kept as reserve a huge surplus. It has been seen that land revenue was levied and collected in the shape of the produce of the land. The question then arises, Was the revenue not paid in money also? Kauṭilya[47] says that taxes, not particularly land revenue, were paid in kind, money, and other forms. It has not been mentioned that land revenue was paid in money. But in view of the fact that in Southern India not very long after the Maurya period, i.e. about the beginning of the Christian era and even earlier, the land tax is stated to have been *payable in money or in kind* at the option of the farmer,[48] it is possible that in Mauryan times also some such practice prevailed.

Broadly speaking, there are two methods of revenue

[47] *Arth.*, Bk. II, ch. 35, *Dhānyapaśuhiraṇyakupyavishṭikarapratikaram*, etc.

[48] *Tamils Eighteen Hundred Years Ago*, p. 112.

collection. Śukra mentions both revenue farming and direct collection by the state. Thus he says that, having determined the land revenue of the village, the king should receive it from one rich man in advance or a guarantee (for the payment) of that by either monthly or periodical instalments,[49] and that the king should appoint officers called *grāmapas* by paying one-sixteenth, one-twelfth, one-eighth, or one-sixth of his own receipts.[50] According to Kauṭilya,[51] the *gōpas*, who appear to have been petty officials in the employment of the government and in charge of five or six villages, collected revenue. But no mention is made of revenue-farming. Nor is information available regarding the practice of paying revenue by instalments. It is not also clear if the land revenue assessment was permanent or was being revised at intervals. Of course, in financial embarrassments a larger percentage was collected.[52] There appears to have been in ordinary years no necessity to change the rate, because the actual revenue varied with the produce of the land, and so the amount actually paid to the state varied though the rate remained the same. Where the land revenue is assessed and paid in money, as in modern India, and the amount paid, being fixed, does not immediately follow the increase or decrease in the yield of the field, a constant revision of the revenue becomes necessary.

THE AMOUNT OF REVENUE

Next arises the question, What part of the produce was paid by the cultivator? V. A. Smith writes:[53] "The normal share of the produce taken by the state as 'land revenue' or crown rent being one-fourth, the amount taken as water rate was approximately equal, varying from one-

[49] *Śukranīti*, iv, 2, 248–50.
[50] *Ibid.*, 251–2.
[51] *Arth.*, Bk. II, ch. 35, *Tatpradishṭaḥ pañchagrāmīṃ daśagrāmīṃ vā gōpāśchintayēt*, etc.
[52] *Infra*, Chapter IX.
[53] *Early History of India*, p. 149; also p. 138.

fourth to one-third." Baden-Powell also writes to the same effect:[54] "It was noticed that in Alexander's time the cultivators were already contributing one-fourth of the grain." This impression seems to originate in an incorrect reading of the Greek accounts. Megasthenes observes:[55] "They pay a land tribute to the king because all India is the property of the crown and no private person is permitted to own land. Besides the land tribute, they pay into the royal treasury a fourth part of the produce of the soil." At first sight it appears as if Megasthenes mentions one-fourth of the produce as the land revenue. Smith and Baden-Powell appear to have overlooked the first words "besides a land tribute" or "rent," which are most important. It may be noticed that Megasthenes does not mention what portion of the produce was paid as land tribute. He only says that it was paid in addition to the one-fourth mentioned.

There is a good explanation for this one-fourth part of the produce paid. It was the water rate which every land had to pay, even though it got its water from natural sources. The question of water rates will be discussed in detail while treating of irrigation.[56] Here, however, it may be noted that water rates varied from one-third to one-fifth of the produce according to the source of the water and the manner of irrigation. One-fourth appears to have been the most common rate, as it was levied on water-lifts worked by bullocks, and on water raised from rivers, lakes, tanks, and wells. It is very probably to this that Megasthenes refers as a payment of a fourth part of the produce in addition to the land tribute.

The land revenue itself appears to have been one-sixth of the produce. Kauṭilya mentions along with the enumera-

[54] *Land Systems of British India*, vol. i, p. 26.

[55] *Diodorus*, ii, 40. In *Strabo*, xv, 1, 40, Strabo writes: "The whole of the land belongs to the crown, and the husbandmen till it on condition of receiving one-fourth of the produce." *Supra*, pp. 55 ff.

[56] *Infra*, pp. 72 ff.

tion of revenue heads an income called *shaḍbhāga,* which probably refers to land revenue.[57] In another place Kauṭilya refers to *dhānyashaḍbhāgaṃ,* i.e. one-sixth of the grains grown as being taken by the king.[58] Even if Kauṭilya had not mentioned this, the custom of taking one-sixth as land revenue had been so firmly rooted in ancient India that, as F. W. Thomas remarks,[59] "the king came to be known as *shaḍbhāgin,* i.e. one whose share is one-sixth." A few instances may be mentioned. According to Manu,[60] a king who affords no protection and yet receives the sixth part of the produce takes upon himself all the sins of his own people. The *Śāntiparva* speaks to the same effect.[61] Gautama[62] and Baudhāyana[63] also indicate one-sixth as the king's maximum tribute. According to Śukra, the king was to realize one-third, one-fourth, or one-half from places which were irrigated by tanks, canals, and wells, by rains, and by rivers respectively, and one-sixth from barren and rocky soils.[64] An explanation is here needed. One-sixth appears to be the pure land tax, but the rates one-half, one-third, and one-fourth seem to include the irrigation cess also. For if the water cess mentioned by Kauṭilya[65] is added to the land revenue of one-sixth we get approximately the rates men-

[57] *Arth.*, Bk. II, ch. 15. Also see *Bhaṭṭaswāmi*, f. 47.

[58] *Arth.*, Bk. I, ch. 13, *Dhānyashadbhāgaṃ paṇyadaśabhāgaṃ hiraṇyaṃchāsya bhāgadhēyaṃ prakalpayāmāsuḥ.*

[59] *Mutual Influence of Hindus and Mohammedans in Law and Religion*, p. 33.

[60] *Manu*, viii, 308. According to Manu (vii, 130) a fiftieth part of the increments on cattle and gold could be taken by the king and an eighth, sixth, or twelfth part of the crops. Manu does not mention at all one-fourth, but one-sixth is the highest. One-fourth of the produce was taken only in items of distress (*op. cit.*, x, 118).

[61] *Śāntiparva*, xxiv, 12; lxxi, 10.

[62] *Gautama*, x, 24.

[63] *Baudhāyana*, i, 10, 18, 1.

[64] *Śukranīti*, iv, 2, 227–9. Also *Vishṇu*, iii, 22–3; *Vaśishṭha*, i, 42, and Bühler's note thereon (*S.B.E.*, vol. xiv, part ii).

[65] *Infra*, pp. 72 ff. One-sixth and one-fifth = eleven-thirtieths, one-sixth and one-quarter = five-twelfths, one-sixth and one-third = one-half.

tioned by Śukra. Of the ancient South Indian kingdoms Kanakasabhai Pillai writes:[66] "One-sixth of the produce on land was the legitimate share of the king, and for water supplied by the state a water cess was levied from the farmers." Yuan Chwang, the Chinese traveller, records[67] that "the king's tenants pay one-sixth of the produce as rent." The Mauryan land revenue also appears to have been one-sixth part of the produce.

In modern India the land revenue differs in different provinces.[68] Roughly, it may be taken to be 8 or 10 per cent of the gross produce, while under Mauryan rule it appears to have amounted to $16\frac{2}{3}$ per cent. It may appear that the revenue exacted by the Mauryas was a little too heavy for the land. But it must not be forgotten that land revenue was the mainstay of Mauryan finance. Moreover, even to-day in some countries, though the land tax is small in amount the total burden on land is much more than it appears at first sight. There are various authorities in the country each of which extracts a share from the land. For instance, in Australia local bodies may, in certain cases, tax land, in addition to the commonwealth and the states. Likewise in New Zealand and Japan.[69]

[66] *Tamils Eighteen Hundred Years Ago*, p. 112.

[67] *Yuan Chwang*, vol. i, p. 176.

[68] "Further and more accurate calculations made by the Famine Commission, 1900–1, show that in the Central Provinces the incidence of the present land revenue is less than 4 per cent of the average value of the produce, that in Berar is about 7 per cent, in Ajmer 10 per cent, in the greater part of the Punjab 7 per cent, in Deccan something over 7 per cent, and in Gujarat over 20 per cent. Calculations recently made for Madras show that the land revenue and water rates of the Ryotwari areas of the Presidency (excluding Malabar South Kanara) fall at an average of about 10 per cent of the gross produce" (*Imperial Gazetteer of India*, vol. iv, p. 217).

[69] *Science of Public Finance*, p. 214. "In Japan an additional tax is also levied by the prefectuses, cities, towns, and villages" (*ibid.*, p. 209). In New Zealand "land holders are liable to income tax in addition to the land tax as in Great Britain" (*ibid.*, p. 215). In India "there is as yet no income tax in addition to the land tax as in Great Britain" (*ibid.*, p. 228).

On the whole, the total burden of revenue taken directly from the cultivator must have been heavier than it is to-day in British India, but this heavy demand may be overlooked if the ideal held out by Kauṭilya,[70] that the king's duty was to "protect agriculture from the molestation of oppressive fines, free labour, and taxes," was realized even to a limited degree.

II. IRRIGATION REVENUE

The water cess (*udakabhāgam*) has been mentioned by Kauṭilya while dealing with crown lands.[71] At first sight, therefore, the tax seems to refer to crown lands. But a closer examination indicates that probably it applies to non-crown lands. For it appears[72] that the crown tenants received one-half of the yield when they employed their own capital and one-fourth or one-fifth when the state supplied the implements and other necessaries. If, in addition to this, they paid the water rate, viz. one-fifth, one-fourth, or one-third as the case was,[73] then practically nothing would be left to them. It must, therefore, apply to non-crown lands, which paid only one-sixth part as land revenue, and the water cess paid by which is not mentioned anywhere else in the *Arthaśāstra*. It is not improbable that the tax is mentioned in chapter 24 while describing crown lands and their cultivation, not because the tax applied to crown lands, but because it is very natural to enumerate it while treating of agriculture, and perhaps also because the cess may have been regulated by the Superintendent of Agriculture, who was a crown officer. Moreover, as discussed on a previous page,[74] Megasthenes also refers to this tax when he remarks:

[70] *Arth.*, Bk. II, ch. 1, *Daṇḍavishṭikarābādhaiḥ rakshēdupahatāṃ kṛishim.*

[71] *Arth.*, Bk. II, ch. 24.

[72] *Ibid.* Compare Gaṇapati Śāstri, *op. cit.*, i, p. 286; Bhaṭṭaswāmi's interpretation, *J.B.O.R.S.*, vol. xii, part 2, p. 137. Compare also *Yājñavalkya*, i, 166.

[73] *Arth.*, Bk. II, ch. 24.

[74] *Supra*, pp. 68 ff.

"Besides the land tribute, they [the cultivators] pay into the royal treasury a fourth part of the produce." In other words, the cultivator paid the land revenue and also another tax, amounting to a fourth part, which proportion was about the average, and perhaps the more commonly paid, amount of water cess. Therefore the water rates mentioned in the *Arthaśāstra* have been considered in this book as those paid by non-crown lands.

The cess was perhaps paid, like land revenue, in the form of produce.[75] Writing of present-day water rates, K. T. Shah observes:[76] "They necessarily vary very much according to the crop irrigated, the quantity of water required and the time at which it is required, the intensity and constancy of demand, and the value of irrigation in increasing the outturn." This could very well apply to the Mauryan days, for there were four classes of rates.[77]

(1) Those who cultivated land, irrigating it by manual labour (*hastaprāvartimaṃ*), appear to have paid one-fifth of the produce. This kind of irrigation implies the consumption of not much water, because wet crops require a continuous supply of water which could not without great difficulty be supplied by manual labour.

(2) Land irrigation by water carried on shoulders (*skandhaprāvartimaṃ*), i.e. water-lifts worked by bullocks,[78] had to pay one-fourth of the produce, because the use of water-lifts and power suggests that the crops require more water.

[75] *Arth.*, Bk. II, ch. 24. Cf. passage beginning: *Svavīryōpajīvinō vā*, etc.

[76] *Sixty Years of Indian Finance*, p. 297.

[77] *Arth.*, Bk. II, ch. 24, *Hastaprāvartimaṃ udakabhāgaṃ pañchamaṃ dadyuḥ Skandhaprāvartimaṃ cha tritīyaṃ Srōtōyantraprāvartimaṃ cha tritīyaṃ Chaturthaṃ nadīsarastaṭākakūpōddhāṭaṃ*. This is the text followed by Jolly and Shāma Śāstry. Gaṇapati Śāstri adds (*op. cit.*, vol. ii, p. 286) *svasētubhyaḥ* before *hastaprāvartimaṃ* which the other two scholars take along with the previous passage. Gaṇapati Śāstri's reading appears better.

[78] According to Bhaṭṭaswāmi, *balīvardapravartitayantrōdakasēka nishpāditaṃ* (*J.B.O.R.S.*, vol. xii, part ii, p. 137).

(3) Where water was supplied by means of water-lifts worked by some mechanical contrivance and probably water from channels,[79] which necessarily implied the consumption of more water and the growth of richer crops, the cultivator had to pay one-third of the produce.

(4) Those who irrigated by raising water from the rivers, lakes, tanks, and wells paid one-fourth of the produce.[80] This rate was exacted even though the source of water was natural, like rivers and lakes, and not constructed by the state. This was so, perhaps, because it was believed that land and water were owned by the state,[81] and perhaps also because the state looked after the natural resources of water.[82] The water rates from works built by the state, i.e. tanks, lakes, and the like (*kaushṭēyaka*), came under the head *rāshṭra*, and were collected by the superintendent of storehouse.[83]

Almost the same rate of tax is mentioned by Śukra.[84] According to him, the king was to realize one-third, one-fourth, or one-half from places which are irrigated by tanks, canals, and wells, by rains, and by rivers respectively, and one-sixth from barren and rocky soil. The figures seem to include land revenue also. The pure water rate would therefore appear to have been one-sixth, one-third, and one-

[79] Bhaṭṭaswāmi, *J.B.O.R.S.*, vol. xii, part ii, p. 138. If this interpretation is accepted, it explains the high water rate of one-third; moreover, if this explanation is rejected, there is no mention in the other groups of water from channels which existed in large numbers.

[80] *Arth.*, Bk. II, ch. 24, *Chaturthaṃ nadīsarastaṭākakūpōddhāṭaṃ*. Shāma Śāstry (*Arth. Trans.*, p. 140) translates this as ". . . paid one-third or one-fourth of the produce." In the Sanskrit original only one-fourth is mentioned. It is not clear on what evidence Shāma Śāstry adds one-third also. Also see Gaṇapati Śāstri, *op. cit.*, vol. i, p. 287.

[81] Compare Gaṇapati Śāstri, *op. cit.*, vol. i, p. 286.

[82] Strabo writes, "Some (magistrates in Pāṭalīputra) superintend the rivers, measure the land as in Egypt, and inspect the sluices by which water is let out" etc. (*Strabo*, xv, 1, 50).

[83] *Arth.*, Bk. II, ch. 15.

[84] *Śukranīti*, iv, 2, 227–9.

twelfth, which compare very favourably with Kauṭilya's rates.

In modern India both these methods, namely, levying in one amount both land and irrigation revenues, and assessing them separately, as Kauṭilya does, are in vogue. According to Baden-Powell,[85] "In some districts the assessment is separated into an assessment of the land in its dry or un-irrigated aspect, and an additional assessment, an 'owner's' rate or a 'water rate,' on account of its being irrigated. In other districts there is a consolidated assessment based on the rental value of the land as irrigated land. The water always belongs to the government."

The water tax collected by the Mauryans varied between 20 per cent and 33 per cent of the produce. The rate in modern India may be taken to be about 6 or 7 per cent of the produce.[86] Even granting that the state was looking after the irrigational needs of the people more than the state is doing now in British India, it must be admitted that the water rates appear to be proportionally much higher under Mauryan rule.

[85] *Land Systems of British India*, vol. i, p. 9.

[86] "On the other hand near Poona, for lands raising sugar-cane, as much as Rs. 50 per acre is paid, but this is exceptional, is confined to every limited area, and is at all possible because the cultivator can raise a crop which pays as much as Rs. 800 per acre" (*Sixty Years of Indian Finance*, p. 326). Though the amount paid may be less in other cases, the produce also being less, this proportion may perhaps be taken as normal.

CHAPTER IV

OCTROIS, TOLLS, AND CUSTOMS DUTIES

The meaning of these terms—Was there foreign trade in Mauryan times?—The *vartanī*—Were there customs duties?—The *dvārādēya*—Treatment of foreign merchants and goods—Forbidden goods—Mauryan octroi duties compared with British Indian customs duties—Kinds of tolls—Road and ferry tolls—Carriage cess—Harbour toll

TAXES on commodities or on consumption may be levied in more than one form: as excise duties on articles produced in the country, as customs duties collected at the part or frontier, and as octrois and tolls levied at the entrance to a town or part of a country and while the articles pass through the land. This chapter deals with customs duties, octrois, and tolls.

At the outset the differences between these three kinds of taxation may be briefly noted.[1] Customs duties are "duties charged by law upon commodities imported into or exported from a country."[2] In other words, the taxes levied when the goods cross the boundaries of a country are called customs duties. No doubt taxes levied upon commodities passing from one province to another and those levied at the gates of cities on the goods produced outside the city —a kind of municipal taxation existing on the European continent—are in the nature of customs duties, and some of them even go by the name of internal customs. But the former may be termed tolls and the latter octrois. Octroi may be defined as "a local tax collected on various articles brought into a district for consumption."[3] It is a duty on articles brought into a city or district from outside, though the goods are of the taxing country itself. Tolls do not

[1] Carl Plehn, *Introduction to Public Finance*, p. 144.

[2] *Dictionary of Political Economy*, vol. i, p. 474.

[3] *Encyclopædia Britannica*, vol. xix, p. 995.

appear to be much different from octrois, for, as the *Encyclopædia Britannica* says, "Goods coming to the market or passing through the borough paid toll; to this extent the practice still exists in various European countries under the name octroi."[4] So also the fee paid for the privilege of making use of a way, ferry, or a bridge is a toll.[5]

It is in these senses that the words are used in the course of this chapter.

To impose customs duties it is necessary that there should be foreign trade in the country. There is abundant evidence to show the existence of foreign trade in the Mauryan period. When we read in the *Arthaśāstra*[6] that spies may spread false news when from one's own country or from another's country merchandise or commodities for manufacture in a manufactory are going to an enemy's country, it is certain that there was foreign trade. Again, Kauṭilya mentions[7] various articles imported into the country from outside. For instance, mention is made of fabrics of China manufacture, cotton fabrics of Madhura (now in the Madras Presidency), woollen products of Pāṇḍya (*Pauṇḍraka*), various articles from *Kāmarūpa* (Assam) and *Simhaḷa* (Ceylon), pearls produced in *Pāṇḍya*, *Simhaḷa*, *Kēraḷa*, Persia, and even *Barbara*, and various other articles from many other countries. Most of these countries were, even at the time of Aśōka, when the Mauryan empire was most extensive, quite independent of the empire. Kauṭilya himself divides[8] articles into foreign (*ātithyaṃ*); external (*bāhyaṃ*), i.e. produced in the country parts; and internal (*ābhyantaraṃ*), i.e. manufactured inside forts. Strabo[9] also says that "large quantities of Indian merchandise were conveyed by

[4] *Encyclopædia Britannica*, vol. xxxvi, p. 1053.

[5] Cohn (*Science of Finance*, p. 391) appears to stand alone in holding that a toll is "a form of taxation usually levied on articles of consumption on their crossing the national boundaries, especially on their import." Thus he identifies tolls with import duties.

[6] *Arth.*, Bk. IX, ch. 6.

[7] *Arth.*, Bk. II, ch. 11.

[8] *Arth.*, Bk. II, ch. 22.

[9] *Strabo*, xi, viii, 3.

it [the Oxus] to the Kaspian Sea," and "it [merchandise] is brought down from Arabia and India to Myos Hormos." According to Pliny,[10] indigo and crystals were imported into Rome from India. *The Periplus of the Erythrean Sea*,[11] though of a later date than the Mauryan times, gives sufficient proof of the foreign trade of India, and mentions that wine was exported to Barygaza (India, Broach). It may therefore be safely concluded that there was foreign trade among countries in Mauryan India and outside, as in later times.[12]

The question then arises as to the commercial policy of the time.

All foreign goods when they entered the country paid at the boundary a tax called *vartanī*.[13] This appears at first sight to be a customs duty, but was very probably only a road toll for the use of the king's highway.[14] It was collected by the officer in charge of the boundary (*antapāla*), who, after examining the goods as regards their quality, sealed and sent them to the octroi house (*śulkaśālā*) for the collection of the duty or *śulka*.[15]

[10] *Pliny*, xxxv, c. 6 (25).

[11] Pp. 34, 42, 287, etc.

[12] See W. Robertson, *An Historical Disquisition concerning the Knowledge which the Ancients had of India.*

[13] *Arth.*, Bk. II, ch. 21, *Antapālaḥ sapādapaṇikāṃ vartanīṃ gṛiḥṇīyāt.*

[14] *Infra*, p. 90.

[15] *Śulka* has been translated by Shāma Śāstry throughout his translation of the *Arthaśāstra* as toll. Such an interpretation is misleading. For the word literally means "a toll, tax, customs duty, particularly levied at ferries, passes, roads," etc. The word appears to have been used in Sanskrit literature in various senses. Bhaṭṭaswāmi explains *śulka* as "*śulkaḥ pañehadaśabhagadidēyaṃ rājñaḥ*" (*J.B.O.R.S.*, vol. xii, part i, p. 122), Śukra (iv, 2, 212) *vikrētṛkretṛto rājabhāgaśśulkamudāhṛitaṃ*, i.e. the king's share received from the buyer and the seller. Macdonell and Keith (*Vēdic Index*, vol. ii, p. 387) observe, "*Śulka* in the *Ṛig Vēda* clearly means price. In the *Dharmasūtras* it denotes a 'tax,' a sense which is found by Muir in a passage of the *Atharvavēda*, where *śulka* is read in the edition with great detriment to the sense." Likewise Bühler (*S.B.E.*, vol. xiv, p. 100) remarks: "I translate the one word *śulka* by 'duties and

The *śulkaśālā* was situated not near the boundary but near the large gate (main entrance) of the city,[16] and the articles evidently paid the tax after their entry into the country and before they could get into the city. But it may be urged that the boundary-keeper sent the foreign goods, perhaps with guards, to the *śulkaśālā* to pay the duties, and that these taxes were levied and collected at the *śulkaśālā* because the boundary-keeper was not the customs officer.

The *śulka* could perhaps have been taken as customs duty had it not been for two circumstances. First, merchandise was divided into three classes:[17] external (*bāhyaṃ*), i.e. arriving from the country parts; internal (*ābhyantaraṃ*), i.e. manufactured inside forts; and foreign (*ātithyaṃ*). All goods had to pay alike when exported and imported, i.e. when entering into or going out of the city.[18] There appears to be nothing to indicate that the duty was paid only when entering the country. The inference, therefore, is that, because the *śulkaśālā* was situated just outside the city, "import" and "export" duties applied to articles that entered or left, not the country, but the city.

This conclusion is supported by the second circumstance, namely, the "importation" of forbidden articles[19] into the

taxes.' The term has a great many different meanings in the law books and is in this verse apparently used in two senses. . . ." Again, he writes (*S.B.E.*, vol. ii, part i, p. 162): "According to Haradatta's commentary as given in P. U. and Mr. U. and printed in the Sanskrit Notes (for the commentary *vide Āpastambha Dharmasūtra,* Mysore Govt. Oriental Library, Series No. 15, p. 256), the *śulka* is the one-twentieth part of a merchant's gain. On account of the *sūtras* immediately following, it is, however, more probable the term is here used as a synonym of '*kara*' and includes all taxes." According to *Manu*, viii, 307, *śulka* excludes *kara*. Compare the interpretations by the six commentators of Manu (*Manusaṃhitā*, vol. ii, p. 1056).

[16] *Arth.*, Bk. II, ch. 21, *Śulkādhyakshaḥ śulkaśālādhvajaṃ cha praṅgmukhaṃ udaṅgmukhaṃ vā mahādvārābhyāśē nivēśayēt.*

[17] *Arth.*, Bk. II, ch. 22, *Śulkavyavahāraḥ bāhyamābhyantaraṃ chātithyaṃ.*

[18] *Ibid., Nishkrāmyaṃ pravēśyaṃ cha śulkaṃ.*

[19] *Ibid.*

forts. These articles were weapons, mail armour, metals, chariots, precious stones, grains, and cattle; and if imported were forfeited and the importer fined. But they could be sold free of *śulka* outside the fort.[20] This indicates that the duty was not levied if the articles were sold outside the city. In other words, the tax was on goods which entered the city. It is not known if foreign articles paid duty merely because they entered the country.

The tax at the *śulkaśālā* appears to have been paid by articles produced in the country but outside the city. For after classifying goods into external, internal, and foreign, Kauṭilya says that all these were liable to pay the tax alike when brought into or taken out of the city.[21] The goods produced in the city had not to pay the "import" tax, because they did not come in from outside, but they paid duty when exported. The external and foreign goods were taxed when coming in, and perhaps the city products also when once they went out of the city, if they were again imported. Likewise the other classes of commodities may have paid the "export" tax. In short, the duty paid to enter the city appears to have been levied on foreign goods as well as on articles produced in the country but outside the city.

Thus the evidence that the *śulka* was probably levied on country-made and foreign goods alike and for purposes of entering the city, and that some forbidden articles when brought in for purposes of sale were allowed to be sold free of *śulka* outside the city gates, strongly suggests that the *śulka* was not a custom but an octroi duty. For, as Plehn observes:[22] "Unless a city or a town forms an independent sovereignty, taxes levied on goods entering a city are not

[20] *Arth.*, Bk. II, ch. 21, *Śastravarmakavachalōharatharatnadhānya-paśūnāṃ anyatamānirvāhyaṃ nirvāhayatō yathāvaghushitō daṇḍaḥ paṇyanāśaścha. Tēshāmanyatamasyānayanē bahirēvochchhulkō vi-krayaḥ.*

[21] *Arth.*, Bk. II, ch. 22, *Nishkrāmyaṃ pravēśyaṃchaśulkaṃ.*

[22] *Introduction to Public Finance*, p. 144.

customs duties, but octrois or imposts, and partake of the nature of excises."

Parallels to this kind of tax are to be found in the Roman empire, where the taxes were known as *vectigalia*, which consisted of *portorium*, "a tax on the entry from or departure to the provinces (those cities which were allowed to levy the *portorium* shared the profits with the public treasury); the *ansarium* or *forcicarium*, a duty levied at the entrance to towns; or the *edulia*, sale of imports levied in markets."[23]

There was also an impost resembling harbour toll. In port towns merchants paid a *śulka*,[24] and, according to Bhaṭṭaswāmi,[25] the rates were 20 or 16½ per cent *ad valorem* according to the custom of the place. Vessels carrying on merchandise spoiled by water were either exempted from *śulka* or paid the impost at half the rate, and "ships that touched the ports on their way also paid the *śulka*."[26] These do not denote customs duty, but tolls, for the tax was collected even when a ship merely touched the port on voyage. These were perhaps akin to the harbour dues of ancient Greece. Boeckh observes:[27] "Besides the fiftieth imposed upon imports and exports, there may, as I conjecture, still a special port charge have been imposed upon all vessels, whether laden or not, for the use of the harbours, which had occasioned so great an expense to the state." In short, the Mauryan *śulka* was perhaps the charge paid by vessels for the privilege of lying in the harbour.[28]

It is not, however, suggested that there were no customs duties at all. For we find similar taxes referred to. Baudhā-

[23] *Encyclopædia Britannica*, vol. xix, p. 994.

[24] *Arth.*, Bk. II, ch. 28, *Paṭṭaṇānuvṛittaṃ śulkabhāgam vaṇijō dadyuḥ.*

[25] *J.B.O.R.S.*, vol. xii, part ii, p. 156.

[26] *Arth.*, Bk. II, ch. 28, . . . *Udakaprāptam paṇyamaśulkaṃ vā kuryāt. . . . Saṃyātīrnāvaḥ kshētrānugatāḥ śulkaṃyāchēta.*

[27] Boeckh, *op. cit.*, p. 427.

[28] *Ibid.*, p. 420.

yana, for instance, says[29] that the duty on goods *imported by sea* was, after deducting a choice article, ten *paṇas* in the hundred, and directs the levy of just duties or other marketable goods according to their intrinsic value without oppression. Kauṭilya has perhaps the customs duty in view when he says[30] that imported salt paid a share to the king. But evidence in the *Arthaśāstra* does not definitely indicate any customs duties except perhaps on salt; and the *śulka* discussed above was in the nature of octrois and tolls.

Octrois exist even in modern times. In continental countries of Europe, says Bastable,[31] everywhere duties have been levied on goods entering into cities. Octroi duties exist in Italy, Spain, Portugal, and in some of the towns of Austria. Although often a municipal tax, the octroi need not be so. For in the Middle Ages in France "the taxes did not remain strictly neutral, for an ordinance of Cardinal Mazarin (1647) ordered the proceeds of the octroi to be paid into the public treasury, and at other times the government claimed a certain percentage of the product, but this practice was finally abandoned in 1852."[32] In the Mauryan times also the octroi appears to have filled the coffers of the state.

In addition to the octroi, goods entering the city had to pay the gate dues (*dvārādēya*), which amounted to 20 per

29 *Baudhāyana*, i, 10, 18, 13–15. It is doubtful if Vishṇu (iii, 29–30) refers to import and export duties when he writes: *Svadēśapaṇyachcha śulkāmsam daśamaṃ ādadyāt. Paradēśapaṇyachcha viṃśatitamam.* Jolly (*S.B.E.*, vol. vii, p. 16) translates it as: "Let him take a tenth part of (the price of) marketable commodities sold in his own country and a twentieth part of (the price of) goods (sold) in another country." In the light of *Arth.*, Bk. II, ch. 16, it appears better to interpret the passage as referring to the lower internal customs duties or octrois or tolls paid by *foreign goods*, the lower duties being levied to encourage foreign intercourse.

30 *Arth.*, Bk. II, ch. 12, *Āgantulavaṇam shadbhāgaṃ dadyāt. Infra*, p. 97.

31 *Public Finance*, p. 542.

32 *Encyclopædia Britannica*, vol. xix, p. 994.

cent of the octroi duties.[33] They were remitted if circumstances required such concession. This kind of double taxation, at least of foreign commodities, was not particular to the Mauryan India. In ancient Athens such a gate duty was found.[34] Even in modern times, in Italy, Bastable observes[35] that "the result is that, in contrast with the French duties, foreign goods already submitted to customs taxation are taxed everywhere over again on their entry within the closed communes." In the Mauryan days indigenous goods also were subjected to double taxation.[36]

Foreign merchants and goods were treated favourably. Mariners and merchants who imported foreign articles are stated to have been favoured with remission of certain imposts (*āyatikshamaṃ*) so that they may get some profit.[37] Bhaṭṭaswāmi explains the concessions as comprising the removal of difficulties such as are caused by forest guards, and countries,[38] and the exemption from paying the *vyāji*. The amount of *vyāji* on commodities sold by cubical measure was $6\frac{1}{4}$ per cent *ad valorem*; that on commodities sold by weight, 5 per cent; and that on goods sold in numbers $9\frac{1}{11}$ per cent.[39] Foreigners, unless trading as asso-

[33] *Arth.*, Bk. II, ch. 22, *Dvārādēyam śulkapañchabhāgam ānugrāhikam vayathā dēśōpakāraṃ sthāpayēt.*

[34] Boeckh, *op. cit.*, p. 432. The author quotes a story and says: "The story suggests at the same time the practice of collecting a duty at the gates and, in fact, a duty collected at the gates in Athens is mentioned. This could hardly have been imposed upon the person. Nevertheless, it is not to be denied that a tax was collected in the market."

[35] *Public Finance*, p. 545.

[36] *Arth.*, Bk. II, ch. 22.

[37] *Arth.*, Bk. II., ch. 16, *Parabhūmijam paṇyamanugrahēṇāvāhayēt. Nāvikasārtha vāhēbhyaścha parihāramāyatikshamaṃ dadyāt.*

[38] *J.B.O.R.S.*, vol. xii, part i, p. 96. Bhaṭṭaswāmi limits the exemptions to the *mānavyāji* of one-sixteenth (*shōḍhaśabhāgamōkshēṇa*), but the exemption appears to extend to the other kinds of *vyāji* also. Gaṇapati Śāstri's interpretation (*op. cit.*, vol. i, pp. 241–2) appears incorrect.

[39] *Bhaṭṭaswāmi*, f. 34.

ciations and partnerships, appear to have been exempted from being sued for debts.[40] This perhaps implies that the merchants could not be sued in the Mauryan courts for debts incurred in foreign countries.

The officer in charge of boundaries (*antapāla*) made good whatever was lost by the merchants. The state thus voluntarily and without premium insured the goods and was responsible for their safety.[41]

The goods were carefully examined and sealed so as to ensure their quality. Some commodities were exempted from paying the octroi duties. Such were commodities intended for marriages, or taken by a bride from her parents' house to her husband's or intended for presentation, or taken for the purpose of sacrificial performance, confinement of women, worship of gods, ceremony of tonsure, investiture of sacred thread, gift of cows made before marriage—any religious rite, consecration ceremony, and other special ceremonials.[42] Articles of great benefit, as well as rare seeds, were not taxed. But things which caused harm or were useless to the country were shut out.[43] Thus foreign goods which were harmful to the country, probably because they competed with indigenous industries, were prohibited from being imported.[44] Some articles were forbidden to be imported into the city, and they were weapons, mail armour, metals, chariots, precious stones, grains, and cattle.[45] Some of these

[40] *Arth.*, Bk. II, ch. 16, *Anabhiyōgaśchārthēshvāgantūnāṃ anyatra sabhyōpakāribhyaḥ*. For a different interpretation see *J.B.O.R.S.*, vol. xii, part i, p. 91.

[41] *Arth.*, Bk. II, ch. 21, *Nashṭāpahṛitañcha pratividadhyāt*. Cf. *Āpastambha*, ii, 10, 26, 8; *Vishṇu*, iii, 66–7.

[42] *Arth.*, Bk. II, ch. 21.

[43] *Ibid.*, *Rāshṭrapīḍākaraṃ bhāṇḍaṃ uchchhindyādaphalaṃ cha yat. Mahōpakāramuchchhulkaṃ kuryādbījantudurlabhaṃ.*

[44] *Ibid.* This was not merely in times of war.

[45] *Ibid.*, *Śastravarmakavachalōharatharatnadhānyapaśūnāṃ anya tamānirvāhyaṃ nirvāhayatō yathāvaghushitō daṇḍaḥ paṇyanāśaścha.* Jayaswal (*Hindu Polity*, part ii, p. 168) interprets this passage as follows: "Certain commodities should not be exported while their imports are to be encouraged by not being taxed at all. They are,

goods—for example, weapons, armour, and chariots—were prohibited perhaps to ensure the stability of the state. As to why grains and cattle came under this group is not clear. It was perhaps to help the local traders from outside competition. Further, this prohibition appears to have been only not to bring them into the city, for the goods were allowed to be sold free of duty outside the city,[46] perhaps because, as Shāma Śāstry suggests,[47] they were usually purchased by the king.

for instance: (*a*) Weapons and armour. (*b*) Metals. (*c*) Military vehicles. (*d*) Rare things. (*e*) Grains, and (*f*) Cattle." This interpretation is opposed to the interpretation followed in this book. For Jayaswal writes of *the prohibition of the export of these articles* and *the encouragement of their imports*, while I have taken it only as the prohibition of imports. He appears to rely on the same edition of the *Arthaśāstra* as this book follows, namely Kauṭilya's *Arthaśāstra* in the Mysore Government Oriental Library, Series 1909. In the footnote (*Hindu Polity*, part ii, p. 168) Jayaswal gives reference to the text as "*śastravarmakavacha . . . anyatamamanirvāhyaṃ*," etc. (*Arthaśāstra*, Bk. II, 21, 39, 111). It will be seen that though quoting from the same edition of the *Arthaśāstra* he reads the text a little differently, i.e. while he gives it as *anyatamamanirvāhyaṃ*, the book published by the Mysore Oriental Library has *anyatamānirvāhyaṃ*. Jayaswal does not explain the difference. Moreover, even if his version is accepted it is doubtful if his interpretation is correct. Further, in view of the immediately succeeding passage in the *Arthaśāstra*—*tēshāṃ anyatamasyānayanē bahirēvōchchhulkō vikrayaḥ*—which means that when any of such commodities were brought in for sale they were to be sold free of toll far outside the fort, it is very probable that the prohibition was applied to imports and that the meaning followed in this book is sound. Thus Jayaswal's interpretation is open to doubt.

Sohrabji (*Notes*, p. 52) suggests a different reading. Instead of *yathāvaghushitaḥ*, Sohrabji suggests *anyathāghōshāyataḥ*. "The *anirvāhya* articles," he writes, "are to be destroyed if the man makes a false statement and he is to be punished. But if he declares the value correctly even then they are not to be allowed into the city but sold outside the *durga*, but free from tax. Of course this only refers to foreign merchants who come into the city."

The original reading appears better.

[46] *Arth.*, Bk. II, ch. 21, *Tēshāmanyatamasyānayanē bahirēvōchchhulkō vikrayaḥ*.

[47] *Arth. Trans.*, p. 133, footnote.

A COMPARATIVE TABLE OF MAURYAN OCTROI DUTIES AND BRITISH INDIAN CUSTOMS DUTIES[48]

Article	Mauryan Octroi Duty	British Indian Customs Duty (1923)[49]
1. Arms[50]	10 % or $6\frac{2}{3}$ %	30 %
2. Fruits and flowers (flowers, fruits, vegetables,[51] roots, bulbous roots)	$16\frac{2}{3}$ %	15 %
3. Dried fish ..	$16\frac{2}{3}$ %	Rate not exceeding 1 rupee fixed by Governor-General
4. Dried meat[52] ..	$16\frac{2}{3}$ %	15 %
5. Precious stones ..	Duty determined by experts on the basis of the time, cost, and finish of the production of these articles	Free if unset, 15 % if otherwise
6. Conch shells ..	Duty determined by experts on the basis of the time, cost, and finish of the production of these articles	15 %

48 The articles given by Kauṭilya have been regrouped here under modern heads for purposes of comparison as well as of convenience.

49 Of the British Indian customs duties only those on articles taxed under the Mauryans are here given. The figures for British India are from K. T. Shah, *Trade, Tariff, and Transport in India*, ch. xiv.

50 "Arms" in the Mauryan time included mail armour and the like. See table of octroi duties and gate dues *infra*, p. 88. It is not certain as to which of the two rates, 10 % or $6\frac{2}{3}$ %, was paid. Even in British India the duty differs as regards different arms, but 30 % applies in most cases.

51 These items are considered here under fruits and flowers.

52 Meat is taken here as coming under "all sorts of food" in the British Indian customs schedule.

A COMPARATIVE TABLE OF MAURYAN OCTROI DUTIES AND BRITISH INDIAN CUSTOMS DUTIES—*continued*

Article	Mauryan Octroi Duty	British Indian Customs Duty (1923)
7. Cotton piece goods (cotton cloth)	10 % or $6\frac{2}{3}$ %	11 %
8. Fibrous garments[53]	10 % or $6\frac{2}{3}$ %	15 %
9. Fibres	5 % or 4 %	15 %
10. Silk	10 % or $6\frac{2}{3}$ %	15 %
11. Wool	10 % or $6\frac{2}{3}$ %	Free
12. Raw materials for fibrous or textile garments[54]	10 % or $6\frac{2}{3}$ %	Free for raw cotton. 15 % for fibrous raw materials
13. Threads[55] ..	5 % or 4 %	15 %
14. All other articles (carpets, curtains)	10 % or $6\frac{2}{3}$ %	15 %
15. Metals[56]	10 % or $6\frac{2}{3}$ %	10 %
16. Medicines ..	5 % or 4 %	15 %
17. Sulphuret of arsenic (red arsenic)	10 % or $6\frac{2}{3}$ %	15 %
18. Dyes (colouring ingredients)	10 % or $6\frac{2}{3}$ %	15 %

[53] This has been taken to denote hemp and the like.

[54] Cotton is mentioned as paying a tax of 4 % or 5 %. As to how cotton is to be distinguished from raw materials (No. 12) is not clear.

[55] Cotton seqing and darning thread has to pay in British India 5 %, while other kinds of cotton threads 15 %. We have taken the item under the latter head.

[56] In British India the duty on metals varies as regards different metals, but that on iron and steel is 10 %. Other metals generally pay 15 %.

A COMPARATIVE TABLE OF MAURYAN OCTROI DUTIES AND BRITISH INDIAN CUSTOMS DUTIES—*continued*

Article	Mauryan Octroi Duty	British Indian Customs Duty (1923)
19. Vermilion ..	10 % or 6⅔ %	15 %
20. Spices	10 % or 6⅔ %	15 %
21. Wine[57]	10 % or 6⅔ %	4½ or 8 rupees per six-quart bottle
22. Liquor[58]	4 % or 5 %	8 annas per six-quart bottle
23. Ferments ..	6⅔ % or 10 %	15 %
24. Skins	6⅔ % or 10 %	Free if raw or salted, 2½ % if otherwise
25. Ivory	6⅔ % or 10 %	15 %
26. Animals	4 % or 5 %	Free
27. Salt	4 % or 5 %	Duty is varying. Now it is R. 1–4–0 per *maund*
28. Sugar	4 % or 5 %	25 %
29. Oil	4 % or 5 %	7½ % or 15 %
30. Grains	4 % or 5 %	2½ %
31. Earthenware[59] (clay pots)	4 % or 5 %	15 %
32. Wood	4 % or 5 %	15 %, 2½ % if fire-wood

[57] The difference in rate in British India depends on quality.

[58] This is coarser kind of liquor.

[59] It is doubtful if clay pots are taxed in British India. Here they have been included as coming under "all other articles" under earthenware.

A COMPARATIVE TABLE OF MAURYAN OCTROI DUTIES AND BRITISH INDIAN CUSTOMS DUTIES—*continued*

Article	Mauryan Octroi Duty	British Indian Customs Duty (1923)
33. Bamboo	4 % or 5 %	15 %
34. Miscellaneous[60] (other commodities)	20 %	15 %

TABLE OF OCTROI DUTIES AND GATE DUES[61]

Article	Octroi Duty (*ad valorem*)	Gate Dues (*ad valorem*)
1. Flowers, fruits, vegetables, bulbous roots, fruits of creepers (*pallikya*), seeds, dried fish, dried meat	16⅔ %	3⅓ %
2. Conch shells, diamonds, precious stones, pearls, corals, and necklaces	Duty determined by experts on the time, cost, and finish of the production of the article	One-fifth of the amount octroi duty determined
3. Fibrous garments, cotton cloths, silk, mail armour,[62] sulphuret of arsenic, red arsenic, vermilion, metals, colouring ingredients, sandal, brown sandal, pungents, ferments, dress, and the like	10 % or 6⅔ %	2 % or ⅓ %

[60] Some other articles taxed under the Mauryas but for which no definite modern parallels are found or which are rather obscure are: Cloths, 5 % or 4 %; Cooked rice, 5 % or 4 %; Dress, 10 % or 6⅔ %; Sandal, 10 % or 6⅔ %; Brown sandal, 10 % or 6⅔ %; Products yielded by worms, 10 % or 6⅔ %.

[61] *Arth.*, Bk. II, ch. 22.

[62] Mail armour mentioned here is forbidden to be imported, as mentioned in a previous chapter, and when brought in for sale was

TABLE OF OCTROI DUTIES AND GATE DUES[61]—*contd.*

Article	Octroi Duty (*ad valorem*)	Gate Dues (*ad valorem*)
Wine, ivory, skins, raw materials for fibrous or cotton garments, carpets, curtains, and products yielded by worms	10 % or $6\frac{2}{3}$ %	2 % or $\frac{1}{3}$ %
Wool and other products yielded by goats and sheep	10 % or $6\frac{2}{3}$ %	2 % or $\frac{1}{3}$ %
4. Cloths, quadrupeds, bipeds, threads, cotton, scents, medicine, wood, bamboo, fibres, skins, clay pots	5 % or 4 %	1 % or $\frac{4}{5}$ %
Grains, oils, sugar, salt, liquor, cooked rice, and the like	5 % or 4 %	1 % or $\frac{4}{5}$ %
5. All other commodities[63]	20 %	4 %

Tolls are of various kinds. Those mentioned by Cohn[64] as existing in the Frankish kingdom are bridge toll, river toll, harbour toll, road toll, wheel toll, packhorse toll, foot-passenger toll, market toll, and the like. Under the Mauryas also there were different kinds of tolls. First, goods which were exported from the city had to pay toll to the extent of the octroi duty mentioned in the foregoing statement. There were, again, tolls in the nature of tolls thorough of modern English law. "Toll traverse is paid for passing

to be sold free of toll outside the city (*supra*, p. 84). It is therefore inexplainable how mail armour could be mentioned here as an article paying duty.

63 The passage (*Arth.*, Bk. II, ch. 22) runs, *pravēśyānāṃ mūlya pañchabhāgaḥ*, and this means the tax on imports is one-fifth of their value. As it is very improbable that the goods had to pay 20 % in addition to the octroi duty and gate dues which themselves sometimes amounted to 15 % or 20 %, the passage has been interpreted to apply to commodities not enumerated above.

64 *Science of Finance*, p. 390.

over a private way, bridge, or ferry. No consideration need be proved. Toll thorough is paid for the use of the highway."[65] Of this kind was probably the Mauryan *vartanī* or road toll collected by the officer in charge of the boundaries on all goods entering the state.[66] The tax may have been levied because of the use made of the king's highway. Perhaps of this kind were the tolls existing in South India in the first century of the Christian era, of which Kanakasabhai Pillai[67] writes: "The principal thoroughfares in the interior of the country were guarded by the king's soldiers, and tolls were levied on these highways"; and, "Tolls were collected on the trunk roads and by caravans, and at the frontier of each kingdom."[68] Another kind of toll was the ferry toll, which was the hire for the use of the government boats in crossing rivers.[69]

The road and ferry tolls may conveniently be brought together in one statement for purposes of comparison (see Table on facing page).

The ferry tolls[70] were double the foregoing amount in case of big rivers. The income went to the state coffers direct, for Kauṭilya says,[71] "The evidence of a ferryman should be given and the daily income should be remitted." Free

[65] *Encyclopædia Britannica*, vol. xxvi, p. 1053.

[66] *Arth.*, Bk. II, ch. 21. *Supra*, p. 77. Cf. Bhaṭṭaswāmi's interpretation (*J.B.O.R.S.*, vol. xii, part i, p. 125).

[67] *Tamils Eighteen Hundred Years Ago*, p. 109.

[68] *Ibid.*, p. 112.

[69] *Arth.*, Bk. II, ch. 28. That the ferry toll was the boat hire is probable from what Manu says (viii, 406): "For a long passage the boat hire must be proportioned to the places and times, know that this (rule refers) to (passages along) the banks of rivers, at sea there is no settled (freight)." Vishṇu (iii, 16) also mentions fares to be paid at ferries. While a Nasik Cave Inscription mentions Ushavadāta as establishing free ferries by boats (*Ep. Ind.*, viii, no. 8, p. 79).

[70] *Arth.*, Bk. II, ch. 28, *Kshudrapaśurmanushyaścha sabhārō māshakaṃ dadyāt. Śirōbhāraḥ kāyabhārō gavāśvañcha dvau. Ushṭramahishaṃ chaturaḥ. Pañchalaghuyānaṃ. Shaḍgōliṅgaṃ. Saptaśakaṭaṃ Paṇyabhāraḥ pādaṃ. Tenabhāṇḍabhārō vyākhyātaḥ. Dviguṇō mahānadīshutaraḥ.*

[71] *Ibid.*, *Kārmikapratyayaṃ dadyānnityaṃ chāhnikamāvahēt.*

passes for exemption from ferry toll were given to ascetics, brahmans, and such others.[72] As in the case of the road toll, here also the state was liable for any loss of goods caused by the loss of the boat on account of heavy loading, sailing at improper time and place, want of a ferryman, or unsoundness of the vessel.[73] Similar tolls were existing at the time of Yuan Chwang, who records[74] that "Tradesmen

ROAD AND FERRY TOLLS

	Road Toll [75]	Ferry Toll [76]
1. A head-load of merchandise ..	1 *māsha*	2 *māshas*
Man with load	—	1 *māsha*
2. Minor quadruped	¼ *paṇa*	1 *māsha*
3. A single-hoofed animal ..	1 *paṇa*	—
Horse	—	2 *māshas*
4. Each head of cattle	½ *paṇa*	—
Cow	—	2 *māshas*
Buffalo	—	4 *māshas*
5. Cartload of merchandise ..	1¼ *paṇas*	—
Small cart	—	5 *māshas*
Medium cart	—	6 *māshas*
Big cart	—	7 *māshas*
6. Camel	—	4 *māshas*

[72] *Arth.*, Bk. II, ch. 28. Compare *Manu*, viii, 407: "But a woman who has been pregnant two months and more, an ascetic, a hermit in the forest, and Brahmans who were students of the *Vēda* shall not be made to pay toll at a ferry."

[73] *Arth.*, Bk. II, ch. 28, *Atibhārēṇāvēlāyāmatīrthē taratas̀cha purushōpakaraṇa hīnāyāṃ asatkṛitāyāṃ vā nāvi vipannāyāṃ nāvadhyakshō nashṭaṃ vinashṭaṃ vā abhyābhavēt.*

[74] *Yuan Chwang*, vol. i, p. 176.

[75] *Arth.*, Bk. II, ch. 21, *Antapālaḥ sapādapāṇikāṃ vartanīṃ gṛihṇīyāt paṇyavahanasya paṇikāmēkakhurasya paśūnāmardhapaṇikāṃ kshudrapaśūnāṃ pādikāṃ aṃsabhārasya māshikāṃ.*

[76] Compare the rates mentioned by Manu (viii, 404–5): An empty cart, 1 *paṇa*; an animal, a woman, ½ *paṇa* each; an unloaded man, ⅛ *paṇa*; carts with merchandise, *ad valorem.*

go to and from bartering their merchandise after paying light duties at ferries and barrier stations."

A carriage[77] cess (*ātivāhikam*) collected by the boundary-keeper is also mentioned, but it is uncertain what this was, because carts with merchandise have already come under road toll and ferry toll. Perhaps this was an additional duty.

Another kind of toll was that paid by ships—the harbour toll. When ships anchored at ports on their voyage they paid the tax.[78] But when the vessels sought refuge in the harbour with goods spoiled by rough seas they were either exempted from paying toll or required to pay half the amount.[79] Likewise, merchants also paid the regulated customary toll in port towns.[80]

Evasion of the payment of tolls was heavily fined, the fines often amounting to eight times the toll, and sometimes even the commodity was confiscated.[81] Thus in Mauryan times the revenue from tolls was derived from the road toll or cess, the ferry toll, the carriage cess, and the harbour toll.

[77] *Arth.*, Bk. II, chs. 16 and 28. Cf. *J.B.O.R.S.*, vol. xii, part ii, p. 160.

[78] *Arth.*, Bk. II, ch. 28. [79] *Ibid.* [80] *Ibid.*

[81] *Arth.*, Bk. II, ch. 21, *Nigūhitaphalgubhāṇḍaṃ śulkāshṭaguṇō daṇḍaḥ. Sārabhāṇḍaṃ sarvāpahāraḥ.* Cf. *Manu*, viii, 400; *Vaśishṭha*, xix, 25; *Vishṇu*, iii, 31.

CHAPTER V

EXCISE AND SALT REVENUES

I. *Excise Revenue:* Duty on prostitutes, actors, etc.—Duty on artisans—Revenue from liquor. II. *Salt Revenue:* In the form of excise revenue, customs duty, consumers tax

I. EXCISE REVENUE

EXCISE is "duty charged on home goods either in the process of their manufacture or before their sale to the consumer."[1] It is an internal tax imposed at some stage in the production of the article. It is usual to regard licence duties and fees as coming under excise. "It is, however, the practice to classify under the general head of excise . . . a large number of *assessed taxes*, being licence duties paid to the state in return for permission to practice or follow certain sports, trades, or occupations, e.g. the dog, game, and gun licences, and the licences on brewers, auctioneers, and pawnbrokers."[2] In this book also licence duties are regarded as excise taxes.

The first of such duties was that on prostitutes, who in the Mauryan period appear to have been under the control and protection of the state.[3] But a prostitute who put herself under the "protection" of a private individual and ceased to attend the king's court paid one and a quarter *paṇas* per mensem to the state.[4] This contribution was

[1] *Encyclopædia Britannica*, vol. x, p. 58.

[2] *Dictionary of Political Economy*, vol. i, p. 787. Also see Bastable, *Public Finance*, p. 505; *Encyclopædia Britannica*, vol. x, p. 58.

[3] *Arth.*, Bk. II, ch. 27.

[4] *Ibid.*, *Aviśantī sapādapaṇāvaruddhā māsavētanaṃ dadyāt.* Bhaṭṭaswāmi (*J.B.O.R.S.*, vol. xii, part ii, p. 152) gives two interpretations of the passage: *Kēchit abhagnabhōgātu saivāvaruddhā niyataikapurushagāminī sapādapaṇaṃ māsavētanam gaṇikāyai dadyāt. Aparētu bhagnabhōgaiva yadā kēnachidapadadhṛitā bhavati tadā karma nikshayārtham gaṇikādhyakshāya dadyāt.* I have followed the first interpretation with the modification that the payment was made to the *gaṇikādhyaksha* and not to the *gaṇika*. Compare *Notes*, p. 61.

imposed on certain classes of persons, perhaps in order to keep them at least under the indirect control of the state by means of a kind of registration.

Actors, dancers, musicians, buffoons, mimics, and such others who came from foreign countries to give exhibitions had to pay five *paṇas* as licence fees or *prēkshāvētana.*[5] Likewise fishermen paid one-sixth of their haul as fee for fishing licence (*naukahāṭakam*),[6] for, as Kauṭilya observes, the king was to exercise his right of ownership with regard to fishing, ferrying, and trading in vegetables, in reservoirs or lakes.[7]

Under the head of forts in the chapter on revenue collection Kauṭilya mentions an income from guilds of artisans and handicraftsmen (*kāruśilpigaṇāḥ*).[8] This was probably a fee for the registration and recognition of the corporations and for the special privileges granted to them as in the Middle Ages, similar to the modern licence fees.[9]

[5] *Arth.*, Bk. II, ch. 27. Compare the practice in other kingdoms of the ancient world. "In Byzantium fortune-tellers who, according to the testimony of Isocrates and Lycian, did a profitable business, quacks, jugglers, and other itinerant practitioners of the magic art paid the third part of their gain for permission to itinerate in the exercise of their arts and persons of the same class in ancient times in other countries were also taxed. Probably Athens likewise collected a tax upon those who practised their arts" (Boeckh, *op. cit.*, p. 442).

[6] *Arth.*, Bk. II, ch. 28, *Matsyabandhakā naukahāṭakam shaḍbhāgaṃ dadyuḥ.*

[7] *Arth.*, Bk. II, ch. 1. *Matsyaplavaharitapaṇyānāṃ sētushu rājā svāmyaṃ gachchhēt.*

[8] *Arth.*, Bk. II, ch. 6.

[9] Compare what Seligman writes: "One of the chief sources of royal income in medieval Europe consisted in the so-called fines for licences, concessions, and franchises. These were payments by individuals and associations for all kinds of special privileges, such as to secure the general favour of the crown to retain or to quit office, to obtain the right of exporting commodities to conduct some business in a particular way, to obtain special jurisdictional privileges, to possess the right of *firma burgi*, and so on. A most common instance can be found in the trading privileges of the guilds, granted chiefly for the sake of the accruing emoluments. Similar to these

In modern states excise revenue is largely derived by taxation of alcoholic drinks. "The tendency of modern legislation has been to throw the largest possible burden of excise taxation on alcoholic drinks, and to exempt, as far as possible, other articles."[10] As a practical example it may be mentioned that in British India in 1924–25, out of a total excise revenue of a little more than 19 crores of rupees, as much as 16½ crores came from liquor and drugs alone.[11]

In the Mauryan time the manufacture and sale of liquor were completely controlled and regulated by the state in forts, country parts, and in camps.[12]

Some revenue was realized from liquor in the form of licence fee. On special occasions like fairs and festivals householders were allowed to manufacture a kind of white liquor (*arishṭa*), used for medicinal purposes, and some other similar drinks; while on some other occasions like festivals, fairs,[13] and pilgrimages allowed to manufacture liquor for four days.[14] A licence fee, however, was collected from such manufacturers.[15]

medieval concessions are the modern licences, especially in the Southern Commonwealths, which are conferred on individuals and corporations alike and in most cases for purely fiscal reasons" (*Essays in Taxation*, p. 222).

10 *Dictionary of Political Economy*, vol. i, p. 787.

11 *Sixty Years of Indian Finance*, p. 261.

12 *Arth.*, Bk. II, ch. 25, *Surādhyakshaḥ surākiṇvavyavahārān durgē janapadē skandhāvārē vā tajjātasurākiṇvavyavahāribhiḥ kārayēt.*

13 These may be the *samājas* referred to by Aśōka, e.g. in *R.E. I*.

14 *Arth.*, Bk. II, ch. 25, *Kuṭumbinaḥ krityēshu śvētasurāṃ aushadhārthaṃ vā arishṭaṃ anyadvā kartum labhēran. Utsavasamājayātrāsu chaturahas saurikōdēyaḥ. Teshvanujñātānāṃ prahvaṇāntam daivasikamatya yamgriḥṇīyāt.*

15 Bhaṭṭaswāmi (*J.B.O.R.S.*, vol. xii, part ii, p. 147; also see Gaṇapati Śāstri, *op. cit.*, vol. i, p. 296) follows the reading *ananujñātānāṃ*. He explains that on festival occasions people were allowed to *drink* without limit and that a fine was collected from those who manufactured liquor on these occasions without licence.

Shāma Śāstry's reading and interpretation (*Trans.*, p. 146) followed along in the text appear better because (1) *Arth.*, Bk. II, ch. 25, does not mention any limitation on drinking, and (2) the chapter prohibits manufacture by unlicensed people. Further, it is probable

Another source of revenue from liquor was a duty of 5 per cent imposed on persons selling foreign stuff.[16] This may be regarded as a licence fee for selling foreign liquor.

Dealers in certain kinds of liquor[17] paid an impost under the name "compensation" (*vaidharaṇa*) because their business deprived the state of the profits that would have accrued to it had the state itself traded.

II. SALT REVENUE

"The salt duty in India," writes K, T. Shah,[18] "is an old item of public revenue, alike instructive in its historical aspect and productive in its fiscal aspect." The principle on which duties on salt and other necessaries of life are levied is that if at all the masses are to contribute to the public purse, it must be largely through taxes levied upon articles of universal consumption.

In Mauryan times there appear to have been three sources of salt, viz. imported salt, that from inland mines and mountains, and sea salt.[19] Pliny observes[20] that "there are mountains also formed of native salt, as, for instance, Ormenus in India, where it is cut out like blocks from a quarry and is continually produced, whence a greater revenue accrues to the sovereigns than those derived from gold and pearls." The manufacture and sale of salt were

that permission to manufacture liquor was given even on the "free" days after payment of fees, while unlicensed manufacturers must have been dealt with otherwise according to law.

[16] *Arth.*, Bk. II, ch. 25, *Arājapaṇyāḥ pañchakaṃ śataṃ śulkam dadyuḥ.*

[17] The liquors were *surākā, mēdaka, arishṭa*; wine, *phalāmla* and *āmlaśīdhū.*

[18] *Sixty Years of Indian Finance*, p. 249.

[19] *Arth.*, Bk. II, ch. 12. Even in modern days 30 per cent of salt is imported by sea.

[20] Bk. xiii, c. 7 (39). There are other references also. Strabo writes (xv, 31): "It is said that in country of Sopiethes there is a mountain of fossil salt which could supply all India"; and (v, ii, 6): "The salt mines in India mentioned by Clitarchus."

controlled by the state through the superintendent of ocean mines.[21] The revenue was derived in three forms, namely, excise duty, customs duty on imported salt, and a consumers tax, just as in British India salt revenue is derived from customs duty, excise duty, and government monopoly of the manufacture and sale of salt.

As regards excise revenue, every person except hermits (*vānaprastha*), who were allowed to manufacture salt without licence, had to obtain a licence to manufacture salt[22] and pay the government either a fixed quantity of salt or a money rent (*prakraya*).[23] If paid in kind, the tax was to be paid in the royal measure, which was 5 per cent larger than the market measure.[24] The state thus obtained 5 per cent extra revenue when its share of salt was sold.

A similar system of licence fee and excise duty prevails in some parts of British India. For instance, in Madras the manufacturer has to pay an excise duty and he is free to sell his salt in the market. But where private individuals take a lease of government salt factories they must obtain a licence before they can manufacture and sell salt.

Secondly, the revenue was derived from customs duty. Imported salt had to pay a tax of one-sixth part or 16⅔ per cent *ad valorem* in the royal measure.[25] Here also, as the royal measure appears to have been 5 per cent more than the market measure, the tariff taken in the royal measure but calculated in the market measure[26] meant an increase

[21] *Arth.*, Bk. II, ch. 12.

[22] *Ibid.*, *Vilavaṇamuttamaṃ daṇḍaṃ dadyāt. Anisṛishṭōpajīvīcha anyatra vānaprasthēbhyaḥ.*

[23] *Ibid.*, *Lavaṇādhyakshaḥ pākamuktaṃ lavaṇabhāgaṃprakrayaṃ cha yathākālaṃ saṃgṛihṇīyāt, vikrayāchcha mūlyaṃ rūpaṃ vyājīṃ.* I have followed Bhaṭṭaswāmi regarding the money rent (*J.B.O.R.S.*, vol. xi, part 3, p. 58).

[24] *Ibid.*

[25] *Arth.*, Bk. II. ch. 12. *Āgantulavaṇaṃ shaḍbhāgaṃ dadyāt. Datta bhāgavibhāgasya vikrayaḥ panchakaṃ śataṃ vyājīm rūpaṃ rūpikam cha.* Compare Bhaṭṭaswāmi's interpretation of *bhāgavibhāga*, *bhāga* meaning the *shaḍbhāga* and *vibhāga* the difference between the royal and market measures (*J.B.O.R.S.*, vol. xi, part 3, pp. 58–9).

[26] *Arth.*, Bk. II, ch. 12. About *vyāji Supra*, p. 32.

of $\frac{5}{6}$ per cent in the duty, that being 5 per cent of $16\frac{2}{3}$ per cent. The actual duty on imported salt, therefore, was $17\frac{1}{2}$ per cent, which is almost a protectionist tariff. In British India, "on imported salt a duty is levied equal approximately to the duty on inland manufacture."

Further, the purchasers of imported salt had to pay two more imposts: one was an internal duty or octroi (*śulka*), and the other compensation (*vaidharaṇa*), to make good the loss which the indigenous manufacturers of salt suffered.[27] Here perhaps the policy of protection was in operation. Trade in indigenous salt was looked upon as the king's commerce, and purchasers of imported salt, as they purchased a foreign commodity, had to make good the loss which the king's commerce suffered. This compensation was to be paid not to the native manufacturers but to the state. If the foregoing taxes were not paid, the purchasers were fined 600 *paṇas*.[28]

There was, moreover, the consumers tax. The state exempted men learned in the *Vēdas*, those engaged in penance, and labourers from paying the tax only when they used salt as food.[29] The labourers were exempted perhaps because of their poverty, and the others because of their caste and occupation. But even these classes could not make use of salt for purposes other than food without paying toll. All others had to pay tax, whatever the purpose for which they used salt and alkalis.[30]

[27] *Arth.*, Bk. II, ch. 12. It is doubtful if the *śulka* does not refer to the customs duty but to a separate impost.

[28] *Ibid.*, *Śulkaṃrājapaṇyāchchhēdānurūpaṃ cha vaidharaṇaṃ dadyāt anyatra krētā shaṭchhatamatyayancha.*

[29] *Ibid.*, *Śrōtriyāstapasvinōvishṭayaścha bhuktalavaṇaṃ harēyuḥ. Atō anyōlavaṇakshāravargaḥ śulkaṃ dadyāt.*

[30] *Ibid.*

CHAPTER VI

MISCELLANEOUS TAXES

Poll tax—Income tax—Excess profits tax—Labour tax—Sales or turnover tax—Trade taxes—Taxes on herdsmen, hunters, etc.—War tax—House tax—Confiscation of unearned increment—Forced benevolences—Gambling—*Bali* —*Kḷripta* and *Piṇḍakara*

UNDER this head will be considered taxes some of which, though important even to-day, cannot be dealt with separately because of the meagre information available about them in Mauryan times.

POLL TAX

A poll tax means a capitation or head tax levied on individuals. It is said to be one of the earliest forms of taxation. In England poll taxes were tried at intervals from 1377 till 1698.[1] Even to-day poll taxes are to be found, but, as Seligman says,[2] they have assumed a political significance, as in Switzerland and in some of the American commonwealths, where the payment of the tax is made a condition of suffrage.

In Mauryan times there appear to have been two kinds of poll tax. One of them had perhaps a political significance. Undesirable foreigners (*bāhirikas*) had to pay a tax to enter the city.[3] This was really a poll tax, and similar to the one found in ancient Athens, where a foreigner who remained in the city beyond a certain period paid a tax "for protection."[4] No doubt the Athenian and the

[1] *Dictionary of Political Economy*, vol. iii, p. 517.

[2] *Essays in Taxation*, p. 10.

[3] *Arth.*, Bk. II, ch. 4, *Nacha bāhirikānkuryāt puravāshṭrōpaghātakān. Kshipējjanapadē chaitān sarvānvā dāpayētkarān.* Compare *ibid.*, p. 57, footnote, for references to *bāhirikas* in *Suyangaga Sūtra* and *Jñātadharma Sūtra*.

[4] Boeckh, *op. cit.*, p. 438: "Among the direct and personal taxes

Mauryan taxes differed from each other in that the former was on all foreigners who remained in Athens beyond a certain period, while the other was on unwelcome foreigners. But they have this in common, that both were on foreigners *because* they were foreigners, thus differing from the modern one mentioned by Seligman, which is a qualification for full citizenship.

In ancient India itself, though of a later period, are found taxes similar to the Mauryan one. Such, for example, is the one on *Ājīvakas* under the Chōḷa kings Kulōttuṅga III[5] and Rājarāja III.[6] The *Ājīvakas* being, like the *bāhirikas*, undesirables had to pay a tax.

The other kind of Mauryan poll tax is mentioned by Megasthenes. He records that of the magistrates in Pāṭalīputra, "the third body consists of those who inquire when and how births and deaths occur, with the view not only of levying a tax, but also in order that births and deaths among both high and low may not escape the cognizance of government."[7] What its amount was and how it was levied is not known. It was perhaps not considered, as in Athens, "most ignominious which none but slaves paid to

that paid by the domiciled alien for protection is the best known. . . . At Athens a foreigner was allowed to dwell a definite number of days without being taxed. If he remained beyond that period he was considered as an alien under the protection of the state or a domiciled foreigner and subjected to the payment of the tax for protection."

[5] *Madras Inscriptions*, p. 74.

[6] *Ibid.*, p. 98.

[7] *Strabo*, XV, i, 50. The registration of families is mentioned by Yuan Chwang (*op. cit.*, vol. i, p. 176) who says: "Families are not registered," thus indicating that registration of families was not unknown. Fahien also writes (*Travels*, p. 42): "They (the people) have not to register their households." Kauṭilya also mentions (Bk. II, chs. 35–6) that one of the duties of the *gōpa* was to register details about families.

This kind of tax is found in later times. The record of Rājanārāyaṇa Śambhava rāya (*Madras Inscriptions*, p. 383) mentions a tax on individuals (*perkkadamai*), while the contribution paid by weavers per head annually in *Ep. Ind.*, v, no. 3, is, as Fleet says, a capitation tax.

the tyrant."[8] The Mauryan tax may have been levied on every member of the family, including children, the tax increasing with every birth and decreasing with every death.[9]

INCOME TAX

The tax on income is no modern invention. It appears to have been known to the Mauryas as well as to the Athenians. The Mauryan income tax was levied on a particular class of people. Even to-day all incomes are not taxed, and some kinds of income are exempted from the tax. Where, for instance, a land tax is levied, often agricultural incomes do not pay the income tax. Apart from taxing a particular class, the Mauryas appear to have adopted the proportional system of income taxation.

The tax was levied on prostitutes, and possibly also on actors, dancers, musicians, jugglers, singers, players on musical instruments, buffoons, mimics, rope dancers, heralds, pimps, unchaste women, and wandering bards.[10] Every prostitute was required to supply information to the superintendent as to the amount of her daily fees, her expected income, and the paramour.[11] The actors, dancers, and others also had to furnish the same information as far as it applied to them.[12] In short, these classes had to submit a statement

[8] Boeckh, *op. cit.*, p. 407.

[9] Were it only on adults, the state had to wait for a number of years and there was perhaps no necessity to register births for levying a tax. The state could have registered only adults.

[10] Some of these classes seem to have been regarded as "undesirables." *Arth.*, Bk. VIII, ch. 3, *Pāṭachcharadyūtakāra lubdhakagāyakavādakaiśchānarthaiḥ saṃyōgaḥ. kāmaḥ.* Compare *Śāntiparva*, lxxxviii, 14–15.

[11] *Arth.*, Bk. II, ch. 27, *Gaṇikā bhōgamāyatīṃ purushañcha nivēdayēt.* Every prostitute's earnings, expenditure, and other details were determined by the Superintendent of Prostitutes. These restrictions appear to have been for political ends also, the state controlling the prostitutes and through them their paramours.

[12] *Ibid.*, *Étēna naṭanartakagāyakavādakavāgjīvanakuśīlavaplavakasaubhikachāraṇānāṃ strīvyavahāriṇāṃ striyō gūḍhājīvāścha vyākhyātāḥ.*

of their income. On this the government collected the tax. Every prostitute was required to pay the government every month twice the amount of a day's earnings,[13] i.e. $6\frac{2}{3}$ per cent of her income. Thus proportional, and not the progressive, system of taxation was operative, because the rate was the same whatever the amount of income. Further, there does not appear to have been a minimum exempted from tax. Another feature is that while in modern days the tax is generally collected once a year, the Mauryas seem to have collected it once a month.

This kind of state control over prostitutes and the collection of the income tax find a remarkable parallel in Athens. Boeckh observes:[14] "According to a passage of Suidas and Zonaras, the *agaronomi* designated the price which each prostitute should take. If this is even incredible, it probably contains the truth, however, that the *agaronomi* determined the amount of this tax, and that as in the ordinance of *batigula*, the rate of which differed according to the difference of their gain or of the class in which they were comprised."

The prostitutes, as stated above, paid the tax in the Mauryan empire. Dancers and actors are not definitely stated to have paid the income tax. But perhaps they also paid, in view of the fact that, like the prostitutes, they also had to submit to the state an account of their income.[15]

EXCESS PROFITS TAX

This tax was adopted by many belligerent countries during the Great War of 1914. Briefly the tax may be explained as follows. Every business concern is assumed to be entitled to a certain amount of profit, which may be called normal or modal profit, and any excess over and above this "normal"

[13] *Arth.*, Bk. II, ch. 27, *Rūpājīvā bhōgadvayaguṇaṃ māsaṃ dadyuḥ.*
[14] Boeckh, *op. cit.*, p. 443.
[15] *Arth.*, Bk. II, ch. 27. Cf. Boeckh, *op. cit.*, p. 442.

standard is to be taxed, or, in Plehn's words,[16] "trimmed away as if it were a noxious growth, or at least made wholesome by a public use."

This tax appears to have been levied by the Mauryan financiers. Under the head "country parts"[17] is mentioned a source of income called *pārśva*, which is "a tax collected when there is some margin left for such collection."[18] Business men were allowed a profit of 5 per cent on local commodities and 10 per cent on foreign produce.[19] The percentage of profit was not determined arbitrarily, but all things worth consideration were taken into account before the price was fixed. The cost of production, the demand and supply, the duties paid, such as the different kinds of toll (*śulka*), road cess (*vartanī*), carriage cess (*ātivāhika*), ferry charges (*taradēya*), *bhāga*, *gulmadēya*,[20] etc., the transport charges, and all other kinds of accessory expenses were calculated.[21] The supply of goods was so regulated that in slack seasons the merchant did not suffer, while in the other seasons the state took care that he did not get undue profits.[22] If there was any profit in excess of the one fixed, which the business man managed to get either by illicit increase of price or by other means, two remedies were adopted. The first was that fines

[16] *Op. cit.*, p. 292.

[17] *Arth.*, Bk. II, chs. 6 and 15.

[18] *Arth. Trans.*, p. 109. P. N. Bannerjea (*op. cit.*, p. 177) refers to this income as royalty. In the light of the discussion in this section, this interpretation appears incorrect. For the meaning of royalty *vide Dictionary of Political Economy*, vol. iii, p. 331. Bhaṭṭaswāmi (*J.B.O.R.S.*, vol. xi, p. 84) explains the words thus: *Pārśvam uchitakaradadhikagrahāṇāṃ kōśahimsārōtaṃ* [(*sic*) *kōśabhissamharaṇōktaṃ*] *prabhutvādēchchhadhigamyamiti*. The exactions were justified in virtue of the sovereignty of the state.

[19] *Arth.*, Bk. IV, ch. 2, *Anujñātakrayādupari chaishāṃ svadēśīyānāṃ paṇyānāṃ pañchakaṃśatamājīvaṃ sthāpayēt. Paradēśīyānāṃ daśakaṃ*. Compare *Yājñavlkya*, ii, 252.

[20] *Arth.*, Bk. II, ch. 16.

[21] *Arth.*, Bk. IV, ch. 2, *Prakshēpam paṇyānishpattiṃ śushkaṃ vṛiddhimavakrayam Vyayānaṇyāmścha saṅkhyāya sthāpayēt arghamarghavit*. Compare *Manu*, viii, 401–2.

[22] *Arth.*, Bk. IV, ch. 2.

were imposed[23] because the law was broken. The second remedy was that the profit was taxed. Kauṭilya does not mention the rate of the tax.

The excess profits tax in the Mauryan empire was not merely a device adopted in great financial difficulties, but was a regular tax in time of peace. A feature of the tax which is hard to justify is the amount of normal profit. The rates of 5 and 10 per cent fixed by the Mauryan state appear too low, and must have hit a little too hard the business men. The state appears to have given the consumers' standpoint too much importance.

LABOUR TAX

To be a tax the compulsory contribution need not necessarily be "one of money or goods, for compulsory military service and forced labour must be reckoned in the category of taxes."[24] This kind of tax is found in some modern states. Adams observes: "Germany imposes a special labour tax for the purpose of procuring military service, and consequently is exempt from the necessity of imposing as large a money tax for the support of the army as would otherwise be the case."[25] "Another illustration of coerced service is found in the practice followed by many states of calling upon individuals to devote a certain number of days to work on the public highways. This is called the 'Road Tax,' and is, in form at least, a labour tax, although it may be converted into a money payment."[26]

[23] *Arth.*, Bk. IV, ch. 2. Plehn believes that "As a source of revenue in times of peace, even in 'piping times of peace,' the excess profits tax is a tax that is difficult to justify" (*op. cit.*, p. 292). This is a disputable view.

[24] *Dictionary of Political Economy*, vol. iii, p. 517.

[25] *Science of Finance*, p. 19. Adams adds: "The merit of this system, regarded from a financial point of view, depends very largely upon the relative burdens of a labour tax on the one hand and a money tax on the other, as well as upon the incidental benefits which accrue from the two plans of military organization."

[26] *Ibid.*, p. 20.

In Mauryan days, according to Megasthenes, the handicraftsmen and the retail dealers had "to perform *gratuitously* certain public services, and to pay tribute from the products of labour."[27] This suggests that there were two kinds of labour tax—the ordinary tax, paid in the form of labour (*simhanika*),[28] and the additional gratuitous performance of public services (*vishṭi*).[29]

As regards the first kind, poor people who could not pay taxes in money or in kind appear to have paid them in the form of service, which was used by the state in its manufactories for pounding, frying, extracting oil, and the like.[30] This was in one sense no gain to the state, because instead of getting the income in the shape of money or kind, it got its due in the form of labour. But it may be pointed out that if the state had refused to accept the labour, it would have been so much the loser for it, as the poor people could not probably have paid their dues in any other shape. This kind of tax has been mentioned by Manu, that *śūdras*, craftsmen, and artisans discharge their dues by work.[31]

The other kind of tax was the gratuitous performance of public services. This does not appear to have been in lieu of any taxes that had to be ordinarily paid, but was in the nature of an additional tax. Its parallels are to be found in the German conscription and the ancient Athenian *liturgiae*. Of the latter, Boeckh observes:[32] "But also personal public services or *liturgiae* which save the state an expenditure to the amount of their cost supplied to that extent the place of a revenue."

This tax was very common in ancient India. Manu[33] writes

[27] Arrian, *Indika*, xii.
[28] *Arth.*, Bk. II, ch. 15. Cf. Bhaṭṭaswāmi's explanation (*J.B.O.R.S.*, vol. xi, part 3, p. 85).
[29] *Arth.*, Bk. I, ch. 4. For other references, *infra*, p. 107.
[30] *Arth.*, Bk. II, ch. 15.
[31] *Manu*, x, 120.
[32] Boeckh, *op. cit.*, p. 584.
[33] *Manu*, vii, 138.

that mechanics, artisans, and others had to work for the king one day every month. Gautama[34] and Vishṇu[35] speak to the same effect. Śukra[36] mentions it as one day in a fortnight. In the *Mahābhārata*[37] forced labourers are said to have accompanied the army. In his famous inscription at Girnār,[38] the Satrap Rudradāman records that the Sudarśana lake was rebuilt "without oppressing the inhabitants of the town and country by taxes, forced labour, and acts of affection." The inscriptions[39] grant villages "with (the right to) forced labour as the occasion for it occurs," or "free of forced labour of very kind." Yuan Chwang[40] remarks that "individuals are not subject to forced labour contributions . . . taxation being light and forced services being sparingly used."

That this was an additional tax finds support in C. V. Vaidya's observation[41] that in epic India "no caste was exempt from this tax of compulsory labour. Even the Brahmans were made to work if they did not follow their own sacred profession and followed the profession of artisans and labourers." According to R. K. Mookerjea,[42] in South India compulsory labour seems to have been employed for the construction of irrigation works, and "even the central government sometimes exploited compulsory labour for its own purpose. The great temple of Tanjore, for instance, was built largely by forced labour."

As noted above, Megasthenes mentions the existence of this tax in the Mauryan period. Free labourers[43] were

[34] *Gautama*, x, 31.
[35] *Vishṇu*, iii, 32.
[36] *Śukranīti*, iv, 2, 241.
[37] lix, 41–3.
[38] *Ep. Ind.*, viii, no. 6.
[39] E.g. *Gupta Inscriptions*, nos. 38, 39, 55, and so on.
[40] *Yuan Chwang*, i, p. 176.
[41] *Epic India*, p. 215.
[42] *Local Government in Ancient India*, pp. 146–7.
[43] "Free" labour is not used here as opposed to slave labour, but means unpaid or gratuitous labour.

employed as pioneers in the Mauryan army, and were under the charge of an officer called *praśasta*.[44] Kauṭilya also mentions it while quoting the opinion of Viśālāksha that free labour (*vishṭi*) is one of the advantages secured from the people.[45] Elsewhere in the *Arthaśāstra*[46] it is mentioned that while an irrigation work was being constructed every person had to co-operate in the task either personally or through servants and bullocks, but could not claim any benefit from the irrigation work.

Forced labour appears to have been much employed in the construction of public works,[47] as was the case in South India and as found in the Girnār edict. And in Adams' words, "the demand of a state for labour or service is, like a demand for land, deducible to a money demand."[48]

SALES OR TURNOVER TAX

The turnover tax levied on the sale of commodities is of two kinds. One is on the sale of particular articles or groups of articles, and this might be termed particular sales or turnover tax; the other levied on sales in general, that is on all commodities, is called the general sales tax.[49] These taxes have existed in the Western World at one time or another since very early days. In Athens the revenue from the markets was derived from the duties imposed upon commodities sold.[50] "It is to be observed," writes Seligman,[51]

44 *Arth.*, Bk. X, ch .1. Compare Mādhava Yajva's explanation, Jolly, *op. cit.*, ii, p. 172. The commentator reads *śāstā* instead of *praśasta*.

45 *Arth.*, Bk. VIII, ch. 1.

46 *Arth.*, Bk. II, ch. 1. In Bk. I, ch. 4, also, free labour is mentioned along with grains, gold, and the like as resulting from the science of *varta*.

47 Compare *The Mahāvaṁśa*, ch. xxx, where the king is stated to have declined to make use of unpaid labour.

48 *Science of Finance*, p. 20.

49 Seligman, *Studies in Public Finance*, ch. vi.

50 Boeckh, *op. cit.*, p. 420. See also pp. 432 ff.

51 *Op. cit.*, p. 125.

"that all through the Middle Ages taxes on the sale of particular commodities, and especially upon the necessaries of life, were common." In Canada a tax on the sale of particular commodities is found even to-day, and Germany and France introduced the general sales tax after the war of 1914.

There appears to have existed a general sales tax of 10 per cent *ad valorem* on the sale price of all articles, imposed and collected on their sale. For Strabo writes:[52] "The sixth and last class consists of those who collect the tenths of the prices of the articles sold. Fraud in the payment of this tax is punished with death." This tax was found in ancient Athens,[53] where, according to one authority, it amounted to 20 per cent. In Byzantine it was 10 per cent, as in Mauryan India. In Rome, too, this was collected on commodities sold at auction or in the public market.[54] As remarked above, even in Germany and France a similar tax was introduced after the Great War.

In ancient India generally this duty appears to have been common. According to Śukra,[55] the tax was to be paid either by the seller or by the buyer according to their gain, and the rate varied from a little more than 3 per cent to $6\frac{2}{3}$ per cent. The Chammak copperplate of Pravarasēna mentions taxes on sale and purchase. An inscription of Vikramā-

[52] *Strabo*, xv, 1, 50.

[53] Boeckh, *op. cit.*, p. 433. Says Boeckh: "Different from the market tax was the duty upon sales, which the grammarians mention from Isacus without having any definite knowledge of its nature. Harpoeration conjectures that it was the fifth, of which as a tax he seems to have obtained information from other sources. So high a tax upon the sale of any article whatever is incredible. The Byzantines imposed even as a measure of necessity a duty upon sales of only a tenth. On the other hand, the account of another grammarian is correct that in the term duty upon sales certain hundreds are comprehended, like the *Centesmia rerum venatium oranctionium*. We know from documents extant that the hundredth was paid upon the sale of landed property, undoubtedly, in all cases, not barely on sales at auction."

[54] *Dictionary of Political Economy*, vol. iii, p. 517.

[55] *Śukranīti*, iv, 2, 216 ff.

ditya VI[56] mentions a sales tax on betel-leaf, while another inscription refers to similar taxes on rubies, grains, betel-leaf, etc.

Likewise, when land and buildings were sold by public auction the highest bidder had to pay under Mauryas a tax on the purchase value.[57] The rate of this tax is not known.

In addition to immovable property, most of the goods were regulated to be sold by public auction.[58] This fact, coupled with the system of taxing some commodities at their source and the statement of Strabo that all articles had to pay the tax, indicates that the duty must have been a universal one levied on goods of all kinds.

The general sales tax has been condemned by many economists and financiers. In the words of David A. Wells, the financial adviser to U.S.A. during the Civil War, "Such a system [i.e. a general sales tax] violates all the fundamental principles of taxation inasmuch as the taxes are neither definite in amount, equal in application, nor convenient of collection."[59] Whenever it has been introduced the tax has had a disastrous effect on business, and has itself ultimately failed to succeed.

Without entering into the ethics of such a tax, it may be noted briefly how far the modern objections against it could have applied in the Mauryan times. That under the Mauryas it was a peace tax, and not merely a resort in great financial crises, is probable.[60]

Seligman adds: "If the tax was adopted, it is exceedingly

[56] *Śukranīti*, xvi, no. 8 (*a*).

[57] *Arth.*, Bk. III, ch. 9, *Vikrayapratikrōshṭa śulkam dadyāt*, etc.

[58] *Arth.*, Bk. II, ch. 21.

[59] Quoted in *Studies in Public Finance*, p. 131. Seligman also is of the same opinion. He writes: "The sales tax, it is evident, sins against every one of these principles" (*ibid.*).

[60] Seligman observes: "The conclusion to be drawn from this historical survey is that the general sales tax constitutes the last resort of countries which find themselves in such fiscal difficulties that they must subordinate all other principles of taxation to that of adequacy" (*ibid.*).

probable that the medieval lesson, as well as the more recent experience of France, would be repeated, and the revenue would be woefully inadequate."[61] How far the Mauryan tax was a success is not known. It was perhaps not a failure, because Megasthenes does not mention the existence of any troubles in its way. As for adequacy of yield, the penalty of death for any evasion in its payment must certainly have produced enough income.

The objection of Le Roy Beaulieu that "the subsidized industries, where the commodity before reaching the final stage of readiness for sale passes through several hands, would have to endure a burden infinitely more heavy than similar industries where all the operations are concentrated in one plant," does not apply with any great force to the Mauryan times, as there were few such large and concentrated industries, so that the burden fell equally heavily on all.

The third objection—administrative in character[62]—is that as the tax applies to all persons who try and sell there is great chance of evasion. This, however, appears inapplicable to a society where, as already observed, fraud and evasion of tax are said to have been punished with nothing short of death.

This, however, does not justify the tax. Nor is it immutable from Seligman's very important criticism that, being a tax on necessaries consumed by the great mass of people, "instead of taxing the man with the higher income more, as we do, you tax the man with the higher income less—not indeed actually less, but relatively less in proportion to his wealth as measured by property or income."[63]

[61] Quoted in *Studies in Public Finance*, p. 132.

[62] Seligman puts it thus: "But in the case of a general sales tax, we are dealing with the totality of the community, with every individual—man, woman, and child—who buys any commodity that is offered for sale . . . what possible devices can be utilized to guard against wholesale fraud and evasion, when it is to the interest of both buyer and seller to avoid the tax" (*op. cit.*, p. 135).

[63] *Op. cit.*, p. 136.

TRADE TAXES

Some minor taxes on trade were to be found in the Mauryan times. Persons could trade in an article only on the payment of a tax. "No one," writes Megasthenes,[64] "is allowed to deal in more than one kind of commodity unless he pays a double tax." Megasthenes appears to suggest that an additional tax was imposed for trading in every additional commodity. Further, traders had to pay every day one *kākaṇi* to the superintendent towards the charge of stamping the weights and measures.[65]

Kauṭilya also mentions[66] "trade taxes" (*āyatikshamaṃ*) which were paid by importers of foreign goods; but it is doubtful if these are identical with the impost mentioned by Megasthenes.

TAXES ON HERDSMEN, HUNTERS, ETC.

According to Arrian,[67] herdsmen were subjected to a tribute which was paid in cattle, while hunters and shepherds also paid taxes and rendered the state prescribed services. According to Kauṭilya,[68] the superintendent of the slaughter-house was to take as tax a sixth of the beasts of prey and about a tenth of birds, deer, fish, and other animals captured, while a sixth of animals caught alive had to be let

[64] *Strabo*, xv, 1, 50. Could this be the same as the revenue from merchants (*vaṇik*) referred to in *Arth.*, Bk. II, ch. 6? *Supra*, p. 29.

[65] *Arth.*, Bk. II, ch. 19, *Prātivēdhanikam kākaṇīkamaharahaḥ pautavādhyakshāya dadyuḥ.*

[66] *Arth.*, Bk. II, ch. 16, *Nāvikasārthavāhēbhyaścha parihāramāyatikshamaṃ dadyāt.* Cf. *J.B.O.R.S.*, vol. xii, part i, p. 65. The trade taxes of ancient South India were perhaps different from these. See *Historical Sketches of Ancient Dekhan*, pp. 343–4, 347.

[67] *Indika*, ch. xi. Taxes on shepherds are mentioned in *South Indian Inscriptions*, vol. ii, nos. 98 and 99. See also *Historical Sketches of Ancient Dekhan*, pp. 343–4.

[68] *Arth.*, Bk. II, ch. 26, *Pravṛittahiṁsānāmaparigṛihītānāṃ shaḍbhāgaṃ gṛihṇīyāt. Matsyapakshiṇāṃ daśabhāgaṃ vādhikaṃ mṛigapaśūnāṃ śulkaṃ vādhikaṃ. Pakshimṛigāṇāṃ jīvatshaḍbhāgamabhayavanēshu pramuñchēt.*

off in state forest. The latter was certainly in the nature of a tax, although the animals were let off, because the state acquired these animals for its forests.

WAR TAX (*sēnābhakta*)[69]

This tax appears to have been collected when the army was marching or preparing for expeditions.[70] It resembles the one mentioned by Śukra,[71] that when the king is preparing to maintain an army to destroy the enemy he should receive from the people special grants of fines, duties, etc. The Mauryan tax was in the form of provisions for the army, e.g. oil, rice, salt, and the like, and was perhaps levied only in times of hostilities and not in times of peace.[72]

HOUSE TAX

As discussed in detail elsewhere,[73] a tax like the English Inhabited House Duty appears to have been paid by houses and other buildings. There may also have existed a tax on vacant building sites. Both these taxes were probably levied only in forts, i.e. towns and cities.[74]

CONFISCATION OF UNEARNED INCREMENT

The taxation and even confiscation of unearned increment in the value of land have been advocated by many economists, including J. S. Mill. Taxation of such increment has been termed by Plehn[75] increment value land tax. In Mauryan India the state seems to have put into operation

[69] *Arth.*, Bk. II, ch. 15.
[70] *J.B.O.R.S.*, vol. xi, part 3, p. 83.
[71] *Śukranīti*, iv, 2, 19–20.
[72] Gaṇapati Śāstri, *op. cit.*, vol. i, p. 230.
[73] *Supra*, pp. 37 ff.
[74] *Arth.*, Bk. II, ch. 6. Compare *Śukranīti*, iv, 2, 256–7.
[75] *Op. cit.*, p. 194.

a similar idea. Lands and buildings appear to have been sold by public auction.[76] When bidders enhanced the value, the increase over the usual price belonged to the State.[77] Other articles also were sold by public auction at the octroi house near the gate of the city, and the enhanced amount of the price, together with any tax on the merchandise, was taken by the state.[78] To quote Kauṭilya: "When under the fear of bidders (enhancing the price) the price of any merchandise is increased beyond its proper value, the king shall receive the enhanced amount or twice the amount of tax on it."[79]

FORCED BENEVOLENCES (*utsaṅga*)[80]

Under the name *utsaṅga*, taxes seem to have been collected on the occasion of the birth of a prince.[81] Bhaṭṭaswāmi, the commentator of the *Arthaśāstra*, observes that some interpret *utsaṅga* to mean presentations to the king, while others regard it as an excess paid by taxpayers over and above the fixed amount.[82] The latter interpretation is probably correct, because presents to the king are mentioned separately as *aupayānika* along with *utsaṅga*.[83] *Utsaṅga* therefore appears to have been a tax collected only occasionally.

[76] *Arth.*, Bk. III, ch. 9.

[77] *Ibid., Svargavāyōrvā mūlyavardhanē mūlyavṛiddhiḥ sa śulkā kōśaṃ gachchhēt.* This disproves the view that in ancient India "the king never claimed the right to the unearned increment of the land" (*Public Administration in Ancient India*, p. 179).

[78] *Arth.*, Bk. II, ch. 21, *Krētṛisaṅgharshē mūlyavṛiddhissaśulkā kōśaṃ gachchhēt. Strabo*, xv, 1, 50.

[79] *Ibid., Pratikrētṛibhayādvā paṇyamūlyādupari mūlyaṃ vardhayatō mūlyavṛiddhiṃ rājā harēt, dviguṇam vā śulkaṃ kuryāt.*

[80] This is Bannerjea's translation (*Public Administration in Ancient India*, p. 177).

[81] *Arth.*, Bk. II, ch. 15.

[82] *J.B.O.R.S.*, vol. xi, part iii, p. 84, *Utsaṅgō rājñaḥ putrajanmādishu paurajānapadadattamiti kēchit. Śālākādikamityapare.*

[83] *Arth.*, Bk. II, chs. 6 and 15. *Infra*, p. 130. Compare the king's benevolences and the "acts of affection" (*praṇayakriyā*) in *Ep. Ind.*, viii, no. 6.

GAMBLING

Gambling was a peculiar source of Mauryan income, yielding revenue in various forms. As there was also a tax on gambling, all forms of revenue from the source will be considered here. The income was derived under the following heads:[84]

(1) A licence fee.
(2) A tax on stakes paid by the winner.
(3) Hire for supplying dice and other accessories of the play.
(4) A fee chargeable for supplying water and accommodation.
(5) Various kinds of fines.
(6) A commission on the transactions of sale and mortgage of things carried on by the superintendent.

The state not only tolerated but even encouraged gambling, and maintained an establishment under a special superintendent (*dyūtadhyaksha*).[85] Gambling was centralized with a view to controlling it so as to find out foreign spies and thieves. If people gambled anywhere other than in the prescribed place a fine of twelve *paṇas* was imposed.[86] Fines were also levied for tricks of hand and cheating at play.[87] The state appears to have maintained gambling houses where private persons played games. Fees were charged for supplying water, accommodation, dice, and other accessories of play.[88] Dice were supplied at the rate of one *kākaṇi* of hire per pair.[89] There was also the licence fee for permission to gamble.[90] Gambling appears to have been at dice play only, though it is not improbable that other games also were allowed.

[84] Compare *Nārada*, xvii, 8; *Bṛihaspati*, xxvi, 1.
[85] *Arth.*, Bk. III, ch. 20, and Bk. II, ch. 6.
[86] *Arth.*, Bk. III, ch. 20, *Dyūtādhyakshō dyūtamēkamukhaṃ kārayēt anyatra dīvyatō dvādaśapaṇō daṇḍaḥ gūḍhājīvijñāpanārthaṃ*. Cf. *Bṛihaspati*, xxvi, 2.
[87] *Arth.*, Bk. III, ch. 20.
[88] *Ibid.*, *Jitadravyādadhyakshaḥ pañchakaṃ śataṃ ādadīta Kākaṇyakshāralāśalākāvakrayamudakabhūmikarmakrayaṁ cha*.
[89] *Ibid.*
[90] *Ibid.*

There was a tax of 5 per cent on the stakes won, which was to be paid by the winner.[91] This tax may have been very fruitful to the state, and as the percentage taken was low, was certainly not intended as a prohibitive duty, so that it was to the interest of the state that the amount of stakes was high.

Lastly, when the losing gamblers wanted to raise funds by sale or mortgage of their properties, the state undertook to see that the transaction was complete, and for its aid must have received a commission.[92]

This active aid of the state with regard to gambling was perhaps on account of the income derived, as well as for political purposes, viz. to find out spies, spendthrifts, and thieves.[93] It may also be that the state permitted its subjects some kind of enjoyment, even as racing and betting are encouraged by modern states, for the evils of gambling were known and recognized.[94] "Lack of recognition of wealth properly acquired, acquisition of ill-gotten wealth, loss of wealth without enjoyment, staying away from answering the calls of nature, and contracting diseases from not taking timely meals, are the evils of gambling."[95] "It is specially due to gambling that assemblies and royal confederacies possessing the characteristics of assemblies are split into factions and are consequently destroyed."[96]

That gambling should be actively encouraged by the state is nothing peculiar to the Mauryan period. In modern civilized Europe are found gambling houses in Monte Carlo. In 1927 the Portuguese government issued a decree legalizing

[91] *Arth.*, Bk. III, ch. 20. It is interesting to note that the Bijapur inscription of Dhavaḷa of Hastikuṇḍi (*Ep. Ind.*, x, p. 19) mentions the grant of *Pellaka-pellaka* (?) by the gambler. This may have been some tax like the one mentioned above.

[92] *Arth.*, Bk. III, ch. 20, *Dravyāṇāmādhānaṃ vikrayaṁ cha kuryāt.*

[93] *Arth.*, Bk. III, ch. 19, *Gūḍhajīvajñāpanārthaṃ.*

[94] *Arth.*, Bk. VIII, ch. 3.

[95] *Arth. Trans.*, p. 384.

[96] *Ibid.*, p. 385. Compare *Manu*, ix, 222, where the king is directed to suppress gambling and betting, which are regarded as open theft.

gambling in Portugal. "The Casinos at Monte Castoril and at Funchal (Madeira)," reported the London *Times* in December 1927, "will be open permanently, and those at various water-places during the season. The term of the concession of gambling rights is for thirty years. The government is to receive 10 per cent of the initial capital, and the entire installation of each casino will revert to the government on the termination of the concession."

Apart from the ethical propriety of allowing and aiding gambling, both modern and the Mauryan states encouraged the vice probably because of the large revenue.

"BALI"[97]

The exact nature of this source of income is doubtful. Shāma Śāstry[98] translates the word as "religious tax." This interpretation finds support in F. W. Thomas's observation[99] that "it is perhaps not superfluous to remark that *bali* properly denotes a religious cess."

But this explanation is not accepted by other commentators, nor does it find support in ancient Indian literature in general. Bhaṭṭaswāmi explains the term thus:[100] *baliḥ shaḍbhāgādanyō yathādēśaprasiddhō daśaviṁśatibaṇḍhādhikaḥ,* i.e. a local tax of one-tenth or one-twentieth other than the ordinary one-sixth. This explanation, in view of the use of the term *shaḍbhāga*, which is usually associated with land revenue, may denote a tax connected with land. Jolly[101] appears to accept this interpretation, but adds:[102] "The law books mention taxes of one-tenth and one-twentieth on home and foreign goods, besides the king's sixth of grain." This indicates that, according to Jolly, *bali* has no necessary connection with land, but is in the nature of an octroi duty, toll, or customs duty, an interpretation which appears

[97] *Arth.*, Bk. II, chs. 6 and 15.
[98] *Arth. Trans.*, p. 109.
[99] *J.R.A.S.*, 1909, p. 467.
[100] *J.B.O.R.S.*, vol. xi, p. 83.
[101] *Op. cit.*, ii, p. 26.
[102] *Ibid.*

to be foreign to Bhaṭṭaswāmi's statement. In the *Kama Jātaka*,[103] *bali* is used in the sense of a tax which, in connection with the land survey mentioned, may connect the tax with land.

In the *Manusmṛiti*[104] the term is used as being different from *kara* and *śulka*: *Yōrakshānbalimādhattē karaṃ śulkaṃ cha pārthivaḥ*. Five commentators of Manu—Mēdhātithi,[105] Sarvajña Nārāyaṇa,[106] Rāghavānanda,[107] Rāmachandra,[108] and Kulluka[109]—explain *bali* as the sixth portion of grain, i.e. land revenue. Kulluka adds[110] that it was the sixth part collected either monthly or in the month of *Bhadrapada* or *Pushya*. Nandana[111] is the only commentator who regards *bali* as consisting of whatever the king enjoys in the shape of cattle, grain, etc. The interpretation of the five commentators appears to be the result of Manu's phrase in the next stanza,[112] "*balishaḍbhāga-hārīṇaṃ*." Nandana,[113] however, explains it thus, "*atra baliśabdaḥ karavachanaḥ*," i.e. *bali* is synonymous with *kara*, meaning probably tax in general.

Bali in the sense of tax in general is used in the *Vēdas*. MacDonell and Keith observe:[114] "*Bali* occurs several times in the *Ṛig Vēda* and often later in the sense of a tribute to the king or offering to a god." Thus in the *Ṛig Vēda*[115] are found phrases such as *balihṛitaḥ*, which, according to

[103] No. 476 (*Fausboll*, iv, p. 169).

[104] viii, 307.

[105] *Mandalik*, vol. ii, p. 1056, *Baliḥ dhānyādēḥ shashṭōbhāgaḥ*.

[106] *Ibid.*, *Baliṃ dhānyādibhāgam*.

[107] *Ibid.*, *Baliṃ dhānyādēḥ shaḍbhāgaṃ*.

[108] *Ibid.*, *Baliṃ dhānyādishaḍbhāgaṃ*.

[109] *Ibid.*, *Baliṃ dhānyādēḥ shaḍbhāgaṃ grāmavāsibhyaḥ pratimāsaṃ vā bhādrapaushaniyamēna grāhyaṃ*.

[110] *Ibid.*

[111] *Ibid.*, *Yadrāshṭrātpaśudhānyādikam viśishṭamāchchhādya rājñāṃ bhujyatē vastu tadbaliruchyate*.

[112] *Manu*, viii, 308.

[113] *Manusaṁhitā*, vol. ii, p. 1057.

[114] *Vēdic Index*, vol. ii, p. 62.

[115] x, 173–6.

Sāyaṇāchārya,[116] means *karasyapradātṛīḥ*. *Bali* thus means taxes[117] or tribute.[118] This general sense is also to be found in the Aśōkan edicts, for example in the passage[119] "*Luṁmini-gāme ubalike kaṭe aṭha-bhāgiye cha*," i.e. "(He) made the village of Lummini free of taxes" (*ubalika* = Sanskrit *udbalika*) "and paying only an eighth share (of the produce)."[120] In some of the *Jātakas*[121] also *bali* appears to be the name of taxes in general. Kāḷidāsa also makes a similar use of the term.[122]

Gaṇapati Śāstri's explanation[123] of *bali* as *upahāraḥ bhikshā va* does not appear to be supported by other interpretations.

It is thus evident that *bali* as the name of a tax has a general and at least one particular meaning. In the *Artha-śāstra* it is used in the particular sense.[124] *Bali* as a particular tax was levied on country parts only, and was different from land revenue, yield of royal domain, tolls, and octroi duties, *kara*, *rajjū* and *chōrarajjū*, *sēnābhakta*, *pārśva*, and *piṇḍakara*. It was collected not by the village and district revenue officers (*gōpa* and *sthānika*), but directly by commissioners appointed by the collector-general (*pradēsh-ṭāraḥ*).[125] This feature appears very significant and suggests that the tax, though perhaps unimportant in yield, was of special importance in some other respect.

116 Max Müller's Edition of the *Ṛig Vēda*, vol. iv, p. 498. Compare the use of the term in the *Aitereya Brahmaṃ*, vii, 29.

117 *Griffith's Translation*, iv, p. 407.

118 *Wilson's Translation*, iv, p. 402.

119 *Cor. Ins. Ind.*, i, pp. 164–5.

120 *Ibid.* Also see *J.R.A.S.*, 1908, pp. 478 ff., 850 ff; 1909, p. 467.

121 *Gagga Jātaka* (*Fausboll*, ii, p. 17); *Mahāssaraha Jātaka* (*Fausboll*, iii, p. 9); *Gandatindu Jātaka* (*Fausboll*, v, p. 98).

122 *Raghuvaṁśa*, i, 18.

123 *Op. cit.*

124 Bk. II, chs. 6 and 15.

125 *Arth.*, Bk. II, ch. 35.

"KLṚIPTA" AND "PIṆḌAKARA"

Another tax mentioned by Kauṭilya is the *klṛipta.*[126] It is explained in the *Arthaśāstra*[127] as being levied on "villages on sea shores or on the banks of rivers and lakes." This explanation, along with the fact that the impost is mentioned in the chapter entitled "Superintendent of Ships," indicates that the tax was probably levied on places which possessed the advantage of being ports and harbours and hence had more facilities for trade.[128]

Another tax perhaps similar to *klṛipta* was the *piṇḍa-kara.*[129] This tax may have been levied on villages,[130] and not on individuals, and collected annually in kind.[131]

[126] *Arth.*, Bk. II, chs. 6 and 28.

[127] Bk. II, ch. 28, *Tadvēlākūla grāmāḥ klṛiptaṃ dadyuḥ*. Some Gupta inscriptions also (*Gupta Inscriptions*, no. 55, for example) mention *klṛipta* along with another tax, *upaklṛipta*. It is doubtful if these also were levied only on villages near the sea, lakes, and rivers.

[128] Compare Bhaṭṭaswāmi's explanation, *J.B.O.R.S.*, vol. xii, part 2, p. 156.

[129] *Arth.*, Bk. II, ch. 15.

[130] Compare Gaṇapati Śāstri's explanation (*op. cit.*, vol. i, p. 230), *Piṇḍakaraḥ tattadgrāmadēyatayā klṛiptaḥ karasamudāyaḥ*. Jolly, *op. cit.*, vol. ii, p. 26.

[131] Bhaṭṭaswāmi explains (*J.B.O.R.S.*, vol. xi, part 3, p. 83), *Piṇḍakaraḥ klṛiptaḥ tadyathāmunā grāmēṇa ētāvaddhānyādikaṃ prativarshaṃ dēyaṃ*. Compare the impost *piṇḍaka* mentioned in *Ep. Ind.*, iv, no. 34, which Kielhorn explains as means of subsistence or payments in kind.

CHAPTER VII

REVENUE FROM GOVERNMENT UNDERTAKINGS

Forests—Mines and manufactures—Mint—
Mercantile marine—Crown lands

FORESTS

FORESTS have been from early times and in many countries an important source of income to the state—in ancient Greece[1] and in modern Germany, and in our own country from time immemorial. In the Mauryan days, as in modern India, they were owned by the state, and were classified into productive and non-productive forests.[2] The latter kind appear to have consisted of game forests, some of which were exclusively for the king's use and others open to all,[3] and yielded little revenue to the state.

Productive forests were under the supervision of a department with a large staff and a superintendent.[4] They yielded revenue in two forms—as elephant forests (*hastivanaṃ*) and as those producing timber and other things.[5] The former, as the source of elephants, were important from the point of view of warfare more than as a source of revenue.[6]

It was perhaps the other kind of forests that yielded the

[1] Boeckh, *op. cit.*, p. 410.

[2] *Arth.*, Bk. II, chs. 2 and 17. In British India forests are classified into reserve, protected, and unclassified forests, all the three being state monopolies.

[3] *Ibid.* Hunting excursions are referred to in *Rock Edict VIII*; *Megasthenes*, Bk. II; *Frag.*, xxvii.

[4] *Arth.*, Bk. II, ch. 17.

[5] *Arth.*, Bk. II, chs. 2 and 17. For elephant preserves see also *Pillar Edict V*. Compare *Vishṇu*, iii, 16, *Ākaraśulkataranagavanēshu āptan niyuñjīta*. Jolly translates *nāgavana* as elephants and forests (*Institutes of Vishṇu*, *S.B.E.*, vol. vii, p. 15). It seems better to take *nāgavanaṃ* as equivalent to *hastivanaṃ* meaning elephant forests.

[6] *Arth.*, Bk. II, ch. 2.

largest income. They were looked after by a forest department with a superintendent, who collected important products such as timber, skins, bones, horns, metals, charcoal, firewood, and fodder.[7] The details enumerated in the footnote give an idea of the income the forests yielded in the shape of various kinds of products. Factories were started both in the forests and outside to manufacture out of the forest products articles of ordinary consumption and for warfare.[8] Among such manufactured articles were colouring materials, oils from seeds, utensils of cane, bark, clay, metallic manufactures, and other things.[9] In British India only a few years ago were erected improved factories for the better utilization of forest produce because of the demand created by the war.

Productive forests were guarded by the Mauryan state very carefully, and damage to them except in calamities was severely punished.[10] Thus the income from forests was

[7] *Arth.*, Bk. II, ch. 17. The chief heads of the products are:

(*a*) Trees of strong timber, e.g. teak and palmyra.
(*b*) Bamboo.
(*c*) Creepers, e.g. cane and betel.
(*d*) Fibrous plants, e.g. hemp.
(*e*) Plants yielding rope-making material.
(*f*) Plants yielding leaves, e.g. birch—a writing material.
(*g*) Plants yielding flowers productive of colouring materials.
(*h*) Medicine.
(*i*) Poisons.
(*j*) Skins of alligator, buffalo, lion, etc.
(*k*) Bones, sinew, horns, hoofs of animals.
(*l*) Metals, e.g. iron, copper, lead, tin, bronze, brass, etc.
(*m*) Utensils of cane, bark, and clay.
(*n*) Menageries of beasts, cattle, and birds.
(*o*) Charcoal and ashes.
(*p*) Firewood and fodder.

[8] *Arth.*, Bk. II, chs. 2 and 17.

[9] Compare *Pliny*, Bk. XV, ch. 7, "The Indians are said to extract oils from the chestnut, sesamum, and rice." Also *Pliny*, Bk. XVIII, ch. 10 (22). Kauṭilya, in *Arth.*, Bk. II, ch. 1, speaks of "Extracting oil by employing shepherds and oil makers," "manufacture of beverages," and "manufacture of sugar from the juice of sugar-cane" by labour done in lieu of taxes due from the people.

[10] *Arth.*, Bk. II, ch. 17.

in the form of elephants, raw products, articles manufactured out of the products, and fines and compensations.

MINES AND MANUFACTURES

"Mines are the source of treasury"[11]—such is Katuilya's opinion of the importance of mines and the revenue from them. The income was derived from two kinds of mines—ocean mines and land mines. The produce of the former consisted of conch shells, diamonds, precious stones, pearls, corals, and salt;[12] and of the latter, minerals like gold, silver, and copper.

Mining, like forests, appears to have been a state monopoly in the sense that all mines belonged to the state, and no private person could work them without a licence from the state,[13] even as it is to-day, but not in the sense that all of them were worked by the state. The state worked those mines which did not require much outlay. Others which needed large investment or which yielded minerals used in the manufacture of vessels were leased out for a royalty.[14] It was the duty of the state to keep old mines in good order and to open new ones.[15] For this purpose a big department was maintained.[16]

The income from mines was derived, according to the *Arthaśāstra*,[17] under ten heads.

[11] *Arth.*, Bk. II, ch. 12, *Ākara prabhavaḥ kōśaḥ kōśāddaṇḍaḥ prajāyate.* Cf. *Vishṇu*, iii, 55, *Ākarēbhyaḥ sarvamadadyāt.* This suggests that the mines were a state monopoly.

[12] *Arth.*, Bk. II, ch. 12. The income from salt has been separately dealt with in detail under a separate head. So also the income from the mint and coinage. [13] *Ibid.* [14] *Ibid.*

[15] *Arth.*, Bk. II, ch. 1, *Ēvam dravyaṃdvipavanaṃ sētubandhamathākarān rakshēt pūrvakṛitānrājā navāmśchābhipravartayēt.*

[16] *Arth.*, Bk. II, ch. 12. Compare Vishṇu (iii, 16), who remarks that the king should appoint officials for the working of his mines: *Bhāṇḍōpakāriṇañcha vyayakriyābhārikamākarañcha bhāgēna prakrayēṇa vā dadyāt. Lāghavikamātmanā kārayēt.*

[17] *Ibid.* Some of these heads, such as coinage, fines, and tolls, should come under heads other than mining. *Vide* Bhaṭṭaswāmi's interpreta tions of these terms (*Bhaṭṭaswāmi*, f. 34; *J.B.O.R.S.*, vol. xi, part 3, p. 60).

(1) The value of the output (*mūla*).
(2) The king's share (*bhāga*).
(3) The premium of 5 per cent (*vyājī*).
(4) *Parigha* (?):[18]
  (*a*) Testing charge of coins (?).
  (*b*) Profits from the manufacture of goods from minerals (?).
(5) A special fine of twenty-five *paṇas* (*atyaya*).[19]
(6) Tolls, octrois, etc. (*śulka*).
(7) Compensation for interfering with royal monopoly (*vaidharaṇa*).
(8) Fines.
(9) Profits of coinage (*rūpa*).
(10) A special premium of 8 per cent (*rūpika*).[20]

The value of the output (*mūla*) consisted of the yield of mines worked by the state, and included gold, silver, copper, oil, bitumen, lead, tin, and the like. When mines were leased out to private persons a royalty[21] (*vibhāga*) was paid in the form of a fixed share of the output.[22] Sometimes, instead of a fixed share a money rent was given.[23] The state received also a premium (*vyājī*), because its share of the minerals was received in the royal weights, which were 5 per cent heavier than the market standards.[24] There were also the fines, tolls (*śulka*), and compensations (*vaidharaṇa*) to be given to the state,[25] because the state lost its revenue by

[18] *Supra*, p. 32. See Gaṇapati Śāstri, *op. cit.*, i, p. 137; Bhaṭṭaswāmi's interpretation, *J.B.O.R.S.*, vol. xi, part 3, p. 60. In view of the omission of the term *parigha* and the mention of *pārīkshika* along with *atyaya*, *rūpika*, and *vyājī* in *Arth.*, Bk. II, ch. 12, it is possible that *parigha* denotes testing charge.

[19] This is Bhaṭṭaswāmi's explanation (*J.B.O.R.S.*, vol. xi, part 3, p. 60) and finds support in Kautilya's phrase, *pañchaviṁśatiśatamatyayaṃ* (*Arth.*, Bk. II, ch. 12).

[20] *Infra*, p. 125.

[21] A licence was necessary, and those who carried on mining without licence were bound with chains and caused to work as prisoners (*Arth.*, Bk. II, ch. 1).

[22] According to *Śukranīti*, iv, 2, 117–18, the royalty was as follows: half of gold, one-third of silver, one-fourth of copper, one-sixth of zinc and iron, one-half of gems, one-half of glass and lead, after the expenses met, i.e. of the net yield.

[23] *Arth.*, Bk. II, ch. 12. [24] *Ibid.*, *Pañchakam śatam vyājīm.*

[25] *Ibid.*, *Rājapaṇyachchedāmurūpaṃ cha vaidharaṇaṃ.*

letting private people work the mines, which were the monopoly of the state.

The state increased the income from mines by manufacturing commodities from copper, lead, tin, mercury, brass, bronze, etc.[26] As Megasthenes writes: "It [the soil] has also underground numerous veins of all sorts of metals, for it contains much gold and silver, and copper and iron in no small quantity, and even tin and other metals, which are *employed in making articles* of use and ornament, as well as the implements and accoutrements of war."[27] Thus the manufacture and sale of articles of mineral products was yet another source of income to the state.

The revenue was also got from the manufacture of other articles. The state maintained a weaving department, where all kinds of cloth and even mail armour were produced.[28] It manufactured sugar, rice, flour, beverages, and a host of other articles, and sold them at a profit. The superintendent of commerce was expected to avoid such large profits[29] as harmed the people, but also a policy which resulted in loss to the state.[30]

MINT

The revenue from this source may not have been much as compared with other sources of income, and the little that was got appears to have been from brassage and seniorage on coins minted. There were three kinds of coins—gold, silver, and copper.[31] There seems to have been free but not gratuitous coinage of gold and silver,[32] and a charge of about 1½ per cent was made for minting bullion into coin. For instance, in minting a gold or silver *suvarṇa* of sixteen *māshas*, one *kākaṇi* or one-quarter *māsha* weight of the metal more was taken towards losses in minting. In modern days

[26] *Arth.*, Bk. II, ch. 12.
[27] *Diodorus II*, 36.
[28] *Arth.*, Bk. II, ch. 23.
[29] *Arth.*, Bk. II, ch. 15.
[30] *Arth.*, Bk. VII, ch. 1.
[31] *Arth.*, Bk. II, chs. 12 and 14.
[32] *Arth.*, Bk. II, ch. 14.

in England, for instance, the small charge for coinage is taken by the mint in the form of adding a small amount of alloy to the sovereign, whereas the Mauryas made extra charge as brassage.

The larger part of the income must have been received from minting token coins and in the form of seniorage. The silver coins appear to have been tokens made of eleven parts of silver, four of copper, and one of any one of the metals *tīkshṇa*, *trapu*, *sīsa*, and *añjana*. Copper coins were made of four parts of an alloy and twelve parts of copper.[33]

There were also other charges of various kinds.[34] The *rūpika*, amounting to 8 per cent, may have been, as Shāma Śāstry suggests,[35] collected as a sort of exchange compensation on payments made to the state as fines, purchase money, etc. According to this interpretation, the actual collections were 8 per cent more than the levy. There was also the *vyājī* of 5 per cent, which was perhaps the extra metal taken from those who wanted bullion to be coined in the mint, the royal weights being 5 per cent heavier than the ordinary ones and the bullion being received in the royal standards. A charge of one-eighth *paṇa* per cent was collected as the testing charge of probably both the bullion and the coins received at the treasury from the public.

MERCANTILE MARINE

Although they have a sort of control over mercantile marine, modern governments do not generally own ships of this type and get revenue from this source. The Mauryan

[33] *Arth.*, Bk. II, ch. 12.

[34] *Ibid.*, *Rūpikamashṭakaṃ śataṃ, pañchakaṃ śatam vyājīm, pārīkshikamashṭabhāgikaṃ śataṃ. Pañchaviṁśatipaṇamatyaṁchāny-atra kartṛikrētṛivikrētṛiparīkshitṛibhyaḥ.*

[35] *Arth. Trans.*, p. 95; also see p. 64. Bhaṭṭaswāmi (*J.B.O.R.S.*, vol. xi, pp. 57 and 60) and Gaṇapati Śāstri (*op. cit.*, i, pp. 206–7) do not explain *rūpika* beyond explaining that it was an income of 8 per cent. Jolly (*op. cit.*, ii, p. 23) regards *rūpika* and *vʎājī* as taxes. Vide re *vyājī*: Kauṭilya's explanation, p. 32 *n* 34

state was peculiar in this respect. Its ships were employed for carrying passengers and commercial goods.[36] The ships were under the control of the admiral of the fleet or *nāvādhyaksha*.[37] Megasthenes confirms what Kauṭilya says. In Strabo's words: "The admiral of the fleet lets out ships on hire both to those who undertake voyages and to merchants."[38] Passengers making use of the king's boats paid a fare (*yātrāvētana*).[39] Those who used the boats for fishing out conch shells and pearls paid a hire (*nauhāṭakaṃ*),[40] while fishermen hiring government boats paid a sixth of their haul as the hire.[41] It is not known what the rates of *yātrāvētana* and *naukahāṭaka* were.

CROWN LANDS[42]

The cultivation of crown lands formed a peculiar function of the government. Not only did the state own private lands,

[36] *Arth.*, Bk. II, ch. 28. [37] *Ibid.*

[38] *Strabo*, xv, 46. McCrindle (*Ancient India as described in Classical Literature*, p. 53, footnote) interprets Strabo's statement as applying only to river traffic. But in view of the mention of ocean traffic in the *Arthaśāstra* and in the *Periplus of the Erythrean Sea*, McCrindle's interpretation is questionable.

[39] *Arth.*, Bk. II, ch. 28, *Yātrāvētanaṃ rājanaubhissaṁpatantaḥ*.

[40] *Ibid.*, *Śaṅkhamuktāgrāhiṇō nauhāṭakān dadyuḥ svanaubhirvātarēyuḥ*. Gaṇapati Śāstri (*op. cit.*, i, p. 307) gives it as *naukābhāṭakam*, while Bhaṭṭaswāmi has *nauvibhāgakaṃ* (*J.B.O.R.S.*, vol. xii, part 2, p. 156).

[41] *Ibid.*, *Matsyabandhakā naukahāṭakaṃ shaḍbhāgaṃ dadyuḥ*. Shāma Śāstry (*Arth. Trans.*, p. 132) interprets *naukahāṭakaṃ* as fishing licence, but Sohrabhji's interpretation (*Notes*, p. 61), accepted by Jolly (*op. cit.*, ii, p. 31) and followed in this book, appears better. Also Bhaṭṭaswāmi explains the word as *rājōnavamakrayaḥ* (*J.B.O.R.S.*, vol. xi, p. 156).

[42] The word *svabhūmi* appears to denote crown lands in *Arth.*, Bk. II, ch. 24. But Kauṭilya uses it in various senses, of which three may be noted here. In the passage *bahuhalaparikṛishṭāyāṃ svabhūmau dāsakarmakaradaṇḍapratikartṛibhiḥ vāpayēt*, etc. (Bk. II, ch. 24), it probably denotes, as Shāma Śāstry interprets (*Arth. Trans.*, p. 138), crown lands. This interpretation, however, is not supported by other scholars. Bhaṭṭaswāmi (*J.B.O.R.S.*, xii, part 2,

but it was itself directly cultivating land.[43] It had a department of agriculture which, in addition to looking after agriculture in general, employed a band of trained assistants, labourers, slaves, and prisoners to cultivate crown lands[44] —wet crops (*kēdāra*), winter crops (*haimana*), and summer crops, according to the supply of labourers and water.[45] Rice, wheat, barley, mustard, sesamum, were among the products. The produce of crown lands was called *sītā*,[46] as distinguished from *bhāga*, which was the portion of the produce payable to the state as regular land revenue by non-crown lands.

The royal domain appears to have been so vast and the supply of labour so limited that lands were sometimes leased out to private cultivators. When fields were unsown for want of labour, half the share of the produce was given as an inducement to farmers.[47] Such a cultivator probably had to employ his own capital.[48] When capital was supplied by the

p. 134), Jolly (*op. cit.*, ii, p. 27), and Gaṇapati Śāstri (*op. cit.*, i, p. 283) explain *svabhūmau* as "in places suitably prepared for them." In this sense the term is used later in the same chapter in the passage beginning *gaṇḍhabhaishajyō . . . yathā svam bhūmishu* . . . and in Bk. II, ch. 18 (*svabhūmau cha sthāpayēt*). A third use of the term is in phrases such as *svabhūmijānāṃ rājāpaṇyānāṃ*, etc. (Bk. II, ch. 16), where *svabhūmi* means own country.

43 *Arth.*, Bk. II, ch. 24.

44 *Ibid.*

45 *Ibid.*, *Karmōdakapramāṇēna kēdāraṃ haimanaṃ graishmikaṃ vā sasyam sthāpayēt.*

46 *Arth.*, Bk. II, ch. 15. Only produce from crown lands appears to have been collected by the superintendent of agriculture, while revenue from non-crown lands was collected by the collector-general. This is confirmed by the words *bhāga* and *sītā* as heads of revenue from country parts (*Arth.*, Bk. II, ch. 6). Here *sītā* means produce from crown lands and *bhāga* means portion of the produce payable to Government as land revenue by other lands. If there were no crown lands there was no necessity for this distinction in the produce. Again, in Bk. II, ch. 24, it is used to denote crown lands.

47 *Arth.*, Bk. II, ch. 24, *Vāpātiriktamardhasītikāḥ kuryuḥ.* Compare the *ardhasītikās* mentioned in *Yājñavalkya*, i, 166.

48 Compare Bhaṭṭaswāmi's interpretation, *J.B.O.R.S.*, vol. xii, part 2, p. 137; Gaṇapati Śāstri, *op. cit.*, i, p. 286.

state and the cultivator supplied his labour, he appears to have received only one-fourth or one-fifth of the produce.[49] Thus the state was very liberal to such farmers, for while the cultivators of ordinary lands[50] obtained in the absence of a previous contract one-tenth of the crops grown, the cultivators of crown lands received a fourth or a fifth of the produce. In fact, the generosity of the state went so far that, according to Kauṭilya, they were allowed to pay only as much as they could without entailing hardship upon themselves. The state was thus receiving revenue both as cultivator and as landlord.

[49] *Arth.*, Bk. II, ch. 24, *Svavīryōpajīvinōvā chaturthapañchabhāgikāḥ yathēshṭam anavasitaṃ bhāgaṃ dadyuranyatra krichchhrēbhyaḥ.* Compare *J.B.O.R.S.*, vol. xii, part 2, p. 137; Gaṇapati Śāstri, *op. cit.*, i, p. 286. As regards the water rates mentioned in *Arth.*, Bk. II, ch. 14, see pp. 71 ff.

[50] *Arth.*, Bk. III, ch. 13, *Karshakassasyānāṃ . . . daśabhāgam asambhāshitavētanō labhēta.*

CHAPTER VIII

MISCELLANEOUS REVENUE

Treasure trove — Presents and royalties — Heirless property — Compensations — Interest — Herds — Fees — Fines

TREASURE TROVE

"TREASURE trove," says Gautama,[1] "is the property of the king; excepting (such as is found) by a Brahman who lives according to (the law)." This was the policy of Kauṭilya[2] also. According to him, when sweepers while *on duty* found any precious thing, two-thirds of the find belonged to the state and one-third to the finder. If the find was of precious stones, the whole of it was surrendered to the king, and a violation of this rule was heavily punished.[3] When any person other than a sweeper on duty discovered mines, precious stones, or treasure troves, he had to inform the state authorities of it immediately.[4] He received a sixth part of the find if he was a private individual and only a twelfth if he was a state employee. But treasure troves valued beyond 100,000 (? *paṇas*) were wholly the property of the state.[5]

[1] *Gautama*, x, 43–4. Also see *Ānanda Rāmāyaṇa*, *Śarakāṇḍa*, iii, 264, *Yadbhūmyaṃ vartatē vittam tanṛipasya na saṁśayaḥ*; *Vaśishṭha*, iii, 13–14; *Vishṇu*, iii, 56 ff. Also see *Jātakas*, nos. 96 and 546.

[2] It is interesting to note that while the law-givers like Vaśishtha and Vishṇu differentiate between castes in the matter of reward for the discoverer of the treasure trove, Kauṭilya distinguishes only a person on duty from one otherwise.

[3] *Arth.*, Bk. IV, ch. 1.

[4] *Ibid.* Compare *Gautama*, x, 44, "Some declare the finder of a non-Brahminical caste even who renounces (his find to the king) shall obtain one-sixth." Also see *Manu*, viii, 33 ff; *Vishṇu*, iii, 56 ff.

[5] *Arth.*, Bk. IV, ch. 1.

PRESENTS AND ROYALTIES

There appear to have been various occasions on which the people gave presents to the king, and such presents were called *aupayānikaṃ*.[6] "When the king washes his hair," writes Strabo, "they celebrate a great festival, and send him great presents, each person seeking to out-rival his neighbour in displaying his wealth."[7] When a prince was born in the royal household the king perhaps received presents in addition to the tax levied on the occasion.[8] There may have been many other such occasions.[9]

Further, Megasthenes mentions a kind of royalty which partakes the nature of presents. People collecting gold from river beds paid a portion of the collection to the state,[10] but what portion is not known.

HEIRLESS PROPERTY

The state inherited unclaimed property,[11] except that which belonged to a woman or a man for whom no funeral rites had been performed, or to a miserly woman or to a *śrōtriya*.[12] It succeeded to all wealth[13] with no direct heir (*aputrakaṃ*) or even a distant heir (*adāyādikaṃ*) or lost and forgotten by the owner (*nashṭa praśṛitaṃ*) or belonging to a person who fled in public disturbances (*ḍamaragatasvaṃ*).[14]

[6] *Arth.*, Bk. II, ch. 15. Cf. *Śukranīti*, ii, 671–2.

[7] *Strabo*, xv, 69.

[8] Compare *Suruchi Jātaka*, no. 489 (*Fausboll*, vol. iv, p. 203), "*Ubhayarattavāsinō sāmi puttassa no khiramulan ti ēkēam kahapaṇam rājāṅganē khipimsu.*"

[9] Perhaps the custom mentioned in the *Kumaspiṇḍa Jātaka*, no. 415, of the citizens making presents to the king on the occasion of the Parosal-festival (*chattamangala divase*) prevailed in the Mauryan times also. Compare *Harshacharita*, p. 111.

[10] *Strabo*, xv, 1, 57.

[11] *Arth.*, Bk. III, ch. 5, *Adāyādakaṃ rājā harēt strīvṛittiprētaka-daryavarjamanyatra śrōtriyadravyāt.*

[12] *Ibid.*

[13] *Arth.*, Bk. II, chs. 6 and 15.

[14] I have followed Jolly, *op. cit.*, ii, p. 18. *Supra*, p. 94.

Likewise, the state inherited the property of a prostitute who died or went abroad without leaving any heir, who could only be her daughter, sister, or another prostitute nominated by the deceased's mother.[15]

COMPENSATIONS

When damage was done by cattle to crops that grew on uncultivated lands, compensation in the form of grain had to be paid to the state.[16] This suggests that crops growing on uncultivated lands belonged to the state,[17] and as the state property was injured compensation had to be paid.

Pedlars who sold the king's merchandise in many markets at a fixed price had to pay compensation (*vaidharaṇam*) in proportion to the loss entailed upon the king's trade,[18] probably on the ground that pedlars by selling the goods got the profits for themselves which the state would have got if it had sold the goods itself. So compensation was to be paid. Likewise compensation was to be paid by those who worked, on private account, mines which were owned by the state.[19]

INTEREST

The Mauryan state appears to have been a kind of banker dealing in grains. While describing the duties of the superintendent of the storehouse,[20] Kauṭilya refers to *the collection of interest on grain* debts and the loan of grain (*āpamityaka*), suggesting that the state was perhaps lending out grain to people on interest, probably with the intention of helping

[15] *Arth.*, Bk. II, ch. 27.

[16] *Arth.*, Bk. II, ch. 15. Bhaṭṭaswāmi gives two interpretations (*J.B.O.R.S.*, vol. xi, part 3, p. 84), *Kēchit pārihīṇikaṃ apakṛishṭāpachyasasyañcha tushādyairvināśitasasyaṃ daṇḍādhigamyamityaparē.*

[17] *Arth.*, Bk. II, ch. 15.

[18] *Arth.*, Bk. II, ch. 16.

[19] *Arth.*, Bk. II, ch. 12.

[20] *Arth.*, Bk. II, ch. 15.

its subjects with seeds or subsistence, but incidentally making profit by the transaction just as modern grain banks.

HERDS (*vraja*)

The revenue from this source was probably different from the tributes paid by the herdsmen which are referred to by Arrian.[21] It was derived by the supervision of the government over private herds. In localities where cattle-lifting was feared, private herds of cattle were left in the care of the state officials, and in return for this service the state received 10 per cent of the dairy produce.[22] The gain to the state from this source was in addition to that got from its own herds and dairy farms.

FEES[23]

There was a passport fee of one *māsha*, like the *visa* fee of to-day.[24] A native without a passport was fined ten *paṇās* if he went out of or entered the country.[25] The superintendent of pasture lands checked the passports.

FINES

There was a host of fines (as many as nearly 350 are mentioned by Kauṭilya),[26] which must have yielded a considerable revenue. When the amount of the fine was less than 100 *paṇās*, 8 per cent more was collected as *rūpa*, and when the amount exceeded 100 *paṇās* 5 per cent was added to it as *vyājī*. These additions were perhaps justified on the

[21] *Indika*, ch. xi. This was in the nature of a tax.

[22] *Arth.*, Bk. II, ch. 29, *Parachakrāṭavībhayādanupravishṭānāṃ paśūnāṃ pālanadharmēṇa daśabhāgaṃ dadyuriti bhāgānupravishṭakaṃ.*

[23] See also under excise revenue.

[24] *Arth.*, Bk. II, ch. 34, *Mudrādhyakshaḥ mudrāṃ māshakēṇa dadyāt.*

[25] *Ibid.*

[26] *Vide Arth. Trans.*, pp. 502–7.

ground that the original sum was unreasonably low.[27] Only one example may be given of the heaviness of fines. For evading payment of tolls and smuggling goods the fines levied amounted to eight times the toll, and often involved forfeiture of the goods.[28]

27 *Arth.*, Bk. III, ch. 17:

> *Daṇḍakarmasu sarvēshu rūpamashṭapaṇaṃ śataṃ*
> *Śatātparē tu vyājīm cha vidyātpañcha paṇam śataṃ.*
> *Prajānāṃ dōshabāhuḷyāt rājñāṃ vā bhāva dōśhataḥ*
> *Rūpavyājyāvadharmishṭhe dharmyānuprakṛitissṃṛitā.*

28 *Arth.*, Bk. II, ch. 21.

CHAPTER IX

REVENUE IN FINANCIAL DIFFICULTIES

I. *Surplus:* Were there public loans? II. *Fresh taxation, etc.:* Demands on cultivators—On merchants—And on herdsmen—Voluntary contributions—Miscellaneous

I. SURPLUS

IF to-day the balanced budget is regarded as the best, in ancient days the state generally accumulated large surpluses. According to Śukra,[1] the treasury should contain money enough for public expenditure for twenty years. Kauṭilya[2] also thinks that the state should lay by for a rainy day. "Justly obtained by inheritance or by self-acquisition, rich in gold and silver, filled with an abundance of big gems of various colours and of gold coins, and capable to withstand calamities of long duration, is the best treasury." The king is directed to fix in accordance with the needs of the country under one-fourth of the total revenue of the state as the charges for maintaining his servants.[3] The civil list given by Kauṭilya after this statement clearly indicates that the servants included most of the employees of the state, including the military. A similar principle is laid down in the *Śukranīti*,[4] viz. that of the public

[1] *Śukranīti*, iv, 2, 25–7:

Sarakshaṇaṃ bhavētsamyak yāvadviśati vatsaraṃ.
Tathā kōśatsu sandhāryaḥ svaprajā rakshaṇā kshamaḥ.

Śukra further observes (*ibid.*, 42–4) that the reserve sufficient for twelve years is *nīcha* (low), that which lasts sixteen is *madhyama* (middling), and that which lasts for thirty years is *uttama* (good).

[2] *Arth.*, Bk. VI, ch. 1, *Dharmādhigataḥ pūrvaiḥ . . . anāyātiṃ sahētēti kōśasampatḥ*. Cf. *Kāmandaka*, iv, 60–1.

[3] *Arth.*, Bk. V, ch. 3, *Durgajanapadaśaktyā bhṛityakarma samudāyapādēna sthāpayēt.*

[4] Śukra's scheme of expenditure is as follows: *Gramapas*, one-twelfth; Army, three-twelfths; Charities, one twenty-fourth; Public Works, one twenty-fourth; Salaries, one twenty-fourth; Personal, one twenty-fourth; Total, six-twelfths.

revenue *one-half* is to be spent on the army, public works, salaries, charities, and royal household, thus having annually a surplus of *half* the income.

The Tamil author, Māmūlanār, refers to the vast wealth accumulated by the Naṅdas, the immediate predecessors of the Mauryas, which they (the Naṅdas) had hidden in the waters of the Ganges and in the earth.[5] In his *Ancient Geography of India*[6] Cunningham observes: "At the time of Aśōka's accession the wealth of Taxila is said to have amounted to 36 *katis*, or 360 millions of some unnamed coin, which, even if it was the silver *tangka* or sixpence, would have amounted to nine crores of rupees or £9,000,000. It is probable, however, that the coin intended by the Indian writer was a gold one, in which case the wealth of this city would have amounted to 90 or 100 millions of pounds. I quote this statement as a proof of the reputed wealth of Taxila within fifty years of Alexander's death." In view of what Kauṭilya says of the best treasury the coin may have been a gold one.

What exactly was the amount of the surplus in the Mauryan treasury is not known. The surplus was probably kept in the form of precious stones, coins, bullion, and materials.[7] The purpose of having such accumulations was to build up a treasury "capable of withstanding calamities of long duration."[8] No doubt additional revenue was raised

[5] *Some Contributions of South India to Indian Culture*, p. 23.

[6] P. 106. Watters, in his *Yuan Chwang*, vol. i, p. 247, writes that the words in the Sanskrit original refer to the inhabitants and not to coins. "This interpretation," he adds, "is supported by two out of the three Chinese translations, the third translation being apparently from a different text."

In the footnote, however, Watters remarks: "In *A-yu-wang-Chean*, ch. 1, and in *Tsa-a-hau-chin*, ch. 1, it is a question of money. The particular form of expression used seems to be susceptible of both interpretations." The latter interpretation is followed here.

[7] *Arth.*, Bk. VI, ch. 1. Compare the Girnār inscription of Rudra dāman (*Ep. Ind.*, viii, no. 6) where it is said the king's treasury "overflows with an accumulation of gold, silver, diamonds, beryl stones, and (other) precious things."

[8] *Arth.*, Bk. VI, ch. 1. Compare *Manu*, vii, 213.

from the people in great financial difficulties,[9] but the surplus was probably used first to meet the calamity.

In the next section the means of raising revenue in financial crises by taxation and such other methods have been described. Here, however, the question of public borrowing may be considered. In ancient India as a whole some kind of public borrowing appears to have existed. In the *Śāntiparva*[10] the king says: "To meet this calamity and dreadful danger, I seek your wealth for concerting measures for your protection. When the danger passes away I will repay you what I now take. Our foes, however, will not return what they (if supposed) will take from you by force." Śukra likewise writes[11] that the "king should receive the wealth of the rich men in times of danger by supplying them wherewith to live, and that when he is free from danger he should return the amount, together with interest." While dealing with public revenue Śukra mentions loans (*auttamarnika*) as one of the forms of wealth,[12] and says that the *sumantra* was to keep accounts of public debts.[13]

In the light of the foregoing it is likely that there was in the Mauryan period also some sort of public borrowing. Kauṭilya says:[14] "When he (the king), however, thinks that 'by taking a repayable income, or loan (*pratyādēya*), I shall cause my enemy's treasury, army, and other defensive resources to dwindle, I shall exploit to impoverishment the

[9] *Infra*, p. 139.

[10] lxxxvii, 29–30.

[11] *Śukranīti*, iv, 2, 21–2.

[12] *Śukranīti*, iv, 2, 326.

[13] *Śukranīti*, iv, 2, 102. It may be mentioned that a record of Rājarāja Chōḷa II (*Madras Inscriptions*, p. 152) refers "to a loan borrowed by the (local) assembly from the temple treasury on account of 'bad time' (famine) and scarcity of grain."

[14] *Arth.*, Bk. IX, ch. 4. Shāma Śāstry (*Arth. Trans.*, p. 406) translates *pratyādēya* as repayable profit; repayable income, i.e. loan, appears better; the words *ādēya* and *pratyādēya* in this chapter appear to denote ordinary income and loans. These meanings have been adopted here in preference to those suggested by Shāma Śāstry. *Vide* Mādhava Yajva's commentary. Jolly, *op. cit.*, ii, p. 135.

mines, timber and elephant forests, irrigational works and roads of traffic of my enemy' . . . then he may take a *pratyādēya* (i.e. repayable income or loan)." Kauṭilya explains[15] *ādēya* as that which is easily acquired and secured without the necessity of its being returned to others, while *pratyādēya* signifies that which is to be returned to others and which is difficult to get; and *pratyādēya* is not recommended, being destructive in effect. In other words, loans even by states were not advocated, perhaps because of inter-state complications, as in the case of modern central American states and the commercial nations like the British Isles and U.S.A.

Another circumstance supports the suggestion that the public loans were probably not unknown. One of the causes of financial trouble, according to the *Arthaśāstra*,[16] arose out of one state leaving revenue in the custody of its neighbour or of a wild tribe.[17] This could not merely be a deposit for safety. The state, as described by Chāṇakya, was too shrewd a banker to lose the interest on its money. To its own subjects it was lending grain and other goods on interest.[18] Lending by the state at interest is advocated in the *Mahābhārata*.[19] Yudhisṭhira is addressed thus: "Grantest thou with kindness loans unto the tillers taking only a fourth of the excess." Śukra remarks[20] that the king should invest the whole, or at least half, of the wealth of a conquered kingdom at interest until it is doubled. It appears therefore improbable that the state did not lend to its neighbours but only kept it as a deposit.

15 *Arth.*, Bk. IX, ch. 4, *Suprāpyānupālyaḥ parēshāmapratyādēya iti ādēyaḥ; viparyayē pratyādēyaḥ, tamādadānastatrasthō vā vināśaṃ prāpnōti.*

16 *Arth.*, Bk. VIII, ch. 4.

17 Compare *Śukranīti*, iv, 2, 45, which says that the king should deposit (surplus) revenue with rich persons so as to get it in times of danger.

18 *Arth.*, Bk. II, ch. 15, *Dhānyamūlyaṃ kōśanirhāraḥ prayōgapratyādānaṃ cha krayimaṃ.*

19 *Sabhāparva*, v.

20 *Śukranīti*, iv, 7, 403.

Still another piece of evidence may be considered. In times of a great famine the state, among other measures, started public works, distributed food, and "sought the help of its friends."[21] This help of the neighbours possibly indicates loans raised in foreign states. It may, however, be noted that in extreme cases the king with his subjects emigrated to the neighbouring kingdom and became its guests.[22] A good country is described by Kauṭilya[23] as one productive of subsistence not only to its own people but also to outsiders on occasions of calamities. It is, however, doubtful if this can be taken as a loan. Perhaps the state which was the guest of another gladly maintained its host under similar circumstances. But it is likely that the passage *mitrāṇicha vyapaśrayēta* denotes loans. The state first helped its subjects with its own accumulated funds; if this was not enough to meet the situation it borrowed from other states, and even if this could not stem the calamity the people migrated to the neighbouring state.

The whole of the foregoing discussion indicates the existence of public debts. A careful examination of the passages quoted above suggests two kinds of loans—internal, i.e. floated within the state, and external, i.e. floated outside the state. Borrowing appears to have been resorted to for productive purposes, such as the exploitation of mines, timber and elephant forests, and the construction of irrigation works and commercial roads,[24] and for unproductive purposes like purchasing the alliance of a neighbouring state, fomenting rebellion among the enemy's subjects, for the maintenance of the army,[25] famine relief,[26] and for financing wars.

[21] *Arth.*, Bk. IV, ch. 3, *Mitrāṇicha vyapaśrayēta.*
[22] *Ibid.*, *Nishpannasasyavishayaṃ vā sajanapadō yāyāt.*
[23] *Arth.*, Bk. VI, ch. 1, *Sthānavānātmadhāraṇaḥ paradhāraṇaśchāpadi svārakshassvājīvaḥ*, etc.
[24] *Arth.*, Bk. IX, ch. 4. Passage beginning "*pratyādēyamādāya* . . ."
[25] *Ibid.*
[26] *Arth.*, Bk. IV, ch. 3.

II. FRESH TAXATION, ETC.[27]

All states some time or other get into great pecuniary difficulties, which may be occasioned by war, famine, trade depression, and such other unforeseen calamities. The Great War of 1914 dragged into financial chaos most European states, and even prosperous countries like England felt the greatest financial shock. Under such circumstances modern states adopt two means—one increasing taxation and similarly exploiting other sources of revenue, and the other, and more important one, resorting to public borrowing. The Mauryas also seem to have employed both these means. The question of public debts has been discussed before. Here will be considered the method of raising revenue by taxation and other means—fair and foul, for, as will be presently seen, some of the measures adopted for getting revenue were at least morally unjustifiable and even degrading.[28]

The ways of raising revenue described by Kauṭilya may be considered under five heads:

1. Demands on cultivators.
2. Demands on merchants.
3. Demands on herdsmen.
4. Voluntary contributions.
5. Miscellaneous.

DEMANDS ON CULTIVATORS

(i) Where agriculture depended on rain and people were rich in grain, the state took one-third or one-fourth of their

[27] *Arth.*, Bk. V, ch. 2. In this whole chapter Kauṭilya systematically and analytically enumerates the various ways of raising income in crises.

In Bk. VIII, ch. 4, Kauṭilya gives a list of financial troubles. "Financial trouble due to two kinds of obstruction and to the molestations described above are stagnation of financial position, loss of wealth due to the allowance of remission of taxes in favour of leaders, scattered revenue, false account of revenue collected, and revenue left in the custody of a neighbouring king or of a wild tribe." Thus the group of financial troubles.

[28] Contrast *Yājñavalkya*, i, 13, 340.

grain according to their capacity. Some persons, however, were exempted from this demand. They were:

(*a*) People living in tracts and cultivating soil of middle quality.[29]
(*b*) Persons who had been of great help in the construction of forts, gardens, buildings, irrigation works, roads, colonization of waste land, exploitation of mines, and formation of forests.
(*c*) People living near the borders of the state.
(*d*) People without enough subsistence.

(ii) The state might demand of cultivators one-fourth of their grain, and one-sixth of forest produce and of such commodities as cotton, wax, fabrics, barks of trees, hemp, wool, sandal, silk, medicines, flowers, fruits, vegetables, firewood, bamboos, and flest. This demand appears to have been a general demand payable by all cultivators, including those mentioned in (i). As stated already, all land paid a land revenue of one-sixth of the produce. This demand of one-fourth does not appear to be in addition to the usual one-sixth but including it. This has Manu's sanction.[30]

(iii) But some of the cultivators who farmed with the aid of rain-water had to pay more than the others. Those who were poor were exempted from this special contribution, because they had not enough to live upon. Besides, persons who had done some service to the state were also exempted. So also were people living near the boundaries of the state, because they occupied a strategic position and lest excess of taxation should drive them to the enemy's camp. Thus it appears that only those who had rich granaries had to pay one-third or one-fourth of the grain. It seems strange that this excess was demanded from persons, however rich, who depended upon unsteady rain; but the explanation may be that others who cultivated by irrigation already paid the regular heavy water rates, while those depending upon rain paid only the occasional excess demanded in great difficulties.

[29] Soil was divided into three grades—best, middle, low, according to quality. *Arth.*, Bk. II, ch. 35.
[30] *Manu*, x, 118.

(iv) Further, the state purchased for gold one-fourth of the produce remaining in the land, deducting the grain required for seeds and subsistence of the people. It might buy up the property of the forest tribes and of Brahmans learned in the *Vēdas*, provided the price was a favourable one.

It is not clear why the state should buy only one-fourth of the remaining produce after making allowance for seeds and subsistence. Perhaps this was in order to allow the people to dispose of the remainder as they liked in trade and commerce. If all the produce was bought up, trade would be stifled and needy people starved.

(v) (*a*) When the revenue thus collected was inadequate, the collector-general induced the cultivators to raise summer crops, threatening that if they disobeyed the state itself would get their land cultivated even in regular seasons. This was nothing short of a threat of confiscation of lands. Similar inducements to raise additional crops were employed by belligerent countries, such as England, Germany, and France, in the World War.

(*b*) The state took away half of all ivory and skins of animals.[31] Trading without licence was punished, and probably a licence involved fees.

DEMANDS ON MERCHANTS

These demands can very well be put in a tabular form (see p. 142).

The property of the goldsmiths was confiscated because they were considered fraudulent traders who pretended to be honest. The tax on dramatists and prostitutes really meant the raising of the income tax from $6\frac{2}{3}$ per cent to 50 per cent. Most of the other items can be classified under trade or occupation taxes.

Thus in hard times, when the king's treasury was in-

[31] Kauṭilya classifies this under "Demands on cultivators." It appears to be better to have it under "Demands on merchants" as trade, ivory, and skins could come under this head.

adequate to meet the emergency, excessive taxation of the people, particularly the rich, was resorted to. This is also evident from Kautilya's statement that in times of famine the state adopted the policy of thinning the rich by exacting

DEMANDS ON MERCHANTS

No.	Items	Amount of Contribution
1	Persons dealing in precious stones, metals, corals, pearls, elephants, and horses ..	500 *paṇas*
2	Persons dealing in clothes, cotton threads, brass, bronze, copper, liquor, sandal, and medicines	400 *paṇas*
3	Dealers in grains, liquids, iron (*lōha*),[32] and carts	300 *paṇas*
4	Traders in glass, and artisans of fine workmanship	200 *paṇas*
5	Artisans of inferior workmanship. Those who keep prostitutes	100 *paṇas*
6	Traders in firewood, bamboos, stone pots, vegetables, etc.	50 *paṇas*
7	Dramatists and prostitutes	Half their wages
8	Goldsmiths	Entire property

excessive revenue or causing them to vomit their accumulated wealth.[33]

DEMANDS ON HERDSMEN

1. Poultry and pig farmers had to surrender half of their stock of animals.
2. Those who reared inferior animals had to give away one-sixth of their stock.
3. Those who kept cows, buffaloes, mules, asses, and camels, surrendered 10 per cent of their animals.

[32] *Lōha* means metals and also iron in particular. As some other metals are mentioned above (e.g. brass, bronze, copper) it appears better to take *lōha* to indicate here iron. Shāma Śāstry, however, translates the word as "metals" (*Arth. Trans.*, p. 293).

[33] *Arth.*, Bk. IV, ch. 3, *Karśanaṃ vamanaṃ vā kuryāt.*

According to Kauṭilya,[34] the foregoing demands had to be made only once and not more often, but it is doubtful how far this was practised.

VOLUNTARY CONTRIBUTIONS

When the foregoing demands were either not resorted to or proved inadequate, the collector-general collected revenue by raising, under the false pretences of carrying on business, subscriptions from the people. "Those who of their own accord or with the intention of doing good," observes Kauṭilya,[35] "offer their wealth to the king shall be honoured with a rank in the court, an umbrella or a turban, or some ornaments in return for their gold." Further, when crops were ripe, the state begged a portion of vegetable and ripe produce, except what is gleaned in the form of vegetables and grains and except grains scattered in harvest fields to be used as offerings to gods and ancestors, to feed cows, or for the subsistence of mendicants and village employees.

Kauṭilya enumerates a long list of miscellaneous ways of raising revenue. Without going into the details may be noticed only the broad outlines of the methods:

Cheating people with the aid of spies; carrying away the property of heretics, temples, and dead men, of religious institutions under the pretence of guarding the property;[36] exploiting the superstition, credulity, and fear of the people;[37]

[34] *Arth.*, Bk. V, ch. 2.

[35] We may compare the gift of war bonds and other things made to the Government in England to help the nation. In ancient Athens also voluntary contributions from citizens formed one of the means of striding over pecuniary embarrassments.

[36] For example, "The superintendent of religious institutions may collect in one place the various kinds of property of the Gods of forfeited cities and country parts and carry away the property" (*Arth.*, Bk. V, ch. 2).

[37] For example, "Or having on some night set up a god or an altar or having opened a sacred place of ascetics, or having pointed out an evil omen the king may collect subsistence under the pretence

cheating merchants as partners or as debtors;[38] confiscating the property of people with the help of prostitutes;[39] and various other false pretences.

In the collection of this revenue, persons who maintained courtesans were required to assist young and beautiful women in the service of the king.[40]

Some of the methods described above are mentioned by Śukra also.[41] He says that in normal times the king should not increase his treasure by augmenting the punishment, land revenues, and duties, and by taking dues from holy places and properties consecrated to divine purposes, implying that in financial difficulties these could be resorted to. A rather peculiar and important feature common to Kauṭilya, Śukra, and the Greeks[42] is getting revenue out of sacred property. Kauṭilya recommends the robbing of temples and religious institutions under the pretext of guarding their wealth.[43] Śukra suggests the taxing of holy places and

of holding processions and congregation (to avert calamities)" (*Arth.*, Bk. V, ch. 2).

One of Kauṭilya's methods in this group was the levy of a tax on people who came to see the appearance of a spirit: this kind of tax was not unknown in ancient India. In the third Sanjan plate of Amōghavarsha I of the ninth century A.D. (*Ep. Ind.*, xviii, no. 26) is found the grant of a village with the (right of) toll "upon the appearance of a spirit" (*sabhūtāpātapratyāyaḥ*). Kauṭilya's ingenuity, however, consisted perhaps in that the state falsely created the opportunity for the sake of revenue.

38 For example, "Or one of the king's spies, in the garb of a merchant, may become a partner of a rich merchant and carry on trade in concert with him. As soon as a considerable amount of money has been gathered as sale proceeds, deposits, and loans, he may cause himself to be robbed of this amount" (*Arth.*, Bk. V, ch. 2).

39 For example, "Prostitute spies, under the garb of chaste women, may cause themselves to be enamoured of persons who are seditious. No sooner are the seditious persons seen within the abode of the female spies than they shall be seized and their property confiscated to government" (*ibid.*).

40 *Ibid., Bandhakipōshakā rājaprēshyābhiḥ paramarūpayauvanābhiḥ kōśaṃ samharēyuḥ.*

41 *Śukranīti*, iv, 2.

42 Boeckh, Bk. II, ch. xx.

43 *Arth.*, Bk. V, ch. 2.

the taking of sacred property. In Greece, borrowing from, and even confiscation of, sacred property was resorted to.[44]

The foregoing instances of the methods give an adequate idea of the various means employed by the Mauryan financiers to tide over pecuniary embarrassments. Many are to be found even in modern days. Viewing these methods financially, one can sympathize with Kauṭilya, who in practice adopted Śukra's maxim[45] that the king should collect funds by hook or by crook and maintain thereby the commonwealth, the army, and the sacrifices. But some of the means employed, e.g. by cheating the people, cannot be appreciated. It is true that these methods were directed to be employed only against the wicked and the seditious, but it is doubtful how far the others were safe from these snares. There appears to be no parallel to these super-Macchiavellian ways of extracting money.[46] Were these practised—nay, even proposed—in modern states, they are certain to be condemned as tyrannical and unbecoming a state worth the name. They are in striking contrast to the method proposed in the *Śāntiparva*,[47] where the king requests the people to give him their wealth for concocting measures

[44] Boeckh, Bk. II, ch. xx, p. 770, "But although the Greeks in general, even at the period of their entire decline, cherished reverential feelings towards the gods, yet the confiscation of sacred property is a Greek conception."

[45] *Śukranīti*, iv, 2, 2.

[46] Compare what Boeckh writes (*op. cit.*, p. 771) of Athens: "There was an appearance of justice in the measure of the tyrant, Hippias, when in order to obtain money he caused those portions which in the upper stories or by juts or by balconies projected over into the street, steps, stairs, and balustrades, extending into the same, and doors opening outward, to be sold, because the street was public property and ought not to be obstructed in that manner. The proprietors bought them and he obtained by the measure a considerable sum of money. At a later date, upon the advice of Ipticrates, the same measure for a similar purpose and with the like result was adopted by an assembly of the people."

[47] lxxxvii, 29 ff.

for their protection and promises to return them after the danger. But Kauṭilya was probably too practical to care for ethics in times of danger. And economically these methods have a great *immediate* advantage.

CHAPTER X

EXEMPTIONS FROM TAXATION AND GRANTS OF REVENUE

It is the recognized right of the state to compel all its subjects to contribute to the common expenses, but there have been always and in every country certain persons and institutions exempted from one or more of the payments to be made to the exchequer. "Exemptions," says Seligman,[1] "were accorded from public rather than private reasons. Even to-day—not to speak of growing crops and working men's tools—ministers' houses, cemeteries, educational and religious institutions are exempt from taxation. The public at large is willing to bear the higher rate of taxation because the exempted classes and institutions are really performing a function which the government would otherwise be called upon to assume."

This was also the case in ancient India in general and the Mauryan days in particular. In theory, as in modern India, every bit of land, especially cultivated land, was liable to pay land revenue and other kindred taxes, but some lands were exempted from paying them. Just as to-day there are *jāghirs* and other grants of land which are revenue-free, so also there were such lands granted to the Mauryan courtiers, to the universities, and Brahmans. Kauṭilya observes[2] that superintendents, accountants, *gōpas, sthānikas,* veterinary surgeons, and messengers should be endowed with lands, which they should have no right to alienate by sale or mortgage. The Superintendent of Accounts had to make note of such grants to the king's courtiers, and remission of taxes was allowed to them often in addition to grant of salaries and provisions.[3]

[1] *Studies in Public Finance*, pp. 139–40.

[2] *Arth.*, Bk. II, ch. 1.

[3] *Arth.*, Bk. II, chs. 7 and 1.

Lands known as *brahmadēya lands*, and exempt from all taxes and fines, were granted to those who performed sacrifices, spiritual guides, priests, and those learned in the *Vēdas*.[4]

Such grants were common in ancient India. Āpastambha observes[5] that a king who, without inconveniencing his servants, gives land and money to Brahmans according to their deserts gains endless worlds.[6]

Many inscriptions[7] in the post-Mauryan period deal with such grants free from the payment not only of land revenue but of all sorts of dues to the state.

The grant of a land seems to have implied the transfer not of its absolute ownership but only of the income from it. Even in the case of crown lands the donee did not get the ultimate ownership of the land, but only the right to all kinds of revenue from it. An inscription of Mahārāja Jayanṫa expresses this idea as follows: "You yourselves (the villagers) shall render to these persons (the grantees) the offering of the tribute of the customary duties (*śulka*), royalties (? *bhāgabhōga*), *kara* (taxes), gold, etc. (*hiraṇyādi*), and shall be obedient to (their) commands."[8]

Apart from this exemption from land revenue as regards Brahmans, courtiers, and others,[9] there were some other

[4] They were known in later days as *sarvamānya* or *sarvanamasya* tenure. *Ep. Ind.*, xv, no. 20; xvi, no. 8, etc. Cf. Gupta, *Land System in South India*, ch. vi.

[5] *Arth.*, Bk. II, ch. 1, *Ṛitvigāchāryapurōhitaśrōtriyēbhyō brahmadēyanyadaṇḍakarānyabhirūpadāyakāni prayachchhēt.* There is also a passage in *Arth.*, Bk. I, ch. 13, indicating that even hermits paid the state a sixth of the grain gleaned by them (*tasmāduñchashaḍbhāgamāraṇyaka api nivappaṅti*). Compare Kāḷidāsa's allusion to a similar contribution (*Śākuṅtalā*, act ii, Kale's Edition, 1925, p. 56).

[6] *Āpastambha*, ii, 10, 26, 1. Also *Vishṇu*, iii, 26–7.

[7] E.g. *Ep. Ind.*, xv, no. 20; xvi, no. 8. *Gupta Inscriptions*, nos. 26, 27, and 28.

[8] *Gupta Inscriptions*, no. 27; also see nos. 26 and 28.

[9] Compare *Vaśishṭha*, xix, 23–4; *Manu*, viii, 394; *Āpastambha*, ii, 10, 26, 12–17.

cases when remissions and exemptions were given.[10] When irrigation works like tanks or lakes were newly constructed by private persons, taxes on their lands below such works were remitted for five years. When ruined or neglected water-works were repaired, the remission of taxes was for four years. For improving, extending, and restoring water-works overgrown with weeds, taxes were remitted for two years. If new works were acquired by mortgage or purchase, lands below such works got a remission of taxes for two years. Taxes were remitted for a like period when uncultivated lands were acquired for purposes of cultivation. Where works of lift-irrigation were constructed, the government was satisfied, perhaps for a fixed number of years, with as much of revenue as did not entail hardship upon the cultivator.

Śukra also mentions such concessions. According to him,[11] when people undertook new industries or cultivated new lands, or constructed irrigation works, the state was not to demand any revenue until they realized twice the sum expended.

The foregoing remissions appear to include the land revenue, the water rate, and other kindred taxes. All remissions had to be recorded by the revenue collectors.[12] Under other circumstances also remissions were made.[13] They were occasional, and in emergencies, or when opening new settlements, only when such remissions tended to "swell the treasury." Thus exemptions and remissions as regards land revenue and other taxes on land were given to Brahmans, courtiers, temples, and villages.

[10] *Arth.*, Bk. III, ch. 9, *Taṭākasētubandhānām nāvapravartanē pañchavārshikaḥ parihāraḥ. Bhagnōtsṛishṭānāṃ chaturvārshikaḥ. Samupārūḍhānāṃ traivārshikaḥ*, etc.

[11] *Śukranīti*, iv, 2, 242–4.

[12] *Arth.*, Bk. III, ch. 15.

[13] *Arth.*, Bk. II, ch. 1, *Anugrahaparihārauchaibhyaḥ kōśavṛiddhikaraudadyāt. Kōśōpapātikau varjayēt. Alpakōśōhi rājā paurajānapadānēva grasate. Nivēśasamakālaṃ yathāgatakaṃ vā parihāraṃ dadyāt.*

Even under British rule "a detailed code, for example, regulating the remission or suspension of revenue on the failure of the crops obtains in all provinces."[14] This situation of remission on the failure of crops never arose in the Mauryan days, as the revenue, being a portion of the produce, adjusted itself automatically to the crops from the land. In British India, permanent agricultural improvements are exempted from any enhanced assessment either temporarily or for a period of years.[15] There are also to-day revenue-free lands like *jāghirs* and *saranjams* belonging to private individuals, as well as a land given to temples and other religious institutions, just like the *brahmadēya* and other lands of the Mauryan days. Because of the existence of such revenue-free land and of persons whose lands, on account of their position or caste, were exempted from all kinds of taxes, the Mauryan state forbade the transfer of revenue-paying lands to such privileged revenue-free landholders, in order to prevent evasion of the payment of revenue to the state. Likewise, to avoid confusion in the collection of revenue, the exempted persons could not transfer their lands to taxpayers.[16]

The Brahmans were exempted from the payment of all contributions to the state.[17] This seems to have been a common practice in ancient India. Manu's dictum[18] is that a king, though dying from want, should not levy a tax on *śrōtriyas*, and no *śrōtriya* residing in his kingdom should perish from hunger. According to Āpastambha,[19] a learned Brahman, women, minors, students, and ascetics were not

[14] *Science of Public Finance*, p. 220.

[15] *Ibid.*, p. 224, "Permanent agricultural improvements, it should be remembered, are expressly exempt from any enhanced assessment in Bombay and Madras for ever, and in other parts of India for a period, irrespective of the term of settlement and sufficient for the capital sunk to be fully recouped from the additional assets created."

[16] *Arth.*, Bk. III, ch. 10.

[17] *Arth.*, Bk. II, ch. 1; Bk. XIII, ch. 5. *Strabo*, xv, 1, 39.

[18] *Manu*, vii, 133.

[19] *Āpastambha*, ii, 10, 26, 10 ff.

to be taxed. In the *Śāntiparva* it is stated that the wealth of persons who perform sacrifices, as also the wealth dedicated to deities, should never be taken. The Greek Bardesanes, of the second century A.D., writes[20] that he was informed by the head of an Indian embassy that "the *Brahmans* pay no taxes like other citizens." The Gupta inscriptions mention that the villages granted to Brahmans and others were free from all taxes.

But the exemption did not apply to all Brahmans, only to *śrōtriyas* or those who were learned, who performed sacrifices and studied the *Vēdas*, i.e. those who were useful to society.[21] Even the Greeks[22] mention that only the philosophers who gave sound advice were exempted. It was even regulated[23] that a *Kshatriya* should take the wealth of such persons as never performed religious rites and sacrifices, and who were, therefore, considered to be equal to robbers.

In addition to *śrōtriyas* and ascetics, labourers,[24] perhaps because of their poverty, were exempted from paying the consumers tax on salt used for purposes of food. The artisan class is stated not only to have been exempted from paying taxes, but to have even received maintenance from the royal treasury.[25]

[20] *Ancient India as described in Classical Literature*, pp. 167, 170.
[21] Cf. *Manu*, vii, 133; *Āpastambha*, ii, 10, 26, 10; *Vaśishṭha*, xxii, 23; *Vishṇu*, iii, 26, 79.
[22] Cf. *Śāntiparva*, cxxxvi, 2.
[23] *Arth.*, Bk. II, ch. 12.
[24] *Ibid.*
[25] *Diodorus*, ii, 41.

PART II

EXPENDITURE

CHAPTER XI

GENERAL CONSIDERATIONS AND CLASSIFICATION OF HEADS OF EXPENDITURE

Principle guiding expenditure—Applicability of modern canons to Mauryan conditions—Classifications of expenditure—Modern classifications—Comparison between Mauryan and British Indian heads of expenditure

PRINCIPLE GUIDING EXPENDITURE

IT has been observed elsewhere that, in contrast with the modern ideal of the balanced budget, the Mauryan financiers —and perhaps all ancient financiers—had a surplus budget as the ideal. Just as taxation was regulated by this principle, so also was expenditure guided by it. Kauṭilya says that the king should fix less than a quarter of the total revenue as the expenditure for maintaining his servants, giving them handsome emoluments so as to inspire them to work well.[1] It is doubtful if all kinds of expenditure are included in this one-fourth of revenue. Perhaps they are not. Kauṭilya probably means that expenses such as salaries, presents, and provisions to government servants and employees, including the military, was met out of this share of revenue. For the list of government servants and salaries given in the same chapter includes military and all other officials of state. An additional share, perhaps one-fourth, was spent on other items of expenditure, such as materials for public works, factories, and arsenals.

According to the *Śukranīti*,[2] salaries of headmen should involve one-twelfth of the public revenue; the army one-

[1] *Arth.*, Bk. V, ch. 3, *Durgajanapadaśaktyā bhṛityakarmasamudāyapādēna sthāpayēt.* This is the text as given by both Shāma Śāstry and Mr. Gaṇapati Śāstri. But Jolly (*op. cit.*, ii, p. 48) reads *Ṣamudāyavādēna*, which Śāstry considers not as good as what he has adopted. Jolly, however, translates the passages as "in accordance with the reports regarding the amount of revenue."

[2] i, 631–5.

fourth; charities one-twenty-fourth; works of public utility one-twenty-fourth; salaries of officials one-twenty-fourth; and royal household one-twenty-fourth. The total expenditure comes to one-half of the revenue, military expenditure itself involving one-fourth of the total expenditure. Perhaps Kauṭilya also had in his mind the same idea of saving one-half of the public income.

APPLICABILITY OF MODERN CANONS TO MAURYAN CONDITIONS

Modern writers on finance enumerate four canons of expenditure, viz. the canons of Benefit, Economy, Sanction, and Surplus.[3]

The Canon of Benefit, or of the greatest social good, is increasing in its importance in modern days owing to the increasing activities and responsibilities of the state, perhaps on account of socialistic influence. Protection of society from external and internal dangers was of course recognized in all ages as the first charge on revenue. In addition to this, beneficial expenditure on social services like education, sanitation, and on essential productive enterprises like the Post Office, is directly beneficial to the state, inasmuch as it either yields more material income, as the Post Office does in India, or lightens the burden of the state by decreasing the number of the unfit.

This principle seems to have been recognized by the Mauryan financiers. Wise public expenditure, according to Kauṭilya,[4] consisted in the building of forts, construction of buildings and commercial roads, opening of new plantations and villages, and exploitation of mines and timber and elephant forests. Again, among the items conducive to financial prosperity, are mentioned[5] public prosperity, abundance of harvest, prosperity of commerce, and absence of troubles and calamities. Expenditure on hospitals, asylums for dumb animals, orphanages, and educational institutions

[3] *Science of Public Finance*, ch. iv.

[4] *Arth.*, Bk. II, ch. 1. [5] *Arth.*, Bk, II, ch. 8; also ch. 7.

have been mentioned by Megasthenes[6] and in the edicts of Aśōka[7] and by later Buddhist travellers.[8] But huge amounts must also have been spent by the royalty in personal extravagance and luxury.

The Canon of Economy with regard to public expenditure is very important because of the dangers of extravagance. The proverb, "What is everybody's business is nobody's," can very well be changed to "What is everybody's money is nobody's." The greatest vigilance and effective financial control is always needed from the highest financial officers of the state.

This kind of control and check under the Mauryas seems to have been not only effective but minute. The chief officer of every department scrutinized its income and expenditure;[9] his accounts were checked and audited by special commissioners who were themselves responsible to the collector-general or the ministers, and above all was the king. Perhaps the most effective check was the system of espionage.[10]

In passing, it may be mentioned that retrenchment was not an unknown weapon.[11]

But an important factor for effective control was probably wanting. Public opinion, which plays the lion's part in modern states, could not be expected in benevolent despotisms like those of the Mauryan times. Possibly the king supplied this want by practising Aśōka's dictum that "All men are my children."[12]

The Canon of Sanction, according to Shirras, "is that no public expenditure should be incurred without proper authority." The Mauryan king, as the head of the state, appears to have been the sanctioning authority in those days.

[6] *Strabo*, xv, 1, 50.
[7] *R.E. II*; *P.E. VII*.
[8] Fahien's *Travels*, p. 79; *Yuan Chwang*, i, p. 298.
[9] *Arth.*, Bk. II, ch. 9.
[10] *Arth.*, Bk. II, chs. 7 and 8.
[11] *Arth.*, Bk. II, ch. 8. *Infra*, Chapter XVI.
[12] *Borderers' Edict*. Compare *Arth.*, Bk. IV, ch. 3, *Sarvatra chōpahatān pitēvanugṛihṇīyāt*. Also *Śukranīti*, i, 150 ff.

The Canon of Surplus mainly implies that there should not be deficits in the budget, though some financiers favour even a moderate surplus. Budgeting in the modern sense probably was unknown in ancient India, but there must have been deficits and surpluses. For when Kauṭilya says that a king with depleted treasury will eat into the vitality of his people, it is clear how fully the danger of deficits was recognized. But it seems to have been the general practice in ancient times to collect more revenue than needed and store the surplus in kind and coin.[13] This surplus was used in times of calamities such as war and famine. The accumulation of a surplus was necessary in those days when public loans were probably rarely resorted to.

CLASSIFICATIONS OF EXPENDITURE

With regard to expenditure, I shall follow the method adopted while dealing with revenue, viz. first consider what the Mauryan financiers have to say on the subject of classification, next consider the classifications given by eminent writers on finance, and lastly compare the various heads of expenditure of the Mauryan budget with those of modern India.

Kauṭilya appears to give two classifications of public expenditure.[14] Expenditure on:

1. The chanting of auspicious hymns during worship of gods and ancestors and on the occasion of giving gifts (*dēvapitṛipūjādānārthaṃ śvastivāchanaṃ*).
2. The harem (*aṅtaḥpuraṃ*).
3. The kitchen (*mahānasam*).
4. The establishment of messengers (*dūtaprāvartimaṃ*).
5. The storehouse (*kōshṭāgāraṃ*).
6. The armoury (*āyudhāgāraṃ*).
7. The warehouse (*paṇyagṛihaṃ*).
8. The storehouse of raw materials (*kupyagṛihaṃ*).
9. Manufactories (*karmāntaḥ*).

[13] *Yuan Chwang*, i, p. 247; *J.A.S.B.*, 1890, nos. iii and iv. Also *supra*, Chapter IX.

[14] *Arth.*, Bk. II, ch. 6. Compare Śukra's classification in *Śukranīti*, ii, 677 ff.

10. Free labourers (*vishṭiḥ*).
11. Maintenance of infantry, cavalry, chariots, and elephants (*pathyāśvarathadvipaparigrahaḥ*).
12. Herds of cows (*gōmaṇḍalaṃ*).
13. Museums of beasts, deer, birds, and snakes (*paśumṛigapakshivyālavataḥ*).
14. Storage of firewood and fodder (*kāshṭhatṛiṇavataḥ*).

If classified under modern heads, the items stand as follows:

1. *Ecclesiastical.*
   (*a*) Chanting of auspicious hymns.
2. *Royal Household.*
   (*a*) Harem.
   (*b*) Kitchen.
3. *Political.*
   (*a*) Messengers.
4. *Military.*
   (*a*) Infantry, cavalry, chariots, and elephants.
   (*b*) Armoury.
5. *Civil.*
   (*a*) Storehouse.
   (*b*) Warehouse.
   (*c*) Storage of firewood and fodder.
   (*d*) Herds of cows.
6. *Public Works.*
   (*a*) Storehouse of raw materials.
   (*b*) Manufactories.
   (*c*) Free labourers.
7. *Educational.*
   (*a*) Museum.

This enumeration of items and expenditure does not do justice to Mauryan public expenditure. It leaves out a host of items which properly came under the Mauryan budget. Therefore the classification of Kauṭilya may be taken, not as an exhaustive enumeration of the heads of public expenditure, but as a casual mention of some of the items.

The second classification[15] is:

[15] *Arth.*, Bk. II, ch. 6, *Nityōnityōtpādikō lābhō lābhōtpādika iti vyayaḥ.* Gaṇapati Śāstri (*op. cit.*, i, p. 141) appears to take the passage to mean four kinds of expenditure. The text, however, does not seem to warrant this interpretation.

1. Daily expenditure.
2. Profitable expenditure, i.e. expenditure on investments yielding profit.[16]

Modern classifications of public expenditure as given by H. C. Adams and Findlay Shirras may now be considered.

Adams' Classification[17]

1. *Protective Functions.*
   (*a*) Military.
   (*b*) Police and court.
   (*c*) Protection against social disease.
2. *Commercial Functions.*
3. *Developmental Functions.*
   (*a*) Education.
   (*b*) Public recreation.
   (*c*) Maintaining equitable conditions for the prosecution of private business.
   (*d*) Public investigations, i.e. collection of social statistics.
   (*e*) Development of the physical basis of the state, e.g. public works like irrigation, forestry, etc.

Shirras' Classification[18]

1. *Primary.*
   (*a*) *Defence.*
      (i) Naval.
      (ii) Military.
      (iii) Air.
   (*b*) *Law and Order.*
      (i) Law and justice.
      (ii) Police.
   (*c*) *Civil Administration.*
      (i) General administration.
      (ii) Cost of collection.
      (iii) Political.

---

[16] See Jolly's Edition, vol. ii, p. 18, and Sohrabji's *Notes*, p. 12. Compare *Śukranīti*, ii, 337. "Expenditure falls under two heads—that which will come back and that which destroys the right for ever."

[17] *Science of Finance*, ch. iii.

[18] *Science of Public Finance*, p. 51.

(*d*) *Debt Service.*
(i) Productive.
(ii) Unproductive.

2. *Secondary.*
(*e*) *Social.*
(i) Education.
(ii) Other social.

(*f*) Government or public undertakings.

(*g*) Miscellaneous.

INDIAN EXPENDITURE [18]	MAURYAN EXPENDITURE CLASSIFIED UNDER MODERN HEADS
Primary Expenditure	*Primary Expenditure*
I. *Defence.*	I. *Defence.*
Army.	Army.
Navy.	Fleet.
Air forces.	—
Military transport, etc.	Transport, etc.
II. *Law and Order.*	II. *Law and Order.*
Police.	Police.
III. *Civil Administration.*	III. *Civil Administration.*
General administration.	General administration.
Political.	Political.
Cost of collection.	Cost of collection.
IV. *Debt Service.*	IV. —
Secondary Expenditure	*Secondary Expenditure*
V. *Social.*	V. *Social.*
Education.	Education.
Medical and sanitation.	Medical and sanitation.
Famine relief, etc.	Famine relief.[19]
Ecclesiastical.	Ecclesiastical.[20]

[18] The classification follows Shirras' reclassification of Indian budget heads in his *Science of Public Finance*, p. 616.

[19] Although there was no amount annually set apart for this purpose, yet in times of necessity and distress the public treasury bore the expenditure of famine relief.

[20] This was probably a very much more important item of expenditure than it is to-day.

INDIAN EXPENDITURE	MAURYAN EXPENDITURE CLASSIFIED UNDER MODERN HEADS
Secondary Expenditure (contd.)	*Secondary Expenditure* (contd.)
VI. *Government or Public Undertakings.*	VI. *Government Undertakings.*
Railways.	—
Irrigation.	Irrigation.
Other public works.	Other public works.
Posts and telegraphs.	—
Mint.	Mint.
Stationery and printing.	—
Forests.	Forests.
Posts and pilotage.	Posts and pilotage.
Scientific and miscellaneous.	Scientific and miscellaneous.
VII. *Miscellaneous.*	VII. *Miscellaneous.*
Refunds, drawbacks, etc.	—
Miscellaneous.	Miscellaneous.

CHAPTER XII

CIVIL AND OTHER SIMILAR HEADS OF EXPENDITURE

I. *Civil Expenditure:* The divisions of the country—The various departments—Scale of salaries—Payment in forms other than salaries. II. *Royal Household:* The harem, etc. —Scale of salaries. III. *Ecclesiastical:* Importance of this item—The state and religious institutions—Royal tours and charity—Public feast

I. CIVIL EXPENDITURE

UNDER this head may be included expenses of general administration, the political department, cost of collection, and such other items.

The accounts of the Greek writers, the *Arthaśāstra*, and the edicts of Aśōka indicate the existence of a well-organized administration. The country was divided into provinces. According to Arrian,[1] from the class of counsellors were chosen governors, provincial rulers, deputy-governors, treasurers, generals of the army, admirals of the fleet, quacestors, and the superintendent of agriculture. Aśōka's edicts[2] contain many references to the provinces. The Girnār inscription of Rudradāman[3] mentions that modern Kathiawar and Malwa were in the charge of Pushyagupta, the provincial governor of Chandragupta Maurya, and later of the Yavana king, Tushāspha, under Aśōka. According to the *Arthaśāstra*, the kingdom was divided into four provinces, each in charge of a *sthānika*[4]; each province was sub-

[1] Arrian, *Indika*, ch. 12.

[2] *Kaliṅga Provincials' Edict II; Kaliṅga Borderers' Edict I; Rock Edict I*, etc.

[3] *Ep. Ind.*, viii, no. 6.

[4] *Arth.*, Bk. II, ch. 35, *Samāhartā chaturthā jānapadaṃ vibhajya*, etc. But this division excluded the capital which perhaps with its immediate surroundings was a province by itself with its own officers.

divided into two *drōṇamukhas*, and each *drōṇamukha* into two *khārvaṭikas*, which comprised many smaller divisions called *saṅgrahaṇas*, consisting of ten villages each.[5] This resembles the organization mentioned by Manu[6] and in the *Mahābhārata*,[7] as well as in *Śukranīti*.[7]

Thus the kingdom was divided into provinces and viceroyalties, including those at Takshaśila, Suvarṇagiri, and Ujjaini, and probably some place in Kaḷiṅga. Tosali, Samapa, and Isila, mentioned in the Aśōkan edicts[9] and the subdivisions in the major provinces, referred ṭo by Katilya,[10] were perhaps administered by governors and deputy-governors. The administration of the capital, a province by itself, was perhaps copied and followed in the various divisions of the country.

As a detailed account of the administrative organization of the Mauryan state is not necessary for the purposes of this book, only the various important officers and the departments of the government may be mentioned.

According to Kauṭilya, there were the following departments in the state:[11]

1. The Department of Forests.
2. The Department of Armoury.
3. The Department of Weights and Measures.
4. The Department of Commerce.
5. The Department of Storehouse.
6. The Department of Goldsmiths (including the mint).
7. The Department of Mines and Manufactures.
8. The Department of Treasuıy.
9. The Department of Tolls, Octrois, etc.
10. The Department of Weaving.
11. The Department of Liquor.

---

5 *Arth.*, Bk. II, ch. 1.

6 *Manu*, vii, 115.

7 *Śāntiparva*, lxxxvii, 3 ff.

8 i, 381 ff.

9 E.g. separate *R.E. I* and *II*. Dhauli and Jaugada texts.

10 *Arth.*, Bk. II, ch. 35.

11 Some of these departments come, strictly speaking, under military expenditure, and others under government undertakings. In *Arth.*, Bk. I, ch. 12, Kauṭilya mentions eighteen government departments (*ashṭādaśatīrtha*).

12. The Department of Agriculture.
13. The Department of Slaughterhouse.
14. The Department of Prostitutes.
15. The Department of Navigation.
16. The Department of Cows.
17. The Department of Horses.
18. The Department of Elephants.
19. The Department of Passports.
20. The Department of Chariots.
21. The Department of Infantry.
22. The Department of Revenue.

According to Megasthenes[12] there were in Pāṭalīputra magistrates divided into committees, looking after industrial arts, foreigners, births and deaths, trade and commerce, manufactures and their sale, and collection of taxes on articles sold. All these magistrates collectively looked after public buildings, temples, and the like. Aśōka's edicts[13] mention viceroys, *rajjukas*, *prādēśikas*,[14] *yuktas*,[15] and *upayuktas*, who were subordinate officials, *lēkhakas*, or secretaries, and a host of other subordinates. There were also the heads of departments and the numerous employees in the various branches of the government, in addition to the royal councillors in the court.[16]

[12] *Strabo*, xv, i, 50.

[13] *Rock Edicts III, IV, V*; *Kaliṅga Borderers' Edict I*; *Pillar Edict IV*, etc.

[14] F. W. Thomas (*J.R.A.S.*, 1914, 393 ff.; 1915, 112) identifies these officers with the *pradēshṭri* mentioned by Kauṭilya (*Arth.*, Bk. II, ch. 24; Bk. III, chs. 6, 10, 12, etc.). Hultzch (*Cor. Ins. Ind.*, p. 5) appears not to accept this identification because of difficulties as regards the derivation of the words and suggests they were high provincial officers.

[15] According to F. W. Thomas (*J.R.A.S.*, 1909, 466–7; 1914, 387–91) *yuktas* and *upayuktas* mentioned in the *Arthaśāstra* denote subordinate officials and Bhandarkar calls them district officers.

[16] The important civil employees mentioned in the *Arthaśāstra* include: Ministers of various types (*amātyas*, *mantris*, and *mahāmātras*), superintendents of the various departments mentioned above, officers in charge of boundaries, waste lands, forts, and country parts, revenue collectors, chamberlains, astrologers, soothsayers, story-tellers, court-bards, women artisans, commissioners, servants, and many others. Compare these officials with those mentioned in

Further, there was the expenditure on the political department, which included envoys, *chargé d'affaires*, messengers and agents, prostitutes used for political purposes, an intensively organized system of espionage, institutes for training various kinds of spies, aged military officers, and reporters. These were also the expenses of political missions.[17]

The expenditure on the civil department was incurred in various ways. Salaries in money were paid to most of the employees. Kauṭilya gives a long list of the pay of government servants.[18] He mentions that the prostitutes had their pay fixed by thousands,[19] and that the courtiers were sometimes paid provisions and salaries in addition to being exempted from taxes and granted lands.[20] Fahien also records[21] that in his days the king's bodyguards and attendants all had salaries.

The scale of the salaries of some government servants was as in Table on page 167.

When money was scarce, a large part of the payments was made in forest products, cattle, or land. But lands were not granted if waste land was to be colonized.[22] Superintendents of departments, accountants, *gōpas*, *sthānikas*, veterinary surgeons, physicians, trainers of horses, and messengers were endowed with lands which they had no right to alienate by sale or mortgage.[23] This practice of granting lands was not unknown in ancient India.[24]

Śukranīti, ii, 168–73, 237–41, 305 ff., etc. Also with those mentioned in some of the inscriptions, e.g. *Ep. Ind.*, xviii, nos. 19, 23; xiv, no. 14; xvii, no. 17.

[17] *Arth.*, Bk. I, ch. 16.

[18] *Arth.*, Bk. V, ch. 3.

[19] *Arth.*, Bk. II, ch. 27.

[20] *Arth.*, Bk. II, ch. 7.

[21] *Travels*, p. 43.

[22] *Arth.*, Bk. V, ch. 3, *Alpakōśaḥ kupyapaśukshētrāni dadyāt, alpaṁ cha hiraṇyaṃ. Śūnyaṃ vā nivēśayituṃ abhyutthitō hiraṇyamēva dadyāt, na grāmaṃ*, etc.

[23] *Arth.*, Bk. II, ch. 1, *Adhyakshasaṅkhyāyakādibhyō gōpasthānīkānīkasthachikitsakāśvadamakajaṅghārikēbhyaścha vikrayādhāna varjaṃ.*

[24] In *Ep. Ind.*, xv, no. 6 (f.) and xviii, no. 22, are mentioned *provision villages*, which are explained by L. D. Barnett as villages specially allotted for the maintenance of officers.

SALARIES OF GOVERNMENT SERVANTS

Officers	Annual Pay	
	In *Panas*	In Pounds Sterling[25]
1. The ministers	Each 48,000	Each 2,400
2. The collector-general	24,000	1,200
3. The chief constable	12,000	600
The officer in charge of the city ..	12,000	600
The superintendent of law or commerce	12,000	600
4. The superintendent of manufactories	12,000	600
Members of the Council of Ministers	12,000	600
The superintendent of country parts and boundaries	12,000	600
5. Commissioners	8,000	400
6. The guards of elephant forests and timber forests	4,000	200
7. Superintendent of departments ..	1,000	50
8. The staff of accountants and writers	500	25
9. Servants in charge of quadrupeds and bipeds	60	3
Workmen doing miscellaneous works	60	3
Procurer of free labourers ..	60	3
10. Miners of mountains	500 to 1,000	25 to 30
11. Messengers	Travelling allowance of 10 *panas* or 10 shillings per *yōjana*	
12. Spies (some)	1,000	50
13. Village servants	500	25
Some spies, poisoners	500	25
Mendicant women	500	25
14. Servants, leading spies	250	12½

[25] *Infra*, p. 195, footnote 2.

Yuan Chwang writes[26] that "of the royal land one part was reserved for the endowment of great public servants. Those who are employed in the government service are paid according to their work. . . . Ministers of state and common officials all have their portion of land and one maintained by the cities assigned to them."

The higher officials appear to have been provided with quarters. Kauṭilya refers[27] to quarters for the officials like the Prime Minister and the priest and others. In view of what Śukra also says,[28] "Dwelling houses for ministers, clerks, and officers should be built separately to the north or east," it is possible that many of the government employees were given quarters by the state, at least in the capital.

Another item of expenditure consisted of the grant of subsistence and wages to dependents of those who died on duty.[29] The herdsmen and hunters received an allowance of grain from the king in return for clearing the land of wild beasts and fowls.[30] There were, again, the expenses of the king's tours, which in Aśōka's days became religious as well as political. Aśōka writes[31] that his predecessors undertook tours for pleasure, while he converted them into pious ones. Such tours were a common feature in ancient India. According to Śukra,[32] the king was to inspect every year the cities, districts, and provinces, know the condition of the people, hear their representations, and test the administration of officers. These administrative tours were undertaken by Harsha also.[33] If the tours were as pompous and expensive

[26] *Yuan Chwang*, vol. i, p. 176. The practice of cities maintaining the officials may not have existed in the Mauryan period.

[27] *Arth.*, Bk. II, ch. 1.

[28] *Śukranīti*, i, 500.

[29] *Arth.*, Bk. V, ch. 3, *Karmasu mṛitānāṃ putradārē bhaktavētanaṃ labhyaṇ*. *Śukranīti*, ii, 832–3.

[30] *Strabo*, xv, 1, 41.

[31] *R.E. VIII*, Kalsi text.

[32] *Śukranīti*, i, 751–2.

[33] *Yuan Chwang*, i, p. 344. The pilgrim writes: "The king also made visits of inspection throughout his dominion, not residing long at any place, but having temporary buildings erected for his residence

in Mauryan days as they were during those of Harsha,[34] they must have told heavily on the public purse. Moreover, officials seem to have been paid travelling allowances.[35] The state undertook the construction and maintenance of roads.[36] This appears to have been common in ancient India.[37]

An idea of what items constituted civil expenditure under the Mauryas can be formed from the foregoing pages, and although there is no evidence to show the amount spent on this head, the civil departments must have cost a considerable sum.

II. ROYAL HOUSEHOLD

Under this head may be considered the harem, the kitchen, and other items, including the salaries of people related to the king or serving in his household.

Kauṭilya devotes a whole chapter to describe the harem.[38] It consisted of the many wives of the king, and all the necessary paraphernalia, including hospitals, parks, attendants, and others. The many departments and people connected with the harem and the palace are well indicated in the following passage: "On one side in the rear of the harem there shall be made for the residence of women compartments provided not only with all kinds of medicine useful in midwifery and diseases, but also with well-known pet herbs and a water reservoir; outside these compartments the residences of princes and princesses, in front (of the

at each place of sojourn, and he did not go abroad during the three months of the rainy season retreat."

[34] See R. K. Mookerjea, *Harsha*, p. 87.

[35] *Arth.*, Bk. II, ch. 8. Jolly's (*op. cit.*, ii, p. 19) interpretation of *piṇḍavisham* is followed here. The word means "fictitious travelling provisions" according to Jolly; "falsified totals" according to Sohrabji; and "inconsistencies in dealing with fixed terms" according to Shāma Śāstry. The mention of fictitious travelling provisions imply *bona fide* travelling expenses.

[36] *Arth. Trans.*, pp. 50, 52, 58, etc., 421. Cf. *Śukranīti*, i, 519 ff.

[37] *Strabo*, xv, 1, 50; *Śāntiparva*, lxix, 53; *Śūkranīti*, i, 526 ff.

[38] *Arth.*, Bk. I, ch. 20.

latter building) the toilet ground, the council ground, the court, and the offices of the heir-apparent and of the superintendent."[39] There were also prostitutes, eunuchs, and others connected with the harem.[40] Royal harems were probably maintained not only in the capital but in the provinces also.[41] It is likely that, as D. R. Bhandarkar observes,[42] Aśōka had women other than queens, and that his *avarōdhana* was not all in Pāṭalīputra, but some of its members stayed in the *moffusil.*

As for the royal kitchen,[43] its hugeness can be imagined by what Aśōka says in *Rock Edict I,* though it is certainly an exaggerated statement. "Formerly, in the kitchen of King Dēvānampriya Priyadarśin, many hundreds of thousands of animals were killed daily for the sake of curries."[44] Kauṭilya mentions along with the harem the kitchen as an item of expenditure. The officials of the royal household and their annual salaries have been enumerated as in Table on page 171.[45]

The salaries were perhaps annual. The number of these officials and others is not known, and therefore the amount of expenditure cannot be known. But the accounts of the Greeks that Chandragupta's palace excelled in splendour those of Susa and Ekbatana, and the description given by Kauṭilya of the royal harem and other

[39] *Arth.*, Bk. I, ch. 20; *Arth. Trans.*, p. 43.

[40] Sohrabji remarks (*Notes*, p. 61) that *rūpājīvās* were ordinary prostitutes as distinct from the *gaṇikās* of the royal court. This appears to be a doubtful interpretation since the prostitutes in the harem are also called *rūpājīvās* (*Arth.*, Bk. I, ch. 20).

[41] E.g. *avarōdhana* mentioned in *P.E. VII.*

[42] *Aśōka*, p. 13.

[43] Compare *Śukranīti*, ii, 315–16.

[44] *Cor. Ins. Ind.*, vol. i, p. 2.

[45] Compare *Manu*, vii, 125–6, "For women employed in the royal service and for menial servants let him fix a daily maintenance in proportion to their position and their work. One *paṇa* must be given (daily) as wages to the lowest, six to the highest, likewise clothing every six months and one *drōṇa* of grain every month." Manu is more liberal than Kauṭilya.

ANNUAL SALARIES OF THE OFFICIALS OF THE ROYAL HOUSEHOLD

Officials	In *Paṇana*	In Pounds Sterling
	Each	Each
1. Sacrificial priest	48,000	2,400
Priest	48,000	2,400
Teacher	48,000	2,400
The heir-apparent	48,000	2,400
The mother of the king	48,000	2,400
The queen	48,000	2,400
2. The door-keeper	24,000	1,200
The superintendent of the harem	24,000	1,200
The chamberlain	24,000	1,200
3. The prince (? princess)	12,000	600
The nurse of the prince	12,000	600
4. The foreteller	1,000	50
The reader of omens	1,000	50
The astrologer	1,000	50
The reader of *Purāṇas*	1,000	50
The story-teller	1,000	50
The bard and the retinue of priests	1,000	50
5. Musicians	250	12½
6. The trumpet-blower	500	25
7. Artisans and carpenters	120	6
8. Attendants upon the royal person bodyguard	60	3
9. Playmate of the king	500 to 1,000	25 to 50
Sorcerer	500 to 1,000	25 to 50
Attendants	500 to 1,000	25 to 50
Teachers	500 to 1,000	25 to 50
Learned men	500 to 1,000	25 to 50
10. Representatives of the king in sacrifices	Twice what is paid to their equals in learning	
11. King's charioteer	1,000	50

departments,[46] suggest that the expenses were perhaps not inconsiderable.

III. ECCLESIASTICAL

In many modern civilized countries the state interferes as little as possible with religion, because citizens may be following various religions and sects.[47] Not much of public funds, therefore, is spent on ecclesiastical items. In British India the budget estimates of 1926–27 showed that this expenditure amounted to a very small part of the total expense.[48] In the Mauryan period, especially in the reign of Aśōka, the state took an active interest in religion, and although the amount expended on this item is not known, yet the various activities indicate that a considerable amount was probably spent on religion.

The expenses were largely in the nature of grants of lands, presents, and sometimes salaries. Persons who performed sacrifices (*ṛitvik*), spiritual guides, priests, and those learned in the *Vēdas* were granted *brahmadēya* lands yielding sufficient produce and exempted from taxes and fines.[49] They were also provided with forests for the performance of penance.

When Aśōka determined upon the propagation of the

[46] *Śukranīti*, i, 435 ff., give a good idea of the elaborate palaces of ancient times.

[47] "It is not necessary here to enter in detail into the question of expenditure on religion, because the amount is not large, and modern thought is in favour of the view that state revenues can on the whole be better devoted to other objects. Experience in the United States and in the Dominions has all pointed in this direction, especially in the former. In Great Britain and on the Continent of Europe, as in France, this enlightened view continues to grow in spite of vested interests. In France no religion is recognized by the state" (Shirras, *Science of Public Finance*, p. 70).

[48] About 36 lakhs of rupees out of the total expenditure of 13,036 lakhs, i.e. about one four-hundred-and-fiftieth.

[49] *Arth.*, Bk. II, ch. 1. Salaries of priests and others have been considered under expenditure on royal household.

dhamma he employed missionaries and special officers for the purpose. It is likely that the existing civil officials undertook a part of this propaganda. But the *Dharma—Mahāmātras*,[50] and perhaps the *Vyustas*, were concerned with religion and morality only. Their constant tours round the country[51] and the despatch of missionaries to far-off foreign lands[52] must have meant expense to the state.

Even during Chandragupta's days the state built places of religious worship and pilgrimage. Kauṭilya says that the king may either himself construct places of pilgrimage (*puṇyasthāna*)[53] and groves (*ārāma*) or help others to construct them. Aśōka appears to have built a great many temples and monasteries. Costly caves in the Barabar Hills near Gaya were dedicated to the use of the non-Buddhist *Ājīvika* ascetics, just as Aśōka's successor, Daśaratha, dedicated caves in the Nāgārjuni Hills.[54] Fahien[55] and Yuan Chwang[56] mention the existence of numerous monasteries or their ruins when they visited India. Yuan Chwang describes Pāṭalīputra in these words:[57] "Of this city the long lapse of time had left only the old foundations. Of monasteries, *dēva* temples, and *topes* there were hundred ruins, but only two or three of the old structures survived." The *Rājataraṅgiṇi*[58] refers to temples which Aśōka restored or built. In short, "the extravagant legend which ascribes to Aśōka the erection of eighty-four thousand *stūpas* or sacred cupolas within the space of three years proves the depth of the impression made upon the popular imagination by the magnitude and magnificence of the Great Maurya's architectural achievements."[59] "The numerous and stately monas-

[50] *R.E. V, VII.*

[51] *R.E. III.*

[52] *R.E. V, XIII*, etc.

[53] *Arth.*, Bk. II, ch. 1.

[54] *Barbara Hill Cave Inscriptions; P.E. VII*; also see Smith's *Āsōka*, p. 40, etc.

[55] *Travels*, p. 43.

[56] Watter, *Yuan Chwang*, vi, p. 86.

[57] *Ibid.*, p. 88.

[58] *Rājataraṅgiṇi*, Bk. I, pp. 101 ff.

[59] V. A. Smith, *Aśōka*, p. 87. Cf. Beal, ii, p. 88.

teries which Aśōka erected at many places in the empire have shared the fate of his palaces, not even one surviving in a recognizable state."[60] Such structures were extremely numerous. Huen Tsiang refers to the ruins of hundreds of *stūpas, saṅghārāmas*, and *dēva* temples.[61] And these numerous monasteries, temples, and others contained a host of people whose expenses were met by the state. Porphyrius quotes Bardesanes, of the third century A.D., to the effect that he founded the houses and temples of the Samanocans and gave a fixed allowance for the support of the inmates.[62]

Again, there was the expenditure on royal tours and charities. Aśōka mentions[63] that his predecessors were undertaking *vihāra-yātras* or pleasure tours, which he converted into *dharma-yātras* or tours of morality. In these tours, says Aśōka,[64] "are practised the beholding of ascetics and Brahmans, with liberality to them, the beholding of elders, largess of gold, the beholding of the country and the people, proclamation of the Law of Piety and discussion of the Law of Piety."

Gifts of gold and other things are mentioned, for example, in *Rock Edicts IX, X*, and *XI*. No doubt Aśōka held the gift of "*dharma*" to be far superior to the gift of worldly goods, but he encouraged and practised the latter also. *Pillar Edict VII* records that the various officers of the state were employed in the distribution of royal alms of Aśōka, his queens, his sons, the princess, and others to promote pious acts. Aśōka is stated to have bestowed great largess at every place except the *stūpa* of Vakkula on his pious tours.

An idea of the expenditure on charities can be got by

[60] V. A. Smith, *Aśōka*, p. 88.

[61] Beal, iv, p. 86. Compare the building of monasteries, *vihāra*, etc., mentioned in the *Mahāvaṁśa*.

[62] *Ancient India as described in Classical Literature*, p. 170. It may be mentioned that *Gupta Inscriptions*, no. 5, mentions that the inmates of the great *vihāra* at Kākanādabōṭa were given the means of subsistence and were made comfortable by Chandragupta II. Also see the Nasik Cave Inscriptions for Ushavadāta's charities.

[63] *R.E. VIII.*

[64] *Ibid.*; Smith's *Aśōka*, p. 124.

what Yuan Chwang says of Vikramāditya of Śrāvasti (seventh century A.D.). According to the pilgrim,[65] this king distributed five lakhs of gold coins among the destitute and desolate on the day he conquered the Indians. Again, a South Indian king, Imayavaramban Nedemkeralathan, is said to have given away as *brahmadēya* the district of Umbarkadu, which consisted of five hundred villages, and assigned part of the revenue of his whole kingdom for thirty-eight years to a Brahman for composing a poem of thirty-four lines.[66] Another king gave away forty lakhs of gold pieces and part of the state revenue to a poet.[67] Whether Mauryan rulers were equally extravagant is doubtful, but it is not improbable that Aśōka was so to a great extent.

There were, again the expenses of the public feasts or *samājas*. The *samājas* were perhaps a mode of public entertainment through feasting and amusements.[68] Khāravēla, king of Kaliṅga, is said to have amused his subjects by celebrating *utsavas* and *samājas*.[69] Kauṭilya also advises the king to imitate the people's attachment to the *samājas*, *utsava* and *vihāra*, and mention is also made of the feeding of the people in festivals and in honour of gods and ancestors. Aśōka's *Rock Edict IV* refers to the display of processional cars, elephants, illuminations, and other spectacles.

In short, Aśōka's efforts to propagate *dharma* were, as V. A. Smith says, "the most comprehensive scheme of

65 *Yuan Chwang*, i, p. 211. The pilgrim continues that when the treasurer remonstrated that the treasury would be exhausted, the king replied that giving to the needy from the surplus of public administration was not a lavish expenditure of the public money on himself and gave the additional five lakhs in largesse to the poor.

66 *Historical Sketches of Ancient Dekhan*, p. 316.

67 *Ibid.*, pp. 316–17.

68 D. R. Bhandarkar, *Aśōka*, p. 20. Could these be the *samājas* mentioned by Kauṭilya in *Arth.*, Bk. II, ch. 25?

69 Public festivals given by the state were common in ancient Athens. "The celebration of public festivals early occasioned in the Athenian state an extravagance which was as unlimited as the expense of the princes who were fond of magnificence for their courts (Boeckh, *op. cit.*, pp. 248, 290).

religious missionary enterprise recorded in the history of the world." The expenditure on such a vast scheme could not have been little. But it is doubtful if there was such a vast amount of money spent on ecclesiastical purposes before Aśōka. No doubt Kauṭilya mentions the chanting of auspicious hymns during the worship of gods and ancestors, and on the occasion of giving gifts,[70] as an item of expenditure, and even states the amount of the salary paid to the priest and his assistants. Still, it appears that Aśōka's predecessors must have spent on this score very much less than Aśōka did.

[70] *Arth.*, Bk. II, ch. 6.

CHAPTER XIII

MEDICINE, POOR RELIEF, ETC.

I. *Medicine and Poor Relief.* II. *Education:* Universities, monasteries, museums, and menageries. III. *Famine Relief:* Were there famines in the Mauryan period?—How the state gave relief

I. MEDICINE AND POOR RELIEF

IN Mauryan India medical relief was organized and controlled by the state. Megasthenes observes: "Should any of them (foreigners) lose his health, they send physicians to attend him, and take care of him otherwise, and if he dies they bury him and deliver over such property as he leaves to his relatives."[1] It is improbable that in a state where foreigners were so readily attended to the local people had no medical aid from the state. Aśōka mentions the medical treatment provided for cattle. The state took such active interest in this direction that wherever there were no herbs that were beneficial to men and cattle they were imported and planted.[2] These curative arrangements were instituted not only in the empire, but even in foreign lands so far distant as Egypt.[3]

V. A. Smith thinks that the free hospital mentioned by Fahien was doubtless a continuation of Aśōka's foundation, and that there may have been animal hospitals. Kauṭilya mentions veterinary surgeons in charge of horses, elephants, and other animals.[4] The evidence therefore indicates the existence of an elaborate system of medical relief both to

[1] *Diodorus*, ii, 42; also *Strabo*, xv, 1, 50.

[2] *R.E. II.*

[3] *Ibid.*

[4] *Arth.*, Bk. II, chs. 30, 31, etc. As for the word *anīkastha* (Bk. II, ch. 1) Sohrabji (*Notes*, p. 1) says; "Shāma Śāstry translates 'veterinary surgeons.' This meaning is not known in the Sanskrit Lexicons." Also see Jolly's Edition, vol. ii, p. 13.

M

a man and beast,[5] even in foreign countries like the Greek kingdoms and the South Indian states.

There also appears to have been a well-organized system of poor relief. The king was to provide with maintenance the orphans, the aged, the infirm, the afflicted, and the helpless, specially helpless pregnant women and the children they gave birth to.[6] The orphans were not only fed and clothed, but were also educated by the state.[7] The edict of Aśōka's second queen, Karuvaki, makes mention of donations made by her to a mango grove, pleasure garden, and charitable hostel (*danagahe*). According to V. A. Smith, the hostel was a rest-house where doles of food and in some cases shelter for a night, were given free to travellers.[8] In *Pillar Edict VII*, Aśōka refers to humanitarian works like mango groves, rest-houses, and watering-places.

This kind of work appears to have been common in ancient India. In the *Mahābhārata*,[9] it is said that the king set up houses for the distribution of food and erected places for the distribution of water, and excavated tanks. These institutions are also mentioned in the *Jātakas*,[10] the *Śukranīti*,[11] and the inscriptions,[12] and by Fahien[13] and Yuan Chwang.[14] The latter pilgrim refers to the existence of

[5] For details about medical relief and sanitation see N. N. Law, *Studies in Ancient Hindu Polity*.

[6] *Arth.*, Bk. II, ch. 1. Compare *Gautama*, x, 9–10. *Śāntiparva*, lxxxvi, 24; xlii, 11.

[7] *Arth.*, Bk. I, ch. 12.

[8] *Aśōka*, p. 198. Compare *Śukranīti*, ii, 337–8.

[9] *Śāntiparva*, xliii, 7 and 11.

[10] Nos. 4 and 96.

[11] i, 207 ff.; ii, 169.

[12] *Ep. Ind.*, v, nos. 3 and 19; vii, no. 6; viii, no. 8; xi, no. 2.

[13] *Travels*, p. 79. Fahien writes: "The heads of the Vaiśya families in them establish in the cities houses for dispensing charity and medicines. All the poor and destitute in the country, orphans, widowers and childless men, maimed people, and cripples, and all who are diseased go to their houses and are provided with every kind of help and doctors examine their diseases." In the Mauryan days, as at other times, these private relief works also were existing, but the main burden was perhaps on the state.

[14] *Yuan Chwang*, i, pp. 288, 328, 344.

numerous rest-houses for the relief of needy distressed travellers, where medicine, food, and other bodily wants were supplied. In ancient Athens[15] much the same system as the Mauryan one was to be found, perhaps with this difference, that there it was confined to citizens and the aid was given in the form of pay also.

In modern India, where there is no system of poor relief, this item of expenditure is absent. In some of the western countries—for example, in England and Germany—is found a systematic and organized administration of poor relief. "In the present position of modern societies," observes Bastable,[16] "a methodized system of public relief is indispensable."

II. EDUCATION

The expenditure under this head falls into two divisions—universities and monasteries, and museums and menageries. In ancient days, "Wherever they (the Buddhist monks) clustered together in monasteries or *vihāras*, a university grew up, and each of these *vihāras* was presided over by a *kulapati* corresponding to the principal of a modern college."[17] There was a host of such monasteries and *vihāras* in the Mauryan period, especially in the reigns of Aśōka and his successors. Brahmans were provided with forests for religious learning.[18] The *brahmadēya* lands appear to have been given to learned Brahmans also in order to enable them to live peacefully so as to spread education to their pupils.

Little information is available about universities of this period. In the University of Takshaśila, which was the centre of learning about the sixth century B.C. and where

[15] "A laudable institution was the provision made for the support of those citizens who on account of the corporal infirmities or weakness were unable to earn a maintenance" (Boeckh, *op. cit.*, p. 337).

[16] *Public Finance*, p. 89.

[17] N. N. Muzumdar's *History of Education in Ancient India*, p. 91.

[18] *Arth.*, Bk. II, ch. 1.

later Kauṭilya was a pupil, the student is said to have paid for his education.[19] This university continued to exist in the Mauryan period, and it may not be too much to assume that it had its own lands granted by the state, especially when one of its own students was the maker of the empire. For it was the habit of kings to present universities with lands. "The land in the possession of the Nālanda University contained more than two hundred villages. They were bestowed upon it by kings of many generations."[20]

"Under the same head, education," writes Bastable,[21] "the cost of museums, libraries, picture galleries, and institutions for promoting science and art generally should be placed." Menageries and museums of animals were not unknown in the Mauryan days. Kauṭilya mentions them as forming one of the items of public expenditure[22] and as being in charge of the superintendent of forest produce.[23] Arrian states that in the palace at Pāṭalīputra there were parks with deer, peacocks, and other animals and birds,[24] and that the people presented the king with tame tigers, panthers, and other beasts.[25] That museums and menageries were found in ancient India is confirmed by Yuan Chwang,[26] according to whom in the Lautakulya country there were beautiful gardens and tanks of clear water, with rarities from strange lands.

[19] Muzumdar, *op. cit.*, p. 90.

[20] *Ibid.* p. 95.

[21] *Op. cit.*, p. 97.

[22] *Arth.*, Bk. II, ch. 6, *Paśumṛigapakshivyāḷa vātāḥ*. As for the phrase *Kāshthhatṛiṇavaṭaḥ* (*ibid.*) Sohrabji (*Notes*, p. 11) suggests if this could refer to a botanical garden, taking *vāṭa* to mean "trees" and *tṛiṇa* to mean "plants" in general.

[23] *Arth.*, Bk. II, ch. 17.

[24] *Aelian*, Bk. XIII, ch. xviii. Compare *Śukranīti*, i, 425–8.

[25] *Aelian*, Bk. V, ch. xiv.

[26] *Yuan Chwang*, vol. i, p. 341. Compare Bāṇa's description in the *Harsha Charita* of the palace grounds, which contained lions, apes, and rare birds in cages.

III. FAMINE RELIEF

The special Orissa Famine Commission of 1867 defined famine as "suffering from hunger on the part of large classes of the population."[27] It is mostly in this sense that the word can apply to the Mauryan period. According to Kauṭilya,[28] famine causes troubles to the whole (of the country) and occasions dearth of livelihood to all creatures.

The question whether at all there were any famines in the period under consideration cannot be answered with certainty. For Megasthenes writes:[29] "It is accordingly affirmed that famine has never visited India, and that there has never been a general scarcity in the supply of nourishing food." This was because, according to him, there were two harvests in the year, and also abundant and regular rains and good irrigation works. He continues: "But, further, there are usages observed by the Indians which contribute to prevent the occurrence of famine among them." Of these usages, one was that the husbandmen were regarded as a class that was sacred and inviolable, so that even during wars they continued their operation unmolested.

There is, however, another piece of evidence which goes to show that there was a great famine. A Jaina inscription (S.B.I.) in Śravaṇa Belagoḷa in the Mysore state,[30] states that Bhadrabāhu, a Jain saint of the time of Chandragupta, "foretold in Ujjayani a period of twelve years of dire calamity or famine," and that Chandragupta, dismayed at the coming troubles, abdicated, and followed Bhadrabāhu. This inscription is, according to Rice,[31] not later than the fifth century A.D.

27 *Report*, para. 79.

28 *Arth.*, Bk. VIII, ch. 4.

29 *Diodorus*, ii, 36.

30 Lewis Rice, *Mysore and Coorg from the Inscriptions*, p. 5 ff. In *Ep. Ind.*, iv, no. 2, Fleet suggests that while Rice takes the word *vaishamya* as famine or dire calamity, it is better to take it as difficulty, as the exact meaning of the word here is doubtful.

31 Fleet and Leuman put it in the seventh century.

Thus, while Megasthenes records that there was no famine, the Jain tradition refers to one which continued for twelve years. These statements are apparently contradictory, and it may appear that, as Megasthenes was a contemporary, his word is more authoritative than an inscription which is at least eight centuries later.

But this contradiction is perhaps only apparent. Both accounts may be true. Megasthenes came to the Mauryan court about the year 302 B.C.[32] and remained there for some time. How long he stayed in India is uncertain, though he had in all probability left India before the end of Chandragupta's reign about 297 B.C. Therefore his record that there were no famines may be accepted as true of the period he remained in India.

No doubt the Jain inscription is of a very late date, being at least eight centuries after the event. But the tradition appears to be of ancient origin. Moreover, the tradition does not say that the twelve years of famine occurred during Chandragupta's reign. The inscription only records that the famine was foretold and the emperor, becoming dismayed at the coming troubles, abdicated. In other words, before the famine began or at least immediately it commenced, the king retired. The famine, therefore, may have commenced at the end of Chandragupta's reign and continued during Bindusara's.

While Megasthenes refers to the period before the abdication of Chandragupta, the Jain tradition speaks of the very end of his reign and the beginning of the next. Thus the two statements can be reconciled as relating to two different periods.

Moreover, the fact that Kauṭilya gives details of famine relief suggests that there were famines in the Mauryan period. Further, throughout the *Arthaśāstra* are found numerous references to famines.[33]

[32] *Cambridge History of India*, vol. i, p. 472.
[33] For example, *Arth. Trans.*, pp. 253, 326, 327, 386, 419, 423.

The state took care to prevent famines, and as the failure of rains is the chief cause for such a calamity, irrigation works were greatly undertaken and also encouraged.[34]

When the preventive measures are insufficient to stop famine and the calamity actually comes down upon the country, relief measures are resorted to. The measures adopted in British India for purposes of relief are broadly five in number, namely:

(*a*) Suspension or remission of land revenue.
(*b*) Granting of Takavi loans more freely.
(*c*) Starting of relief works.
(*d*) Establishment of poor houses and gratuitous relief.
(*e*) Granting of loans to buy cattle, seeds, ploughs, etc.

As regards suspension or remission of land revenue, in modern India the method of assessment and the rigidity of the demand are a great inconvenience in times of stress, for the land revenue is a fixed sum of money for a particular year irrespective of the produce, and unless it is remitted the *ryots* have to borrow from the moneylender in order to pay the tax. And in times of distress an express remission is necessary. But in the Mauryan days such a remission was automatic as the revenue was a part of the produce.[35]

There is little evidence to show the granting of any loans during famines. But, as mentioned on a previous page,[36] there seem to have existed a kind of grain loans known as *apamityaka*. Whether these loans were given during calamities is not certain. It is possible that both in ordinary times and during famine these loans were granted.

[34] *Infra*, Chapter XIV.
[35] *Arth.*, Bk. IV, ch. 3. The relief works mentioned by Kauṭilya are: *Durbhikshē rājā bījabhaktōpagrahaṃ kṛitvā anugrahaṃ kuryāt. Durgasētukarmavā bhaktānugrahēna bhaktasaṃvibhāgam dēśanikshepaṃ vā. Mitrāṇi vā vyāpāśrayēta. Karśanam vamanam vā kuryāt. Nishpannasasyamanyavishayaṃ vā sajanapadō yāyāt. Dhānyaśākamūlaphalāvāpān sētushu kuryāt. Mṛigapaśupakshivyālamatsyārambhān vā.* In the second sentence Shāma Śāstry reads *durgatakarma*, while Jolly (vol. ii, p. 42) has *durgasētukarma*.
[36] *Supra*, p. 131.

As part of relief works the state resorted to the construction of fortifications and irrigation works,[37] probably with the idea of giving employment and wages or provisions to the sufferers. As for poor houses and gratuitous relief, the king was required to distribute his own collection of provisions or the hoarded income of the rich among the people.[38] Moreover, the state provided the people with seeds and provisions.

The rich were thinned of their excessive wealth and the poor helped.[39] The state also sought the aid of the neighbouring states, and the king and his subjects even emigrated to another kingdom where harmony and plenty were found.[40] The state also helped its subjects to migrate to another part within its boundaries, like seashores, banks of rivers, and lakes, where water and fish were available, and where vegetables, grains, roots, and fruits could be grown. The king even hunted to provide his people with wild beasts, fish, and the like.[41] In short, the king had to protect the afflicted among his people as a father protects his sons.[42]

There does not seem to have existed any system of budgeting for famine relief in the same way as we have it now. No doubt irrigation works were undertaken by the state. There was also the accumulated surplus in the treasury. But there were not sums annually set apart particularly for relief works to be used in times of distress. Yet if what Kauṭilya lays down was followed fully by the state, then its activities and the interest it took in preventing famine and in relieving distress appear to have been more vigorous than in modern days.

[37] *Arth.*, Bk. IV, ch. 3. *Infra*, pp. 187 ff.
[38] *Arth.*, Bk. IV, ch. 3.
[39] *Ibid.*
[40] *Ibid.*
[41] *Ibid.*
[42] *Ibid.*, *Sarvatrachōpahatān pitēva anugṛihṇīyāt.*

CHAPTER XIV

GOVERNMENT UNDERTAKINGS, INCLUDING IRRIGATION WORKS

I. *Irrigation Works:* Importance paid to irrigation works—Works constructed by the state—Encouragement given by the state to private irrigation works. II. *Other Government Undertakings:* Agriculture — Mining — Manufacturing — Trade and commerce—Banking

I. IRRIGATION WORKS

THE importance and necessity of works of irrigation, especially in a predominantly agricultural country like India, can hardly be exaggerated. This was completely recognized by the Mauryas. "Irrigational works," says Kauṭilya, "are the sources of crops; the results of a good shower of rain are ever attained in the case of crops below irrigational works."[1] Megasthenes remarks that India has "vast plains of fertility. . . . The greater part of the soil, moreover, is under irrigation, and consequently bears two crops in the course of the year."[2] To quote Kauṭilya again: "Of irrigational works [*sētubandhaḥ*] that which is of perennial water is better than that which is fed with water drawn from other sources; of works containing perennial water, that which can irrigate an extensive area is better."[3] The existence of water rates and the details given below, as well as in the chapter on "Irrigation Revenue," strongly suggest the extensive use of irrigation.

In the Mauryan days it was the recognized duty of the

[1] *Arth.*, Bk. VII, ch. 14, *Sētubandhaḥ sasyānāṃ yōniḥ nityānuśaktō hi varshaguṇalābhaḥ sētuvāpēshu.*

[2] *Diodorus*, ii, 35. *Strabo*, xv, 1, 20. Strabo also mentions the great fertility of the soil.

[3] *Arth.*, Bk. VII, ch. 12:

Sētubandhayōrapi āharyōdakātsahōdakaśrēyān.
Sahōdakayōrapi prabhūtavāpasathānaḥ śrēyān.

state to get irrigation works constructed. The king had to construct reservoirs filled with water, either perennial or drawn from some other source,[4] and in barren tracts was advocated the construction not only of tanks, buildings for shelter, and wells, but also flower gardens and fruit gardens.[5]

The Girnār inscription[6] records that the lake Sudarśana was constructed by Pushyagupta, the provincial governor of Chandragupta Maurya, with well-provided conduits, drains, and means to guard against foul matter, and was further improved by Tushāspha, a governor under Aśōka in a manner worthy of a king. Rudradāman adds that it cost him a vast amount of money to repair a breach "420 cubits long, just as many broad, (and) 75 cubits deep." Another inscription[7] also mentions that the lake Sudarśana again burst, and that it cost Chakrapālita, a governor of Saurāshṭra under the early Guptas, "an immeasurable expenditure of wealth" to rebuild the dam, the breach this time being "a hundred cubits in all in length, and sixty and eight in breadth, and seven men's height in elevation . . . of two hundred cubits," etc.

The dimensions of the dam, especially those given by the Girnār edict, even if they are exaggerated, give an idea of the vastness of the reservoir and suggest the huge expenditure for building it. The fact that the state got the Sudarśana lake constructed in such a remote corner as Kathiawar gives rise to the belief that many more such works must have been undertaken in the other parts of the kingdom also. What the Famine Commission of 1880 recommended, namely, the restoration and reconstruction of sundry irrigational works in addition to the construction of new works, was put into practice by the Mauryas more than two thousand years ago.[8]

[4] *Arth.*, Bk. II, ch. 1, *Sahōdakamahāryōdakam vā sētum bandhayēt.*

[5] *Ibid* ch. 34, *Anudake kūpasetubandhōtsān sthāpayēt pushpaphalavāṭāṁścha.*

[6] *Ep. Ind.*, viii, no. 6.

[7] *Gupta Inscriptions*, no. 14.

[8] *Arth.*, Bk. IV, ch. 3.

Irrigation seems to have been regarded as a primary consideration of the state in ancient India. In the *Mahābhārata*,[9] for example, the king is enjoined to multiply the number of tanks and wells, while Śukra[10] directs that there should be many canals, wells, tanks, and ponds in the kingdom. The inscriptions also refer to the works undertaken by the state. For instance, King Khāravēḷa of Kaliṅga is said to have strengthened the embankments of springs and lakes.[11] So also Viśvavarman of Mālva[12] built irrigation wells and tanks. The like was the case in South India.[13]

In addition to the state constructing and repairing both major and minor works, private persons were encouraged to build and restore irrigation works. The state provided sites, roads, timber, and other necessary materials to persons who constructed reservoirs of their own accord.[14] In such undertakings neighbourers were required to co-operate and send bullocks and servants to carry on the work.[15] Remission of taxes were made for some years in favour of persons who constructed or repaired tanks, lakes, and wells.[16] Some of the private irrigation works, even lakes and tanks, were allowed to be transferred by sale.

The care bestowed by the state on irrigation may be understood from Strabo's observation that "some [magistrates in Pāṭalīputra] superintend the rivers, measure the land, as is done in Egypt, and inspect the sluices by which water is let out from the main canals into their branches, so that every one may have an equal supply of it."[17] Rudradāman confirms the existence of sluices and canals. "This lake

[9] *Śāntiparva*, lxxxvi, 15.

[10] *Śukranīti*, iv, 4, 125–9.

[11] *J.B.O.R.S.*, vol. iii, pp. 361–2. Also see V. A. Smith, *Early HIstory of India*, p. 219 and footnote.

[12] *Gupta Inscriptions*, no. 17.

[13] *Ep. Ind.*, v, no. 9. See also *Historical Sketches of Ancient Dekhan*, pp. 365 and 367.

[14] *Arth.*, Bk. II, ch. 1, *Anyēshām vā bandhatāṃ bhūmimārgavṛikshōpa karaṇānugrahaṃ kuryāt.*

[15] *Ibid.*

[16] *Arth.*, Bk. III, ch. 9. *Supra*, p. 149.

[17] *Strabo*, xv, 1, 50.

Sudarśana . . . constructed without gaps, as they are of stone, [clay], . . . furnished with a natural dam, [formed by ?] . . ., and with well-provided conduits, drains, and means to guard against foul matter."[18] The existence of numerous channels is mentioned by Kauṭilya also, who says that they were used in agriculture.[19]

Thus in the Mauryan days the state, as well as private persons, constructed, restored, and repaired both major and minor works of irrigation. The description of the great fertility of the land given by the Greeks leads to the belief that irrigation was widespread. The expenditure incurred by the state must have been great, and the state had realized centuries ago what the Famine Commission of 1880 recorded, that the irrigation works are a great advantage to the state, regarded merely from the direct financial return on the money invested, in increasing the wealth of the country in ordinary years and in preventing or mitigating famine in years of drought.

II. OTHER GOVERNMENT UNDERTAKINGS

On a previous page government undertakings have been considered from the standpoint of revenue.[20] In the present chapter they will be considered from the side of expenditure.

The state in Mauryan times undertook trading, agriculture, mining, and manufacturing. As observed elsewhere,[21] mines were regarded as the source of the treasury, and the state had a monopoly of mining and commerce in minerals. Not only did the state own mines, but it even worked those which did not involve much outlay.

[18] *Ep. Ind.*, viii, no. 6.

[19] *Arth.*, Bk. II, ch. 24. Dion Chrysostom of the first century A.D. writes that there were many channels to convey water from the rivers, "some of them large and others which are smaller and mingle with each other" (*Ancient India as described in Classical Literature*, p. 175). Though this does not refer to the Mauryan times, yet it shows the widespread system of irrigation about two centuries after the fall of the Mauryas.

[20] *Supra*, Chapter VII.

[21] *Ibid.*

Manufactories were a source of expenditure to the state.[22] "A king shall carry on *mining operations and manufactures*," observes Kauṭilya,[23] "exploit timber and elephant forests, offer facilities for cattle-breeding and commerce." Of the sections in the accounts department, one was in charge of the work carried on and of the results obtained in manufactories; others looked after the financial side of the business; still others were concerned with the status, wages, and conditions of the employees; and others with fresh investments.[24] Again, to give one example, the state had its own weaving department, wherein were manufactured various kinds of cloths with the labour women, especially widows, girls, and cripples.[25] It also carried on the manufacture of goods from tin, copper, bronze, brass, etc.[26]

That agriculture also was undertaken by the state is evident from the discussion about crown lands on a previous page.[27] There was an agricultural department which looked after this kind of work.[28] Nor was trade neglected by the state. Commerce in minerals was a state monopoly. There was a department in charge of commerce.[29] Lastly, the government appears to have been a banker also,[30] lending grain at interest. Thus the state was itself a big business man, undertaking many kinds of enterprises. This must have meant a great deal of expenditure.

[22] *Arth.*, Bk. II, ch. 1.
[23] *Supra*, Chapter VII.
[24] *Arth.*, Bk. II, ch. 7, *Tatrādhikāriṇānāṃ saṁkhyā* . . ., etc.
[25] *Arth.*, Bk. II, ch. 23.
[26] *Arth.*, Bk. II, ch. 12.
[27] *Supra*, Chapter VII.
[28] *Arth.*, Bk. II, ch. 24.
[29] *Arth.*, Bk. II, ch. 15.
[30] *Arth.*, Bk. II, ch. 16.

CHAPTER XV

EXPENDITURE ON THE MILITARY, JUSTICE, AND POLICE

I. *Military:* The fleet—The army: the commissariat—Different kinds of combatants: the infantry, cavalry, chariots, and elephants; kinds of infantry troops: standing army of hereditary fighters, soldiers contributed by local bodies, armies of allies—The probable strength of the Army—Scale of salaries—An estimate of the expenditure. II. *Justice and Police*

I. MILITARY

IN an extensive empire like the Mauryan, and especially with independent and warlike states bordering, and perhaps conquered states within, the empire, always on the alert to shake off the imperial yoke—which actually happened after Aśōka's death—it is only natural to find a huge and highly organized army. Even in British India, where there is little likelihood of internal disturbance and not much chance of external trouble, a large[1] army is maintained.

The Mauryan forces of defence consisted of the navy and the army. As regards the navy, Megasthenes mentions a fleet and its admiral, as well as ship-builders. He remarks that one division of magistrates in Pāṭalīputra was appointed to co-operate with the admiral of the fleet.[2] Kauṭilya also mentions[3] ships under the control of an admiral (*nāvā-dhyaksha*). Alexander the Great is said to have utilized the

[1] We are not concerned here with the question as to how far the huge army and the huge expenditure are necessary and justifiable. K. T. Shah does not appear to be justified in throwing the blame for the existence of the problem of defence on modern commercial civilization (*Sixty Years of Indian Finance*, p. 62). The question of military preparedness has existed ever since men organized themselves into different states, and was found even in such a kingdom as Aśōka's.

[2] *Strabo*, xv, 1, 50.

[3] *Arth.*, Bk. II, ch. 28.

Indian navy for crossing the Indus. As V. A. Smith observes,[4] considering Aśōka's relations with Ceylon and even more distant powers, we may credit him with a sea-going fleet as well as an army.

The army consisted of the commissariat and the combatants. Of the commissariat, Strabo writes[5] "One division of magistrates in Pāṭalīputra was appointed to co-operate with the admiral of the fleet, another with the superintendent of the bullock trains which are used for transporting engines of war, food for the soldiers, provender for the cattle, and other military requisites. They supply servants who beat the drum and others who carry gongs; grooms also for the horses, and mechanists and their assistants." These details of the commissariat—bullock trains, food, fodder, mechanists, engines, and so forth—are confirmed by Kauṭilya. He says that "destruction or protection of the commissariat (*vivatha*)" is one of the duties of cavalry;[6] that the camp requisites of an army are surgeons with medicine and instruments, women (? nurses), foodstuffs, grass, bedding, etc.,[7] as well as hunters with dogs and pioneers under the *prasta*, consisting of carpenters and free labourers.[8]

Asses, camels and horses,[9] bulls, mules, and carts,[10] trainers of horses and elephants, grooms, veterinary surgeons, cooks, etc., formed part of the non-combatant forces.[11] Kauṭilya's references to the examination of camps, roads, bridges, wells, and rivers, carrying the machines, weapons, armour, instruments, and provisions, carrying away the men that are knocked down, along with the weapons and armour,[12] to the guarding of camps, transports, supplies, and also the roads of communications,"[13] clearly

[4] *Edicts of Aśōka*, Introduction, p. viii.
[5] *Strabo*, xv, 1, 50.
[6] *Arth.*, Bk. X, ch. 4.
[7] *Arth.*, Bk. X, ch. 3.
[8] *Arth.*, Bk. X, ch. 2.
[9] *Arth.*, Bk. IX, ch. 1.
[10] *Arth.*, Bk. X, ch. 4.
[11] *Arth.*, Bk. II, chs. 30–3. Also Megasthenes; *Frag.*, xxxiv, 13–15.
[12] *Arth.*, Bk. X, ch. 4.
[13] *Arth.*, Bk. XIII, ch. 4.

indicate the existence of a well-organized commissariat and transport service.

The combatants were of four kinds. The Greek ambassador observes: "The third division has charge of the foot soldiers, the fourth of the horses, the fifth of the war chariots, and the sixth of the elephants."[14] This division of the army into infantry, cavalry, chariots, and elephants mentioned by Megasthenes was common in ancient India.[15] One of the items of public expenditure, according to Kauṭilya,[16] was the maintenance of infantry, cavalry, chariots, and horses.

The infantry consisted of six kinds of troops—hereditary troops, corporations of soldiers, and the army of friendly or unfriendly kings, and of wild tribes.[17]

The *maulabala* or hereditary troops appear to represent the standing army,[18] for, according to Śukra,[19] the *maula* army is that which has been existing for many years. This perhaps mainly consisted of the Kshatriyas.[20] For, according to Hindu *śāstras* and usage, the Kshatriyas were the heredi-

[14] *Strabo*, xv, 1, 50.

[15] *Diodorus*, ii, 41; Pliny, *Hist. Nat.*, vi, 21; *Strabo*, xv, 1, 50.

[16] *Manu*, vii, 1, 50. *Tamils Eighteen Hundred Years Ago*, p. 130. *Yuan Chwang*, i, p. 171. *J.B.O.R.S.*, vol. iii, p. 462 (Khāravēla's inscription). *Arth.*, Bk. II, ch. 6.

[17] *Arth.*, Bk. II, ch. 33. *Étēna pattyadhuakshō vyākhyātaḥ samaula-bhṛitaśrēṇimitrāmitrāṭavībalānāṃ sāraphalgutāṃ vidyāt.* Also see Bk. X, ch. 2. These four wings of infantry are mentioned in the Ganesaghad plate (No. 1) of Dhruvasēna I of the sixth century A.D. (*Ep. Ind.*, iii, no. 46). *Maulabhṛitamitraśrēṇibalavātma rājyasrīh*, etc., which is translated by Hultzch as "who acquired the glory of royalty by the strength of a devoted body of hereditary servants, hired soldiers," thus taking *śrēṇibala* to mean devoted body of hereditary servants, etc., and not the corporation of soldiers. Cf. *Kāmandaka* xix, 28, 3 ff. *Maula* and *bhṛitya* troops are also mentioned in *Ep. Ind.*, i, no. 28.

[18] *Kāmandika*, xix, 28, 12.

[19] *Śukranīti*, iv, 7, 22. Śukra adds that one's own army is maintained by salary.

[20] Kauṭilya considers (*Arth.*, Bk. IX, ch. 2) an army of the Kshatriya cast as the best army. But the army sometimes included other castes also, e.g. *vaiśyas* and *śūdras*.

tary warriors. Moreover, Yuan Chwang says: "The National Guard (lit. warriors) are heroes of choice valour, and as the profession is hereditary they become adepts in military tactics."[21] The standing army in ancient India therefore appears to have been formed of hereditary troops.

According to Arrian, "The fifth caste among the Indians consists of the warriors, who are second in point of numbers to the husbandmen, but lead a life of supreme freedom and enjoyment. They have only military duties to perform. Others make their arms, and others supply them with horses, and they have others to attend on them in the camp, who take care of their horses, clean their arms, drive their elephants, prepare their chariots, and act as their charioteers. As long as they are required to fight they fight, and when peace returns they abandon themselves to enjoyment—the pay which they receive from the state being so liberal that they can with ease maintain themselves and others besides."[22] Megasthenes refers to these troops when he observes that the King of Pāṭalīputra "has in his pay a standing army of 600,000 foot soldiers,"[23] etc.

In Kauṭilya's opinion the hereditary army was the best of all kinds of troops because it depended for its existence upon the existence of its master and was constantly drilled.[24] This indicates a standing army regularly trained and paid by the state. There is evidence in the *Arthaśāstra* which proves the existence of standing divisions of chariots, elephants, and cavalry.[25] The royal horse and elephant stables were under the care and control of the state. The animals were given special military training by experts and were kept mainly for purposes of war. The superintendent of chariots looked after the chariots. There can thus be little

[21] *Yuan Chwang*, vol. i, p. 171.

[22] Arrian's *Indika*, xii; *Strabo*, xv, i, 47. See also *Ancient India as described in Classical Literature*, p. 53.

[23] Pliny, *Hist. Nat.*, vi, 22.

[24] *Arth.*, Bk. IX, ch. 2; *Kāmandaka*, xix, 28, 4, 11.

[25] *Arth.*, Bk. II, chs. 30–3.

doubt of the existence of a standing army under the Mauryas.

The second branch of infantry consisted of hired troops, who were perhaps mercenaries enlisted at the time of hostilities. Elephants, chariots, and cavalry could not be hired or contributed by corporations because of the cost of their maintenance in times of peace, and perhaps because private persons were forbidden to keep these. This may be the reason why the *Arthaśāstra* mentions only infantry as hired or contributed. There were also the armies of friends and of wild tribes.

Neither Kauṭilya nor the Greeks give details of the strength and number of either the fleet or the commissariat.[26] About the army, however, full particulars are obtainable from the Greeks. Pliny writes:[27] "Their king (i.e. of the people of Pāṭalīputra) has in his pay a standing army of 600,000 foot soldiers, 30,000 cavalry, and 9,000 elephants." These figures do not appear to include the

[26] Kauṭilya, however, writes (*Arth.*, Bk. X, ch. 5) that "there must be three men to oppose a horse, fifteen men or five horses to oppose a chariot or an elephant, and as many as (fifteen) servants (*pādagōpa*) for a horse, a chariot, or an elephant should be maintained." This means that each horse, chariot, and elephant was attended by fifteen men, like the Spartans, who in battle were attended upon by seven helots. If the figure given by Kauṭilya is correct it means that these attendants alone number 705,000, which figure is almost incredible. Again, this statement is contradicted by another of Kauṭilya himself (*Trans.*, p. 431), "thus in an array of chariots, the number of chariots amounts to forty-five: two hundred and twenty-five horses, six hundred and seventy-five men, and as many servants to attend upon the horses, chariots, and elephants—this is called an even array of troops." Obviously this indicates that each horse, chariot, and elephant had one attendant. Compare Arrian's *Indika*, c. 12, where Arrian states that the warriors received such liberal pay that they maintained others besides themselves and kept servants to attend on them in the camp, to clean their arms, and to take care of their horses, elephants, and chariots.

[27] *Hist. Nat.*, vi, 22. *Solin*, 52. 6–17, however, gives different figures. "Their king keeps in his pay at all times 60,000 foot, 30,000 horse, and 8,000 elephants." The difference in figures is not clearly explainable. Perhaps the smaller figures are a mistake.

hired and contributed troops and the troops of allies, for, according to the *Arthaśāstra,* they were called upon only in

DETAILS OF ARMY PAY

Name of Officer	Pay (in *Paṇas*)	Approximate Equivalent in Modern Currency (Pounds Sterling)[28]
1. The commander of the army	48,000	2,400
2. The commander	24,000	1,200
3. The chiefs;		
Elephants	8,000	400
Horses	8,000	400
Chariots	8,000	400
Infantry	8,000	400
4. The superintendent of—		
Infantry	4,000	200
Cavalry	4,000	200
Chariots	4,000	200
Elephants	4,000	200
5. The chariot driver	2,000	100
The physician of the army	2,000	100
The trainer of horses	2,000	100
The carpenter	2,000	100
Those who rear animals	2,000	100
6. Trained soldiers	500	25
The staff of accountants and writers	500	25
7. Elephant driver	500 to 1,000	25 to 30

times of war, while Megasthenes definitely mentions the figures as applying to the standing army. The forces at the

[28] The equivalent in modern currency is a rough calculation on the basis of V. A. Smith's statement (*Early History of India*, p. 137, footnote) that the "value of the silver *paṇas* (146 grains of impure silver) may be taken as about a shilling." It is given solely to get an idea of the pay. It must be carefully noted that in a comparison of a modern budget with an ancient one, there are a host of other considerations to be calculated, e.g. the value of money, income of other kinds, etc.

time of hostilities would therefore have been enormous, as they included the war troops also.

We shall, however, consider the standing army only. Megasthenes observes that the entire force of men-at-arms, war horses, war elephants, etc., was maintained at the king's expense.[29] Kauṭilya also writes that one of the items of expenditure was the maintenance of infantry, cavalry, chariots, and elephants.[30] Arrian says that the soldiers received such liberal pay that they maintained others beside themselves and kept servants to attend upon them in camp.[31]

Kauṭilya gives (p. 195) details of the pay of the army from the commander-in-chief to the ordinary soldiers.[32]

It is not known whether the pay was annual or monthly. The probability is that it was annual. Assuming that a *paṇa* was equal to about a shilling and that the pay was what was actually paid, the total expenditure would amount to the following sum:

Infantry	600,000 at £25 each soldier	=	£15,000,000
Cavalry	30,000 at £25 each soldier	=	750,000
Elephants	9,000 at £25 to £50 each	=	337,500
Charioteers	8,000 at £100 each	=	800,000
Total		=	£16,887,500

Roughly this may be taken at £17,000,000. This calculation omits the following items:

1. The figures given by Megasthenes have been assumed to include officers also.
2. Even on this assumption, we must remember that officers had higher pay. For instance, the chiefs, the commanders of infantry, cavalry, etc., were getting £4,000 and £2,000 each. Their number is not known. Yet not only have they been included in the number given by Megasthenes, but their pay also has been assumed as equal to that of an ordinary soldier, i.e. £25.
3. The figures show the pay of the combatants only. We have to consider the maintenance of the elephants, horses,

[29] *Diodorus*, ii, 41. [30] *Arth.*, Bk. II, ch. 6.
[31] *Indika*, ch. xii. Also see *Strabo*, xv, 1, 47.
[32] *Arth.*, Bk. V, ch. 3.

and other animals. According to Kauṭilya the animals were kept in the royal stables under royal care.[33] Strabo also says: "There are royal stables for the horses and elephants and also a royal magazine for the arms, because the soldier has to return his arms to the magazine, and his horse and his elephant to the stables."[34]

4. No allowance has been made for the expenses of the fleet.
5. Further, it is known from Megasthenes that able and trustworthy overseers and courtesans were employed for the inspection of the army.[35] In the *Arthaśāstra* also prostitutes, spies and inspectors are mentioned as employed in the army.[36]
6. Lastly we have to add the expenditure on the armoury, the arsenal, and other similar departments. The armoury department is mentioned[37] by the Mauryan minister as being under a superintendent who employed wage-earners to manufacture weapons and instruments of warfare like mail armour, bows, arrows, moveable and immoveable machines, etc. Arsenals,[38] ornaments and other things for elephants, horses, and chariots are also mentioned in detail in the *Arthaśāstra*. For the manufacture of chariots a huge department was maintained employing permanent as well as temporary hands and distributing pay in money and provisions.[39] Megasthenes confirms this statement. "But the armour-makers and shipbuilders receive wages and their victuals from the king, for whom alone they work."[40]

II. JUSTICE AND POLICE

There is to-day little controversy about the expenditure on the administration of justice and the police. "The maintenance of a judiciary is not merely a symbol of sovereignty, it is indispensable under the existing social organization."[41]

[33] *Arth.*, Bk. II, chs. 30–3.

[34] *Strabo*, xv, 1, 50.

[35] *Strabo*, xv, 1, 48.

[36] *Arth.*, Bk. V, ch. 3, *Satriṇaśchāyudhīyānām vēsyāḥ kārukuśīlavaḥ; Daṇḍavṛiddhāścha jānīyuḥ śauchāśauchamatandritāḥ.*

[37] *Arth.*, Bk. II, ch. 18.

[38] *Arth.*, Bk. IV, ch. 9.

[39] *Arth.*, Bk. II, ch. 33.

[40] *Strabo*, xv, 1, 46. Kauṭilya mentions (*Arth.*, Bk. II, ch. 1) quarters for the civil officials like the prime minister and the priest, but it is natural to expect quarters for soldiers which are mentioned in the *Mahābhārata* (*Śāntiparva*, lxix, 54–5). It enumerates "arsenals, camps, and quarters for soldiers, trenches, etc." This item of expenditure on military quarters should perhaps also be included.

[41] *Sixty Years of Indian Finance*, p. 104.

In Mauryan times this judiciary appears to have been well organized. For every ten villages there was a court, another—perhaps of appellate and wider jurisdiction—for every four hundred villages, and a third with greater powers for every eight hundred villages; in addition to inter-district courts, probably to settle disputes between districts as well as to deal with questions arising over the borders there were both civil and criminal courts are mentioned,[42] at the head of which was the king, the fountain of justice (*dharmapravartaka*),[43] and final court of appeal.

This close attention to the administration of justice is confirmed by the statements of Megasthenes and the edicts of Aśōka. The Greek ambassador mentions the existence of assessors and tribunals of justice.[44] He also says:[45] "The Judges also decide cases in which foreigners are concerned, with the greatest care, and come down sharply on those who take unfair advantage of them." Aśōka also makes mention of a well-established organization. In the Kaliṇga edicts the government officials are stated to have been in charge of justice also. According to Hultzch,[46] the *nagala vyavahārikas* mentioned in the first separate Jaugada edict were judicial officers of the city[47] and were comparable to the *pauravyavahārikas* mentioned in the *Arthaśāstra*. In the light of this evidence it is probable that, as Kauṭilya writes, there were about eighty courts in every *drōṇāmukha*, presided over by judges who were salaried government servants.

It is not certain as to what kind of police organization the Mauryas had. Three commissioners and three ministers,

[42] *Arth.*, Bk. II, ch. 1; Bk. I, ch. 10, *Tatra dharmopadhāśuddhān dharmasthīyakaṇṭakaśodhanēshu sthāpayēt.*

[43] *Arth.*, Bk. I, ch. 1.

[44] *Strabo*, xv, 1, 48.

[45] *Diodorus*, ii, 42.

[46] *Cor. Ins. Ind.*, i, 95.

[47] D. R. Bhandarkar, however, suggests (*Aśōka*, p. 56) that the *nagala vyavahārika* was a judge of district towns only, but of the status of a viceroy.

observes Kauṭilya,[48] "shall deal with measures to suppress disturbances to peace (*kaṇṭakaśōdhanaṃ*)." The commentator explains *kaṇṭaka* to mean artisans, and the succeeding passages in the chapter also indicate to the same effect. But in view of the verse[49] at the end of the chapter that traders, artisans, musicians, beggars, buffoons, and other idlers who were thieves in effect though not in name, should be restrained from oppression in the country, it is probable that the commissioners were doing police duty, as the term is now understood, and that their duty was not restricted to a particular class. Elsewhere[50] we find that the detection of thieves and evil characters was done by the city superintendent with his army of spies, and by a special commissioner (*pradēshṭri*) assisted by *gōpas* and *sthānikas*.

Moreover, the *chōrarajjukas*[51] were police officers who were stationed in some parts of the country, and who were responsible for loss in their jurisdiction when there was no superintendent of pasture lands. These appear to be special police officers, because they were only in charge of some places only, and the ordinary police duty was performed by the city superintendent and the *pradēshṭri*, with their subordinates in the city and in the country respectively. The practice of the state being responsible through its officers for the loss of goods is advocated by early lawgivers. Āpastambha says[52] that the officers appointed to look after villages and towns must be made to pay what is stolen within their jurisdiction." Likewise Gautama says[53] that if the stolen property is not recovered the state shall pay its value out of the treasury.

There were also jails maintained by the state. They are often referred to in the *Arthaśāstra*.[54] Aśōka also in his edicts

[48] *Arth.*, Bk. IV, ch. 1.

[49] *Svam chōranachōrākhyān vanikkarukasilaram*
Bhikshukānkuhukaṁśchanyān vārayēt dēśa pīḍanāt.

[50] *Arth.*, Bk. IV, ch. 6.

[51] *Supra* Appendix.

[52] *Āpastambha*, ii, 10, 26, 8.

[53] *Gautama*, x, 46–7.

[54] *Arth.*, Bk. I, ch. 14; Bk. II, ch. 36; Bk. IV, ch. 9.

refers to prisoners and jails.[55] The jails had superintendents and other officers in charge of them.[56]

Thus the Mauryan state appears to have had an organized judicial administration as well as a police department and jails. If Megasthenes' statement[57] that the ancient Indians were extremely honest and that in the vast camp of Chandragupta the amount of thefts was 200 *drachmae* is true, then the expenditure to the state on the score of jails must have been very little. But the description of the judicature and the police as given by Kauṭilya suggests that a considerable sum must have been spent on the departments.

[55] *R.E. V*; *P.E. V*.

[56] *Arth.*, Bk. IV, ch. 9.

[57] *Strabo*, xv, 1, 53–6.

CHAPTER XVI

FINANCIAL ADMINISTRATION

The classification of villages—The unit of financial administration—The *gōpa* and his duties—The *sthānika* and the *pradēshṭāra*—The responsibility of the heads of departments—The accountants—Retrenchment and economy—Punishment for defaults

IN every well-administered state there ought to be a well-organized and trustworthy financial machinery. In the Mauryan days there appears to have existed a good system of financial administration.

The kingdom was divided into four parts, which comprised smaller divisions. These were further divided into villages, which were classified into three grades according to their importance,[1] and were brought under one of the following heads:[2]

1. Those that are exempted from taxation (*pārihārika*). These were probably completely free from taxation, contributing not even soldiers.

2. Of those that paid taxes in some form:

(*a*) some supplied soldiers in lieu of the ordinary taxes (*āyudhīya*);
(*b*) others paid taxes in the form of grains, cattle, gold, or raw material;
(*c*) still others contributed free labour and dairy produce.

The unit of financial administration was a group of five or ten villages,[3] and every such unit was under the charge of the *gōpa*, who looked after the accounts as ordered by

[1] *Arth.*, Bk. II, ch. 3. [2] *Ibid.*

[3] *Ibid.* Compare the *daśagrāmikas* mentioned in *Ep. Ind.*, iv, no. 34. Also the *daśādhyakshas*, *śatādhyakshas*, and *dēśādhyakshas* referred to in *Vishṇu*, iii, 8–10. Also *Manu*, vii, 115.

the collector-general.[4] The *gōpa* appears to have been a maid-of-all-work and his duties were manifold. He

(*a*) numbered fields and classified them as cultivated wet-lands, gardens, plains, forests, irrigation works, and so forth, and
(*b*) fixed the boundaries of villages, fields, forests, and roads;
(*c*) registered gifts, sales, charities, and remission of taxes regarding fields;
(*d*) classified houses as tax-paying and non-tax paying;
(*e*) registered the number of inhabitants of all castes in each village (i.e. the duty of a census register);
(*f*) kept an account of the number of cultivators, cowherds, merchants, artisans, labourers, and slaves, and bipeds and quadrupeds;
(*g*) fixed the amount of free labour tolls and other duties, gold and fines that could be collected from each village; and
(*h*) kept an account of the number of young and old men, their history, occupation, income, and expenditure.

Superior to the *gōpa* was the *sthānika* or district officer, who attended to the accounts of the district. This person appears to have been a revenue official only, while the *rāshṭramukhya*[5] was probably a political officer. Neither the *gōpa* nor the *sthānika* was empowered to collect the tax known as *bali*.[6] The collection of this tax, as well as of arrears of revenue and the inspection of the work of the *gōpa* and the *sthānikas*, were undertaken by special commissioners (*pradēshṭāra*), who were appointed by the collector-general.

According to F. W. Thomas,[7] the *pradēshṭāra* was identical with the *pradēśika* of the edicts of Aśōka, and this official was charged with the executive duties of revenue collection and police. Kauṭilya gives the impression that this officer was a kind of government auditor in addition to being in charge of collecting certain kinds of revenue and superintending the work of the *gōpa* and the *sthānika*. He checked the affairs of other departments also.

At the head of the finance department (country branch) was the collector-general.[8]

[4] *Arth.*, Bk. IX, ch. 3. [5] *Ibid.* [6] *Supra*, p. 118.
[7] *J.R.A.S.*, 1914, pp. 395 ff.; 1915, p. 112. *Supra*, p. 165.
[8] Compare *Śukranīti*, ii, 204 ff.

The *gōpa* and *sthānika* were found in the cities also. The former kept accounts of ten, twenty, or forty households. His duties were, as in the country, those of recording the caste, occupation, and other details of the people, and of ascertaining their income and expenditure. The *sthānika* who had charge of the city had the same functions as his rural colleague.[9] At the head of these was the city superintendent and the customs officer under the control of the collector-general.

The final authority in the matter of finance, as in everything else, was the king, one of whose daily duties was to attend to the accounts of receipts and expenditure.[10] This may have been purely formal so far as the details were concerned, as it is impossible for any person, however able, to look into details. The king perhaps superintended the general policy.

As for the expenditure of public revenue, the departmental officers appear to have been primarily responsible. The chief officer of each department thoroughly scrutinized the real amount of the work done, the receipts and the expenditure relating to his department, both in detail and in the aggregate.[11] Every department had its own accountant, treasurer, and others,[12] and each minister was responsible for the finances of his department. "When employed as a minister," observes Kauṭilya,[13] "he (the courtier) shall show the net revenue that remains after all kinds of expenditure are met with." This indicates individual responsibility. But the ministers were to present their accounts together,[14] and

[9] *Arth.*, Bk. II, ch. 36. It is probable that the *sthānika* was only the revenue officer, while the *nāgarika*, who was his superior, had other functions as well.

[10] *Arth.*, Bk. I, ch. 19. Compare *Yājñavalkya*, i, 13, 327.

[11] *Arth.*, Bk. II, ch. 9, *Tasmādasya yō yasminnadhikaraṇē śāsansathaḥ sa tasya karmaṇō yāthātathyāmāyavyayau cha vyāsasamāsābhyāmāchakshīta.*

[12] *Ibid.*

[13] *Arth.*, Bk. V, ch. 5, *Niyujitaḥ karmasu vyayaviśuddhamudayaṃ darśayēt.*

[14] *Arth.*, Bk. II, ch. 7.

this was perhaps in order to make an economic and wise minister an example to others. The ministers were chosen from among the courtiers noted for their great ability and trust,[15] and yet they were checked by the king.[16]

The heads of departments and the ministers were assisted by accountants. When the accountants submitted accounts they were not permitted to mix with one another, lest there be confusion of accounts.[17] Irregular and untimely accountants were punished. Their superintendent had to receive and check the accounts of the clerks, and if he failed in his duty he was punished.[18] Thus the system of checks was well developed, and at the head of all was the king himself.

Retrenchment and economy also appear to have been familiar to the Mauryan financiers. Kauṭilya directs that the service of some government servants should be dispensed with when not conducive to financial prosperity.[19] Economy was practised through a system of rewards and punishments. The rewards took various forms. One of them was that temporary hands in the departments were made permanent if the officials worked loyally and well.[20] Money rewards were also given. For example, when the superintendent of a department increased the net revenue, either by increasing the receipts or by decreasing the expenditure, he was rewarded eight times the increase.[21] Promotions were also made.[22]

Punishments were not equally heavy. The Mauryan financiers recognized that "just as it is impossible not to

[15] *Arth.*, Bk. II, ch. 9; Bk. I, chs. 8, 9, and 10. Compare *Śukranīti*, ii, 220 ff.

[16] *Arth.*, Bk. I, ch. 19.

[17] *Arth.*, Bk. II, ch. 7.

[18] *Ibid.*

[19] *Arth.*, Bk. II, ch. 9:

> *Na bhakshayaṅti yē thvarthāṇnyayatō vardhayanti cha.*
> *Nityādhikārāḥ kāryāste rajñaḥ priyahitēratāḥ.*

[20] *Ibid.*

[21] *Arth.*, Bk. II, ch. 7, *Yachchāgrādāyasyāntaravarṇe nīvyā vardhēta, vyayasya vā yatparihāpayēt, tadashṭaguṇamadhyaksham dāpayēt.*

[22] *Arth.*, Bk. II, ch. 9.

taste the honey or poison that finds itself on the tip of the tongue, so it is impossible for a government servant not to eat up, at least, a bit of the king's revenue."[23] The conduct of all employees of the state was therefore watched by spies. Espionage was made complete use of in all its forms. When the guilty officers were found out, their ill-earned hoards were confiscated and they were transferred to other departments.[24] Fines were imposed for loss of revenue or increase of expenditure.[25]

The accounts were submitted at the close of the month of Āshāḍha,[26] which marked the end of the financial year. On the new year's day the accounts were carefully audited and revenue and expenditure items were examined in detail, and the surplus also was scrutinized.[27]

This system of financial administration indicates the highly organized system of government existing in India long before the Christian era.

Kauṭilya mentions some checks to expenditure.[28] The first of them is investment of capital. This perhaps means that if money is invested it is locked up, and so will not be available to be spent and so checks expenditure. The second check is "relics of a wretched undertaking." This perhaps means that the failure of an undertaking prevents the state

[23] *Arth.*, Bk. II, ch. 9:

Yathā hyānāsvādayituṃ na śakyaṃ,
Jihvātalasthaṃ madhu vā vishaṃ vā
Arthastathā hyarthacharēṇa rājñaḥ,
Svalpōpyanāsvādayituṃ na śakyaḥ.

[24] *Ibid.*:

Āsrāvayēchchōpachitān viparyasyēchcha karmasu,
Yathā na bhakshayantyarthaṃ bhaksitaṃ nirvamanti vā.

[25] *Arth.*, Bk. II, ch. 7. [26] *Ibid.* [27] *Ibid.*

[28] *Arth.*, Bk. II, ch. 6, *Vikshēpavyādhitāntarārambhaśēshaścha vyayapratyayaḥ.* Jolly (*op. cit.*, vol. ii, p. 18) translates this passage as follows: "Investment, an undertaking naturally weak, and the balance of an outlay, are heads of expenditure." This translation appears incorrect. It is difficult to understand how the balance of an outlay can be an item of expenditure.

from spending any more on such dangerous undertakings, and expenditure on such enterprises is therefore checked. The third check is "savings from an estimated outlay." Whatever sum of money is allotted for some purpose and it is more than is actually required, the next time when money is given for the same purpose the amount which was actually required the previous time and the savings therefore act as a check on the sanction of that amount of extra money.

BIBLIOGRAPHY

PRIMARY SOURCES

Arthaśāstra of Kauṭilya.

(*a*) Edited by R. Shāma Śāstry (Mysore, 1924). This is the text followed by me except where otherwise indicated.

(*b*) Edited by T. Gaṇapati Śāstri. 2 vols. (Trivandrum).

(*c*) Edited by J. Jolly and R. Schmidt (Lahore, 1923).

Translation and Commentaries on the Arthaśāstra.

(*a*) Translation by R. Shāma Śāstry (Mysore, 1923).

(*b*) *Śrī Mūlam*, by T. Gaṇapati Śāstri, published in his edition of the *Arthaśāstra* (Trivandrum).

(*c*) *Pratipadapañchika*, by Bhaṭṭaswāmi. The extant commentary is from Bk. II, ch. 8, to end of Bk. II. This has been printed in *J.B.O.R.S.*, vols. xi and xiii, but this contains misprints and incorrect readings. So wherever mistakes were found I have given reference to the copy of the Manuscript in Mysore Government Oriental Library, No. A 207. The Manuscript in grantha characters (Mysore Government Oriental Library, No. 3231) has also been consulted.

(*d*) *Nayachandrikā*, by Mādhava Yajvan or Misra. This commentary exists from Bk. VII, ch. 7, to Bk. XII, ch. 3, and has been printed in Jolly and Schmidt's edition of the *Arthaśāstra*, vol. ii.

(*e*) *Notes on the Adhyakshapracāra, Bk. II of the Kauṭilīyaṃ Arthaśāstraṃ*, by I. J. Sohrabji (Allahabad, 1914). Based chiefly on Bhaṭṭaswāmi's commentary.

(*f*) Notes by J. Jolly in vol. ii of his edition of the *Arthaśāstra.*

(*g*) *Jayamangala* (author unknown). This is an exceedingly brief summary of the *Arthaśāstra*.

McCrindle, J. W. *Ancient India as described by Megasthenes and Arrian* (Bombay, 1926).

Ancient India as described in Classical Literature (Bombay, 1877; Edinburgh, 1901).

Corpus Inscriptionum Indicarum, vol. i (containing the *Edicts of Aśōka*), edited by F. Hultzch (Oxford, 1925).

Also *Inscriptions of Aśōka*, edited by D. R. Bhandarkar and S. N. Mazumdar (Calcutta, 1920).

Edicts of Aśōka, by V. A. Smith.

ORIGINAL BUT SECONDARY SOURCES

(*These are immensely useful for purposes of comparison and as supporting evidence.*)

Śukranītisāra, edited by G. Oppert (Madras, 1882). Translated by B. K. Sarkar (*Sacred Books of the Hindus*, vol. xiii. Allahabad, 1914).

Kāmandakīya Nītisāra, edited by T. Gaṇapti Śāstri (Trivandrum, 1912). Translated by M. N. Dutt (Calcutta, 1896).

Bṛihaspaty Sūtra, edited and translated by F. W. Thomas (Lahore, 1921).

Rājanīti Ratnākara of Chandisvara, edited by K. P. Jayaswal (Patna, 1924).

Vaiṣampāyana Nitiprakāśika, edited by G. Oppert (Madras, 1882).

Yuktikalpataru, edited by I. J. Śāstry (Calcutta, 1917).

Mānava Dharma Śāstra, edited by V. A. Mandalik (Bombay, 1886). This contains the commentaries of Medhātithi, Sarvajnanārāyana, Kulluka, Rāghavānanda, Nandana, and Rāmachandra. The editions by J. Jolly (London, 1887) and by Gangānātha Jhā (Calcutta, 1921–23) have also been consulted. Translated by G. Bühler (*S.B.E.*, vol. xxv, Oxford, 1886) and by A. C. Burnell and W. Hopkins (London, 1884).

Yājñavalkya Smṛiti, with Vijnanēśvarai's *Commentary*, edited by Pansikar (Bombay, 1909). Translated by S. C. Vidyāranya (Allahabad, 1918).

Bṛihaspati Smṛiti (Ānandāṣrama Series, Poona). Translated by J. Jolly (*S.B.E.*, vol. xxxiii, part 1, Oxford, 1889).

Vishnu Smṛiti, edited by J. Jolly (Calcutta, 1881). Translated by J. Jolly (*S.B.E.*, vol. vii, Oxford, 1880).

Gautama Dharma Śutra, with *Maskari bhashya*, edited by L. Srinivasacharya (Mysore, 1917). Translated by G. Bühler (*S.B.E.*, vol. ii, Oxford, 1879).

Āpastambha Dharma Sūtra, with Haradatta's *Ujjvala*, edited by A. Mahadeva Śāstry and K. Rangācharya (Mysore, 1898). Translated by G. Bühler: *Āpastambha's Aphorisms of the Sacred Law* (*S.B.E.*, vol. ii, Oxford, 1879).

Vasishṭa Dharma Sūtra, edited by A. Führer (Bombay, 1883). Translated by G. Bühler (*S.B.E.*, vol. xiv, part 2, Oxford, 1882).

Baudhāyana Dharma Sūtra, with the *Commentary* of Govindasvamin, edited by L. Srinivasacharya (Mysore, 1907). Translated by G. Bühler (*S.B.E.*, vol. xiv, part 2, Oxford, 1882).

Dharma Śāstra Sangraha, edited by Jīvānanda Vidyasāgara (Calcutta, 1876).

Sarasvati Vilāsa, edited by R. Shāma Śāstry (Mysore, 1927). This contains extracts from various *Dharma sāstras*.

Ṛig Vēda Samhita, with Sāyaṇācharya's *Commentary*, edited by Max Müller (London, 1890–92). Translated: by H. H. Wilson (London, 1850); by R. T. H. Griffith, *The Hymns of the Ṛig Vēda* (Benares, 1889).

Atharva Vēda Samhita, with Sāyaṇācharya's *Commentary*, edited by S. P. Pandit (Bombay, 1895–98). Translated by R. T. H. Griffith (Benares, 1895).

Aitereya Brāhmaṇa, edited and translated by Naug (Bombay, 1893).

Mārkandēya Purāṇa, edited by Kanhaiya Lal (Bombay, 1910). Translated by H. H. Wilson (London, 1864–70).

Matsya Purāṇa (Ānandāṣrama Series, Poona, 1907). Translated by "A Talukdar of Oudh" (Allahabad, 1917).

Brahma Vaivarta Purāṇa, edited by K. S. Krishnadās (Bombay, 1909). Translated by R. N. Sen (*Sacred Books of the Hindus*, Allahabad, 1920).

Dhammapada, edited by S. S. Thera (London, 1914). Translated by Max Müller (*S.B.E.*, vol. x, Oxford, 1881).

Dīpavamśa, edited and translated by Oldenburg (London, 1879).

Mahāvamśa, edited and translated by W. Geiger (London, 1908 and 1912).

Jātakas, edited by V. Fausboll (London, 1877–97). Translation by E. B. Cowell and others (Cambridge, 1895–1913).

Divyāvadhāna, edited by E. B. Cowell (Cambridge, 1888).

Vinaya Texts. Translated by Rhys Davids and Oldenburg (*S.B.E.* vols. xii, xvii, xx, Oxford, 1881–85).

Buddhacharita of Asvaghōsha.

Dandin: *Daśakumāracharita*, edited by G. Bühler and Peterson (Bombay, 1888 and 1891).

Mudrārākshasa of Visākhadatta, edited by M. R. Kale (Bombay).

Harsha Charita of Bana, edited at the Nirnaya Sagar Press (Bombay, 1886). Translated by Thomas and Cowell (London, 1897).

Raghuvaṃśa of Kāḷidāsa, edited by M. R. Kale (Bombay).

Abhijñāna Śākuntalā of Kāḷidāsa, edited by M. R. Kale (Bombay, 1894).

Rājataraṅginī of Kalhana, edited by M. A. Stein (Bombay, 1892).

Kathāsaritsāgara of Somadeva: The Ocean of Story, translated by C. H. Tawney and edited by N. M. Penzer (10 vols., London, 1924).

Pañchatantra, edited by K. P. Parab (Bombay, 1896).

Schoff, *The Periplus of the Erythranean Sea* (London, 1912).

Ancient India as described by Ktesias the Knidian (Calcutta, 1882).

Ancient India—its Invasion by Alexander the Great. Translated by McCrindle (Edinburgh, 1893).

Cunningham, A. *The Coins of Alexander's Successors in the East* (London, 1873).

Beal, S. *Buddhist Records of the Western World* (London, 1906).

Legge, J. *A Record of the Buddhist Kingdom* (containing the *Travels of Fahien*) (Oxford, 1886).

Giles, H. A. *The Travels of Fa-hsien* A.D. 399–419), or *Record of the, Buddhistic Kingdoms* (Cambridge, 1923).

Watters, J. *On Yuan Chwang's Travels in India* (London, 1904).

Takakusu, J. *I-Tsing—A Record of the Buddhist Religion as Practised in India and the Malay Archipelago* (Oxford, 1896).

Epigraphia Indica.

Epigraphia Carnatica.

South Indian Inscriptions, edited by Hultzch and others. (Madras, 1892).

Inscriptions of the Early Gupta Kings, edited by F. J. Fleet (*Corpus Inscriptionum Indicarum*, vol. iii, Calcutta, 1888).

Inscriptions of the Madras Presidency, edited by V. Rangacharya (Madras, 1919).

SECONDARY AND CONTROVERSIAL LITERATURE

Baudhōpādhyāya, N. C. *Kauṭilya*, vol. i (Calcutta, 1927).

Development of Hindu Polity and Political Theories (Calcutta, 1927).

Economic Life and Progress in Ancient India (Calcutta, 1925).

Bannerjea, P. N. *Public Administration in Ancient India* (London, 1916).

Bannerjea, G. *India as known to the Ancient World* (London, 1921).

Beni Prasad. *Theory of Government in Ancient India* (Allahabad, 1927).

The State in Ancient India (London, 1928).

Bhandarkar, D. R. *Aśōka* (Calcutta, 1925).

Lectures on the Ancient History of India (Calcutta, 1919).

Bhandarkar, R. G. *Early History of the Dekhan* (Bombay, 1895).

Chakladhar. *Social Life in Ancient India* (Calcutta, 1929).

Das, A. C. *Ṛig Vēdic India* (Calcutta, 1921).

Das, S. K. *Economic History of Ancient India* (Calcutta, 1925).

Dikshitar, V. R. R. *Hindu Administrative Institutions* (Madras, 1929).

Studies in Tamil Literature and History (London, 1930).

Mauryan Polity (Madras, 1932).

Fick, R. *Social Organization in North-East India in Buddha's Time*. Translated by S. Maitra (Calcutta, 1920).

Ghoshal, V. N. *A History of Hindu Political Theories* (Oxford, 1927).

Hindu Revenue System (Calcutta, 1929).

Gupta, K. M. *The Land System in South India* (Lahore, 1933).

Gupta, N. C. S. *Sources of Law and Society in Ancient India* (Calcutta, 1913).

Jayaswal, K. P. *Hindu Polity* (Calcutta, 1924).

Kanakasabhai Pillai, V. *Tamils Eighteen Hundred Years Ago* (Madras, 1904).

Keay, F. E. *Ancient Indian Education* (London, 1915).

Kṛishṇaswāmi Iyengar, S. *The Beginnings of South Indian History* (Madras, 1918).

Some Contributions of South India to Indian Culture (Calcutta, 1923).

Ancient India (Madras, 1911).

Law, N. N. *Studies in Ancient Hindu Polity* (London, 1914).

Aspects of Ancient Indian Polity (Oxford, 1921).

Inter-State Relations in Ancient India (London, 1920).

Macdonell, A. A., and Keith, A. B. *Vēdic Index* (London, 1912).

Mazumdar, N. N. *History of Education in Ancient India* (1916).

Mazumdar, R. C. *Corporate Life in Ancient India* (Calcutta, 1919).

Mookerjea, R. K. *History of Indian Shipping and Maritime Activity* (London, 1912).

Local Government in Ancient India (London, 1920).

Harsha (London, 1927).

Aśōka (London, 1928).

Oppert, C. *On the Weapons, Army Organization, and Political Maxims of the Ancient Hindus* (Madras and London, 1880).

Pran Nath. *A Study in the Economic Condition of Ancient India* (London).

Rapson, E. J. *Cambridge History of India*, vol. i. Edited by Rapson (Cambridge, 1922).

Ancient India (Cambridge, 1914).

Raṅgaswāmy Aiyengar, K. V. *Considerations on Some Aspects of Ancient Indian Polity* (Madras, 1916).

Rice, B. L. *Mysore and Coorg from the Inscriptions* (London, 1909).

Robertson, W. *An Historical Disquisition Concerning the Knowledge which the Ancients had of India* (Calcutta, 1904).

Samaddar, J. N. *Economic Condition of Ancient India* (Calcutta, 1922).

Glories of Magadha (Calcutta, 1924).

Sen, A. K. *Studies in Hindu Political Thought* (Calcutta, 1926).

Shāma Śāstry, R. *Evolution of Indian Polity* (Calcutta, 1920).

Smith, V. A. *Early History of India* (Oxford, 1924).

Aśōka (Oxford, 1909).

Srinivasiengar, P. T. *Life in Ancient India in the Age of the Mantras* (Madras, 1912).

Subrahmanya Aiyar, K. V. *Historical Sketches of Ancient Dekhan* (Madras, 1917).

Thomas, F. W. *Mutual Influence of Hindus and Mohammedans in Law and Religion* (Cambridge, 1892).

Warnington, E. H. *Commerce between the Roman Empire and India* (Cambridge, 1928).

Winternitz. *Some Problems of Indian Literature* (Calcutta, 1925).

Vaidya, C. V. *History of Mediaeval India* (Poona, 1921).

Epic India (Bombay, 1907).

Viśvanātha, S. V. *International Law in Ancient India* (London, 1925).

JOURNALS, WORKS OF REFERENCE, ETC.

Journal of the Royal Asiatic Society (London).

Journal of the Bihar and Orissa Research Society (Calcutta).

Journal of the American Oriental Society.

Journal of the Asiatic Society of Bengal (Calcutta).

Sir Aśutosh Mookherjea Silver Jubilee, vols. ii and iii.

Śabdakalpadruma, by Rajakanta Dev, 5 vols. (Calcutta, 1808).

Sanskrit–English Dictionary, by Monier-Williams (Poona).

Sanskrit–English Dictionary, by V. S. Apte (Poona).

INDEX

C

D

E

H

I

J

K

S

U

V

W

Y

For Product Safety Concerns and Information please contact our EU
representative GPSR@taylorandfrancis.com
Taylor & Francis Verlag GmbH, Kaufingerstraße 24, 80331 München, Germany

www.ingramcontent.com/pod-product-compliance
Ingram Content Group UK Ltd.
Pitfield, Milton Keynes, MK11 3LW, UK
UKHW020159200926
475702UK00004B/539
9781041381532